CapitaLogic Limited Emp...

Managing Credit Risk
Under The Basel III Framework
(Third Edition)

应用巴塞尔资本协议三管理信贷风险
(第三版)

Jointly authored by:

Dr. Yat-fai LAM, Doctor of Business Administration,
CFA, CAIA, CAMS, FRM, PRM

Mr. Edward Tak-wah KWAN, Master of Laws

Prof. Kin-keung LAI, PhD in Transportation Engineering
and Operations Research

Printed in the United States of America.

Yat-fai LAM
Edward Tak-wah KWAN
Kin-keung LAI

       Managing Credit Risk Under The Basel III Framework (Third Edition).

       ISBN-13: 978-1719599702
       ISBN-10: 171959970X

       1. Credit   2. Risk management   3. Basel III

Course design

This book is developed for teaching a one semester course in credit risk management at postgraduate and advanced undergraduate levels as the first university course in financial risk management. Under the assumption that one credit is equivalent to fourteen lecture hours, subject to the number of credits carried, the course may cover the chapters proposed in the following table:

Part	Chapter	Title	Number of credits			
			3	2	1.5	1
I. Credit risk theories	1	Credit risk factors and measures	*	*	*	*
	2	Credit products	*	*	*	*
	3	Homogeneous debt portfolios	*	*	*	
	4	Heterogeneous debt portfolios	*	*	*	
	5	Credit quality monitoring	*	*	*	
	6	Credit risk controls	*	*	*	
II. Credit assessments	7	Credit ratings and FICO scores	*	*	*	*
	8	Corporate credit analysis	*	*	*	*
	9	Credit scoring	*	*	*	*
	10	Practical issues in credit assessments	*	*	*	
III. Credit derivatives	11	Credit default swaps	*	*		
	12	CDS indices	*			
	13	Credit linked notes	*	*		
	14	Collateralized debt obligations	*	#		
	15	Financial tsunami 2008	*	*		
IV. Credit regulations	16	The IFRS 9	*			
	17	The Basel III framework	*			
	18	Internal ratings based approach	*			
	19	Regulatory IRB validation	*			
	20	Regulatory credit exposures	*			

* Full chapter.
# Selected critical sections in the chapter.

Excel work examples

Over 140 Excel work examples were developed to illustrate the implementation of credit risk management techniques in real life lending operations. These Excel work examples operate on a personal computer installed with Microsoft Excel 2007 or its successors.

These Excel work examples are packaged as four password protected zip files which can be downloaded from the book website:

> https://sites.google.com/site/crmbasel

The **sixteen-digit passwords** to open the zip files are listed on the **last page** of this book.

Presentation slides

Over seven hundred presentation slides were developed to facilitate the teaching of credit risk management in conjunction with this text book. The Internet version of these presentation slides can be accessed from the book website:

> https://sites.google.com/site/crmbasel

The full set of presentation slides are also compiled in the book "Managing Credit Risk Under The Basel III Framework: The Presentation Slides" which can be purchased separately from Amazon.com.

Question bank

A question bank comprising a number of examination questions and answers developed by the authors is ready to be accessed by qualified university teachers who adopt this book as one of the core text books of their financial risk management courses. Interested teachers may enquire for the access to the question bank by sending their official course syllabus to the publisher with the e-mail address:

> crmbasel@gmail.com

Prerequisites

Efforts have been made to minimize the fundamental knowledge that is required to go through this book. In general, readers are assumed to have completed:

- a three-credit undergraduate course in quantitative methods for finance; and
- a three-credit undergraduate course in financial management or corporate finance.

Students in business schools usually enroll these two courses during the first year of their study.

Kindle version

To facilitate this book to be published on the Amazon's Kindle platform, the book is re-organized into four parts which can be purchased separately at a lower list price per part.

Third edition

The third edition of this book is developed with only **ONE** objective:

> to improve the teaching quality in credit risk management.

Contemporary contents have been added, including the IFRS 9 new accounting standards for debt investments and regulatory model validation.

Moving forwards

After completing this book, readers are able to manage the credit risk of a financial institution in accordance with the Basel III framework. Readers who wish to further advance their knowledge in credit risk management may proceed to the study of the official curriculum in credit risk management set forth by the Global Association of Risk Professionals for the Financial Risk Manager examinations. The official curriculum is highly fragmented and assumes a great deal of prior knowledge. Therefore, this book also serves as a bridge for the candidates who seek to attempt the Financial Risk Manager examinations.

Preface

This book is developed for teaching a one semester course in credit risk management at postgraduate and advanced undergraduate levels as the first university course in financial risk management. Readers are assumed no prior knowledge in financial risk management. This revolutionary approach aims to broaden the lectures on credit risk management to the majority of students who intend to work in the financial industry.

Recognizing that credit risk is the largest risk exposure in financial institutions, this book also seeks to answer the questions that are often raised by practitioners who actually work in the field of credit risk management. Riding on the Basel III framework, the solutions are delivered by contemporary techniques conforming to the latest regulatory standards. This fills immediately the gap between the working requirements in the office and the academic knowledge in the laboratory. Simply speaking, this book answers specifically the common questions of "how to" in the field of credit risk management.

It is well understood that time is precious and simplicity is beautiful. Only the most important and contemporary topics are included to ensure that the contents can be well covered in one semester. In addition, the critical topics are highlighted with "★★★" next to the section titles. During the drafting of this book, much effort was spent to:

- make the book be self-contained to avoid any prior knowledge in derivatives and/or fixed income securities;
- use intuitive words instead of technical jargons;
- use tables and figures instead of lengthy paragraphs;
- use simple algebra instead of calculus;
- use free financial data over the Internet instead of from paid financial information services; and
- use Microsoft Excel instead of expensive computer programmes.

A pilot run of a credit risk management course with the first draft of this book was conducted at City University of Hong Kong in spring 2013. The course was well received with all key performance indicators outperforming the departmental and university averages during the course evaluation. Many constructive comments were received and incorporated in the design of the final version. In general, the contemporaneity and practicality are highly appreciated by students who, after taking the course, carry much stronger competitive advantages than their peers in career development.

Special thanks must be made to CapitaLogic Limited. Ms. Fiona NG and her team spent countless hours on the quality assurance of the book and in consultation with industry practitioners on the applicability of the contents. Without their contributions, this book would remain as a to-do item on the authors' wish lists.

About the authors

Dr. Yat-fai LAM (林日辉 博士)

Dr. Yat-fai LAM is the Director of CapitaLogic Limited and Adjunct Professor of Finance, City University of Hong Kong. He has worked for bank regulator, international bank and sovereign wealth fund, specializing in the areas of credit risk management, anti-money laundering and structured products.

Dr. LAM graduated from City University of Hong Kong with a Doctor of Business Administration degree in finance and holds the CFA, CAIA, CAMS, FRM and PRM professional designations. He is honoured with the "PRM Award of Merit 2005" by PRMIA for his outstanding results in the PRM examination.

Mr. Edward Tak-wah KWAN (关德华 律师)

Mr. Edward Tak-wah KWAN is a solicitor and has practised laws for over twenty years. He is well versed with commercial laws and quality management in law practices. Moreover, Mr. KWAN is very interested in the application of the legal and compliance approach to credit risk management.

Mr. KWAN holds a Master of Laws degree from The University of London and a Bachelor of Science degree from The Chinese University of Hong Kong.

Prof. Kin-keung LAI (黎建强 讲座教授)

Prof. Kin-keung LAI received his PhD degree in Transportation Engineering and Operations Research at Michigan State University, United States. He was the Chair Professor of Management Science at City University of Hong Kong. He was also the Director of the Invesco-Great Wall Research Unit on Risk Analysis and Business Intelligence at the College of Business. Prior to his academic life, Prof. LAI was a Senior Operational Research Analyst at Cathay Pacific Airways and an Area Manager on Marketing Information Systems at Union Carbide Eastern.

In addition to his positions at City University of Hong Kong, Professor LAI was also the Adjunct Professor of: (i) School of Management, Key Laboratory of Management, Decision and Information Systems, and Institute of System Sciences, Chinese Academy of Sciences, Beijing; (ii) Huazhong University of Science and Technology, Wuhan; (iii) Jinan University, Guangzhou; and (iv) North China Electric Power University, Beijing.

Contents

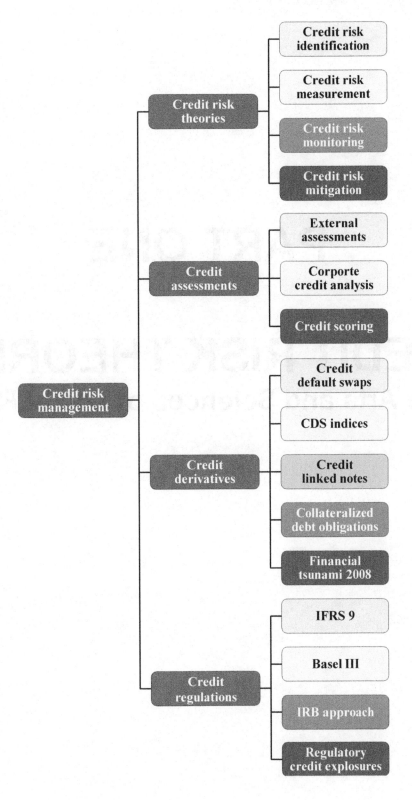

Road map

PART ONE

CREDIT RISK THEORIES
The Arts and Sciences of Credit Risk

Credit Risk Factors and Measures

KEY CONCEPTS

- Credit
- Default risk

- Risk factor
- Risk measure

1.1   Introduction

Credit risk is by far the largest risk exposure in the banking industry.   Thus the management of credit risk is critical to the success of a bank.   This chapter starts with an introduction to the contemporary approach of credit risk management in a bank.

1.1.1   Funding source

Lending is one of the core businesses of a bank.   Through lending and deposits taking, a bank generates profits from the spread between the higher interest rate that the bank charges borrowers who collect monies from the bank and the lower interest rate that the bank pays depositors who place monies into the bank.

Individual persons borrow from banks in the forms of term loans, credit cards, mortgages, etc..   In addition to traditional bank lending, corporations can raise funds by issuing bonds to debt investors.   Bonds are essentially tradable loans with transferable ownership. Thus loans and bonds are collectively referred to as debts.   In this regard, borrowers and bond issuers are collectively referred to as debt issuers while lenders and bond investors are collectively referred to as debt investors.

1.1.2   Credit

Central to "credit" is the idea that a borrower, either an individual person or institution, uses other people's monies in pursuit of his[1] financial needs.   Credit enables a borrower to spend with a lender's monies today but pay the lender in the future.   In return, the lender charges the borrower interest: (i) to compensate the time value of monies over the lending period; (ii) to cover the potential loss if the borrower defaults; and (iii) as a service charge for arranging temporary funds to the borrower.

---

[1]   To simplify the presentation in this book, the pronouns "he", "him" and "his" are used when referring to any gender.

1.1.3   Time value of money

Monies depreciate over time as a result of inflation. If a lender plans to lend to a borrower in an economy at an inflation rate 3 percent, to maintain the purchasing power of the loan amount at maturity, the lender must charge the borrower a normal yield higher than 3 percent regardless whom the borrower is.

1.1.4   Default

When a borrower fails to pay to the lender the interest and/or principal in full on schedule, the borrower is considered in default. Debt collection efforts will then be initiated by the lender upon default of the borrower to recover the whole or part of the principal plus interest.

1.1.5   Credit risk[2]

In this book, the term "credit risk" means the uncertainty of loss to a lender caused by the default of a debt owned by the lender. The lender invests with an intention to hold the debt until maturity or for a medium to longer period of time, i.e., one year or longer.

To compensate for taking the credit risk, a lender invariably demands that a borrower pay a nominal yield higher than the risk-free rate. The larger the credit risk, the higher the nominal yield the lender will seek from the borrower.

1.1.6   Credit risk management ★★★[3]

Under the Basel III framework, credit risk management comprises four building blocks:

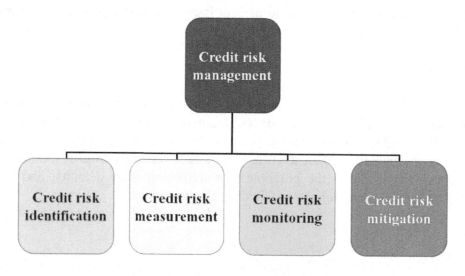

Figure 1.1   Credit risk management

---

[2] In the broadest sense, credit risk comprises default, rating migration and credit spread risks.
[3] Critical sections in this book are highlighted with "★★★" next to the title.

- Credit risk identification: The credit risk of a single debt is driven by four factors: exposure at default ("EAD"), loss given default ("LGD"), probability of default ("PD") and residual maturity ("RM"). In addition, the credit risk of a debt portfolio is driven by two more factors: concentration of debts and default dependency.

- Credit risk measurement: The credit risk of a single debt is measured by the expected loss ("EL") and/or one-year expected loss ("1-year EL") which increases with increasing EAD, LGD, PD and RM. The credit risk of a debt portfolio is measured by the extreme case loss ("XCL") which increases with increasing EAD, LGD, PD, concentration of debts and default dependency.

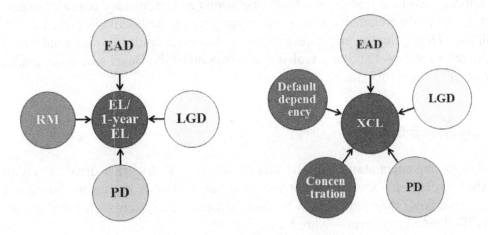

Figure 1.2   Credit risk measures

- Credit risk monitoring: Practically, the credit risk of a single debt is monitored by tracking regularly the credit quality of the borrower. In addition, the credit risk of a debt portfolio is monitored by tracking regularly the relevant systematic financial market monitoring factors in the lending universe and the credit quality of those borrowers with large outstanding debt amounts.

- Credit risk mitigation: The credit risk is mitigated by implementing pre-lending and/or post-lending controls to reduce the impacts from the factors that drive the credit risk of a single debt or debt portfolio.

1.1.7   Basel Accord

While banks endeavour to manage their credit risks to reduce potential losses, they are bound by regulatory requirements to adopt prudent lending practices to maintain the confidence of the stakeholders and procure the stability of the banking system.

The Basel Committee on Banking Supervision ("BCBS") develops standards and guidelines for internationally active banks to shore up their risk management practices. The BCBS has promulgated the Basel Accord, an international standard in the form of "pillars", to manage risks in banking practices.

The first Basel Accord was published in 1988. Through the decades, the BCBS continues to enhance the Basel Accord, taking into account the rapid evolution of the global banking market. In late 2010, the BCBS published the latest version of the Basel Accord, referred to as the Basel III framework, which has incorporated the lessons learnt from the financial tsunami in 2008 and the European debt crisis in 2010. Overall, the Basel III framework aims at improving a bank's ability to absorb shocks as a result of financial and economic stresses.

This book follows largely the Basel III framework when introducing the theories and practices of credit risk management. The methodologies incorporate the building blocks from finance, accounting, statistics, bank operations and regulatory considerations. It is by far the most comprehensive credit risk management methodology with international recognition. Depending on the nature of the business, a lender in other industries may adopt the relevant subset and/or a scaled down version of the Basel Accord to manage the credit risk of his debt investments.

1.2   Credit risk factors

Credit risk management starts with the identification of factors that drive the credit risk. Under the Basel III framework, credit risk of a single debt is driven by four credit risk factors. This allows the credit risk to be modelled effectively across major types of debts with a unified set of explanatory variables.

The credit risk of a single debt is characterized by four factors, namely: the EAD, LGD, PD and RM.

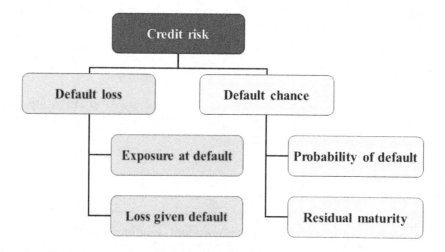

Figure 1.3   Credit risk factors of a single debt

1.2.1   Exposure at default ★★★

The EAD is the amount that a borrower owes a lender when the borrower defaults. For many types of debts, like term loans, mortgages and corporate bonds, the EAD is the sum of the principal and interest. For a revolving loan subject to a credit limit, like credit card and credit line, with the outstanding loan amount varying over time, the EAD is the sum of the expected drawdown amount and interest upon default of the borrower. This EAD is bounded below and, in general, approaches the credit limit of the revolving loan.

1.2.2   Loss given default   ★★★

The LGD is the default loss expressed as a percentage of the EAD, after the borrower has recovered part of the EAD through the collaterals and/or debt collection actions mandated in the lending agreement.

Many credit products are designed in a way such that the lender will request at origination the borrower to pledge certain collaterals to the lender. When the borrower defaults, the lender will convert the collaterals into cash in order to recover the whole or part of the EAD. For the credit products which are not supported by collaterals, the LGD is driven primarily by the debt collection actions.

This essentially polarises the LGD into two extremities: loans with collaterals exhibit a smaller LGD, ranging from 0 to 20 percent, with 10 percent as a typical estimate due to the excessive amount of collaterals over the EAD demanded by lenders; and loans without collaterals exhibit a larger LGD, ranging from 80 to 100 percent, with 90 percent as a typical estimate.

The simplest LGD estimation method is to calculate the historical average LGD of a group of defaulted debts with similar characteristics and then assume that this historical average LGD also represents the LGD of similar debts that may default in the near future. Statistics from Moody's Investors Service demonstrated that the historical average LGD of a senior unsecured bond was around 62.3 percent over the 24-year period from 1983 to 2016.

1.2.3   Probability of default   ★★★

The PD is the chance that a borrower will default in the following **ONE** year. The PD looks into the credit quality of a borrower and ranges from 0 percent (if the borrower will surely survive in one year) to 100 percent (if the borrower will definitely default in one year). A higher PD means a higher chance for a borrower to default in the following year.

The simplest PD estimation method is to calculate the historical average annual default rate of a group of borrowers with similar characteristics and then assume that this historical average annual default rate also represents the PD of similar borrowers in the near future. Statistics from Moody's Investors Service demonstrated that the historical average PD of an investment grade borrower was around 0.096 percent over the 24-year period from 1983 to 2016.

1.2.4   Residual maturity ★★★

The RM is the remaining time horizon over which a debt will generate cash flows to a lender. Obviously, the longer the RM, the more time for a borrower to default.

1.3   Credit risk dimensions

When selected credit risk factors are combined logically, a credit risk dimension is formed to characterize the combined effect from these selected credit risk factors along a particular dimension.

1.3.1   Default loss

The default loss is the net loss amount to be incurred upon the default of a borrower. According to the definition of the LGD:

$$\text{Default loss} = \text{EAD} \times \text{LGD}$$

1.3.2   Default chance

The default chance [4] measures the chance that a borrower will default during the remaining lending period RM years.

For a borrower to survive within a period of RM years, he must survive in each of these RM years, then:

$$1 - \text{Default chance} = \left(1 - \text{PD}\right)^{\text{RM}}$$

The default chance in this RM-year period thus becomes:

$$\text{Default chance} = 1 - \left(1 - \text{PD}\right)^{\text{RM}}$$

1.3.3   Bernoulli distribution

The default of a borrower can be modelled statistically by a Bernoulli random variable characterized by the default chance. The Bernoulli random variable returns a:

- zero with a probability equal to 1 - default chance; and
- one with a probability equal to default chance.

---

[4] Default chance is also referred to as cumulative probability of default.

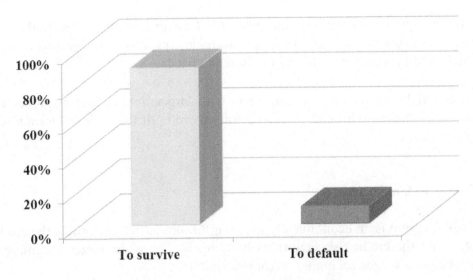

Figure 1.4   Bernoulli distribution

1.3.4   Risk map

Risk map is a graphical presentation to visualize credit risk. With a risk map, the credit risk of a debt is presented as a point on a two dimensional space where the vertical axis exhibits the default loss and the horizontal axis exhibits the default chance.

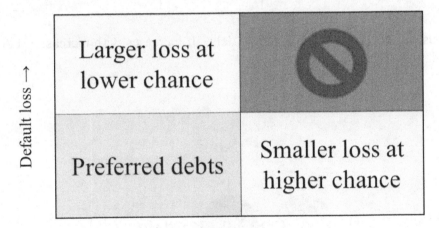

Figure 1.5   Risk map

The risk map divides the credit risk characteristics into four regions:

- The lower left region presents the debts with smaller default loss at lower default chance. Professional lenders prefer to lend in this region;

- The upper left region presents the debts with larger default loss at lower default chance. Only lenders who can afford the larger default loss may lend in this region;

- The lower right region presents the debts with lower default loss at higher default chance. Risk tolerant lenders lend in this region by charging borrowers a higher nominal yield to compensate the higher default chance;

- The upper right region presents the debts with larger default loss at higher default chance. No lenders will lend in this region where both the default loss and default chance are large.

1.4   Credit risk measures

A credit risk measure is an economically meaningful metric that quantifies the credit risk of a debt, using the credit risk factors as building blocks. The larger magnitude of a credit risk measure suggests a higher credit risk of a debt.

1.4.1   Expected loss ★★★

The EL is defined as the default loss weighted by the default chance, i.e.:

Expected loss = Default loss × Default chance

$$EL = EAD \times LGD \times \left[1 - \left(1 - PD \right)^{RM} \right]$$

The EL measures the credit risk of a single debt. It increases with increasing EAD, LGD, PD and RM.

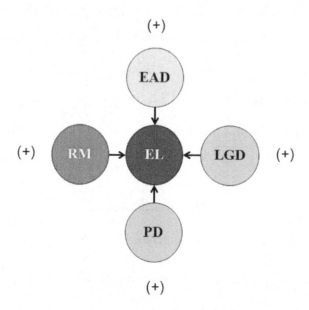

Figure 1.6   The EL vs four credit risk factors

In general, the EAD, LGD and PD can be estimated with sufficient accuracy for a debt with a short to medium RM. Therefore, practically, the EL is a good credit risk measure of a short to medium term debt.

In a real bank lending operation where the PD and RM are relatively small, e.g., when the PD and RM are below 3 percent and five years respectively, the EL can be approximated conveniently as:

$$EL \approx EAD \times LGD \times PD \times RM$$

1.4.2 One-year expected loss ★★★

For a longer term debt with a remote maturity day, it is difficult to estimate a set of reliable EAD, LGD and PD throughout the remaining life of the debt. Under such situation, the EL becomes a less meaningful credit risk measure.

Inline with the general lending practices in the financial industry, for a debt with maturity longer than one year, it is assumed that a lender will review and control the credit risk of the debt at the end of the following one year, the latest, and the risk horizon is reduced to one year. Then: (i) the RM is set artificially to one year; and (ii) the 1-year EL, defined as the EL in one year, is utilized to measure the credit risk of a debt subject to year end credit risk review and control.

For a debt with maturity below one year, since the review and control of the credit risk will not take place within its life, the 1-year EL is simply identical to the EL.

Therefore, the 1-year EL of a debt with any RM can be expressed mathematically as:

$$\text{1-year EL} = EAD \times LGD \times Min\left[1 - (1 - PD)^1, 1 - (1 - PD)^{RM}\right]$$

$$= EAD \times LGD \times Min\left[PD, 1 - (1 - PD)^{RM}\right]$$

$$\approx EAD \times LGD \times PD \times Min\left[1, RM\right]$$

For a revolving loan with on-going drawdown and re-payment transactions, there is no fixed maturity day. Theoretically, the maturity can be extended to infinite as long as the requirement of minimum payment is satisfied. Following the same principle applied to the debts with longer maturity, it is assumed that a lender will review and control the credit risk of the revolving loan at the end of the following one year and the RM is set artificially to one year, leaving the EAD, LGD and PD as the only three credit risk factors. Then the 1-year EL is simply calculated as:

$$1\text{-year EL} = \text{EAD} \times \text{LGD} \times \text{Min}\left[1 - (1 - \text{PD})^1, 1 - (1 - \text{PD})^\infty\right]$$

$$= \text{EAD} \times \text{LGD} \times \text{Min}\left[\text{PD}, 1 - (1 - \text{PD})^\infty\right]$$

$$= \text{EAD} \times \text{LGD} \times \text{PD}$$

Although the EL and 1-year EL are defined in a similar way, for a debt with the RM longer than one year, they essentially carry very different economic meanings in terms of the existence of year end credit risk review and control. Conversely, for a short term debt with the RM shorter than one year, both the EL and 1-year EL are identical. The EL of a short term debt also represents the EL in one year because the default chance will not increase after the maturity.

A lender focusing on short to medium term debts may use the EL to measure the credit risk of his debts. A lender must use the 1-year EL to measure the credit risk of a debt with longer maturity or without a fixed maturity day. A lender investing in debts with a wide range of maturities should use the 1-year EL as a unified credit risk measure.

1.5   A simple loan ★★★

The following example exhibits the credit risk factors, credit risk dimensions and credit risk measures of a simple loan:

1.	Exposure at default	EAD	USD 10,000
2.	Loss given default	LGD	90%
3.	Probability of default	PD	3%
4.	Residual maturity	RM	3 years
5.	Default loss		USD 8,000
6.	Default chance		8.7327%
7.	Expected loss	EL	USD 786
8.	One-year expected loss	1-year EL	USD 270

Table 1.1   A simple loan

From a lender's perspective, this simple loan is equipped with the following characteristics:

Functional purposes

- The borrower needs immediate cash; and
- The lender has spare cash that could be put aside for three years and desires to seek an excess return over the risk-free rate.

Cash flows

- The only cash outflow occurs at origination when the principal is lent to the borrower; and
- The only cash inflow occurs at maturity when the principal and interest are paid to the lender.

Default

- Default occurs when the interest and/or principal are not paid in full to the lender at maturity; and
- Debt collection actions will be initiated by the lender to recover the whole or part of the principal plus interest.

Appendix 1.1   Cumulative standard normal distribution function[5] ★★★

The cumulative standard normal distribution function $\Phi(x)$ is defined as:

$$\Phi(x) = \frac{1}{\sqrt{2\pi}} \int_{-\infty}^{x} \exp(-\frac{\tau^2}{2})d\tau$$

When x increases from -∞ to ∞, $\Phi(x)$ increases from 0 to 1. Given a value x, $\Phi(x)$ can be calculated easily in Microsoft Excel with the function Normsdist(…).

The inverse cumulative standard normal distribution function $\Phi^{-1}(x)$ is defined implicitly as:

$$x = \frac{1}{\sqrt{2\pi}} \int_{-\infty}^{\Phi^{-1}(x)} \exp(-\frac{\tau^2}{2})d\tau$$

The value $\Phi^{-1}(x)$, when substituted into the cumulative standard normal distribution function, will result in the quantity x. When x increases from 0 to 1, $\Phi^{-1}(x)$ increases from -∞ to ∞. Given a value x, $\Phi^{-1}(x)$ can be calculated easily in Microsoft Excel with the function Normsinv(…).

Throughout the study of credit risk management, these two functions are utilized frequently to perform the conversion between a standard uniform random variable and a standard normal random variable.

A standard normal random variable, in general, has more convenient mathematical properties, including among others:

- A standard normal random variable can be any real number from -∞ to ∞;
- A standard normal distribution function is a simple continuous, differentiable and integrable function;
- The sum of N independent standard normal random variables is a normal random variable with mean zero and standard deviation N;
- The average of several independent standard normal random variables is a standard normal random variable;
- The dependency between any two standard normal random variables is well characterized by a correlation coefficient; and
- The dependencies among N standard normal random variables are well characterized by an N × N correlation matrix.

---

[5] Readers with less experience in credit risk management are advised to **SKIP** most appendices during the first time when they read this book, except Appendices 1.1, 2.1, 8.1, 8.2, 8.3 and 17.1 which are marked with "★★★" next to the appendix title.

Appendix 1.2   Probit transformation

Since a PD is defined only on the range from 0 to 100 percent, mathematically it is less convenient to work with. Therefore, a transformation is proposed to convert a PD into a more convenient variable Probit in order to facilitate the development of the PD models.

The Probit of a PD is a real number between -∞ and ∞ which, when substituted into the cumulative standard normal distribution function, will result in a value equal to a given PD.

$$PD = \frac{1}{\sqrt{2\pi}} \int_{-\infty}^{Probit} \exp(-\frac{\tau^2}{2})d\tau$$

Given a Probit, the corresponding PD can be calculated in Microsoft Excel with the function Normsdist(…).

   PD = Normsdist(Probit)

Conversely, given a PD, the corresponding Probit can be calculated in Microsoft Excel with the function Normsinv(…).

   Probit = Normsinv(PD)

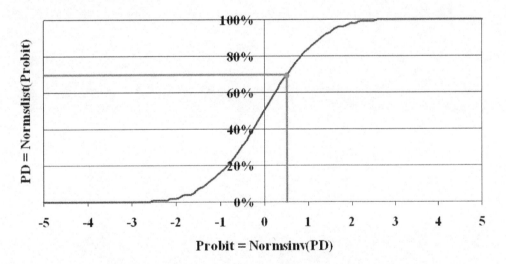

Figure 1.8   Relationship between the PD and Probit

Appendix 1.3   Similarities between credit and market risk measurements

Credit risk measurement of debts and market risk measurement of equities share some similarities, as compared in Table 1.2.

Item	Credit risk of debts	Market risk of equities
Expectation	1-year EL rate = LGD × PD	Expected return
Exposure	EAD	Equity value
Probability distribution	Bernoulli	Normal
Distribution parameter	PD	Standard deviation
Dependency	Copula correlation coefficient	Beta
Portfolio risk measure	1-year 99.9th percentile extreme case loss	10-day 99th percentile value-at-risk

Table 1.2   Credit risk measurement vs market risk measurement

Credit Products

2

KEY CONCEPTS

- Term loan
- Credit card
- Mortgage
- Corporate bond

2.1 Lending business

A lending business is originated through demands from borrowers who need cash and supplies from lenders who have spare cash that could be put aside for some time and desire to seek a return higher than the risk-free rate.

Over the years, many credit products have been developed to serve various financial needs of the community, taking into account the risk-return preferences and investment horizons of the lenders, and the payment amounts and schedules affordable by the borrowers. This chapter introduces four common credit products: term loan, credit card, mortgage and corporate bond, by referencing the following dimensions:

- Functional purpose: Why do a borrower need and a lender design this credit product?
- Cash flow: What are the cash outflows and inflows from a lender's perspective?
- Risk measurement: What are the credit risk factors and credit risk level?
- Actions upon default: What actions will a lender take when a borrower defaults?

Among the four credit risk factors, the EAD, LGD and RM are properties of a credit product. They are controlled largely by a lender who designs the credit product. Conversely, the PD relates solely to the characteristics of a borrower.

2.2 Term loan

With a term loan, a lender advances a principal to a borrower at loan origination. This is the only cash outflow from the lender. The borrower promises to: (i) return the principal to the borrower at maturity; and (ii) pay the borrower a fixed amount of interest on scheduled days, usually on a monthly basis. Since the lender faces the risk that the borrower may default during the lending period, he must demand a nominal yield higher than the risk-free rate in order to compensate the credit risk.

In case a borrower does not pay the interest and/or principal in full on a payment day, the borrower is taken to be in default. Upon the default of a borrower, which can only be observed on a payment day, the lender carries out debt collection actions to recover the principal and interest that remain outstanding.

Therefore, the EAD is equal to the sum of the principal and monthly interest.

$$EAD = Principal + Monthly\ interest$$

The debt collection actions can be taken by the lender himself or a professional debt collection agency who charges the lender a service charge from 40 to 60 percent of the collected amount.

When a borrower defaults on a term loan, neither the lender nor the professional debt collection agency has recourse to collect the EAD, except to keep on warning and then take liquidation actions against the borrower. Therefore, the LGD of a term loan is relatively high, at a typical estimate of 90 percent.

The lending period of a term loan, i.e., the initial RM, is determined by referencing: (i) how fast the borrower can release his financial burden and accumulate certain wealth to pay back the principal; and (ii) the investment horizon of the lender. The lending period usually ranges from one year to five years. This short to medium term lending period ensures that the LGD and PD of a term loan can be estimated with sufficient accuracy.

A term loan is generally considered as a credit product with moderate risk due to its higher LGD. As such, even at a lower interest rate environment in 2016 when the medium term US treasury rates were typically below 2 percent, the normal yield of a term loan demanded by a bank was often over 12 percent.

2.3   Credit card

In essence, a credit card represents a revolving loan up to a certain amount (credit limit) advanced by a card issuer (lender) to a consumer (borrower). When a consumer buys a good or enjoys a service with his credit card, the card issuer pays on behalf of the consumer and becomes the lender to the consumer. The more utilization on the credit card, the larger the amount that is owed by the consumer to the card issuer, noting that the outstanding amount, after incorporating the interest, must not exceed the credit limit agreed upon previously by the card issuer.

The transaction amounts are accumulated and summarized as a statement balance on a monthly basis and conveyed in a monthly statement to the consumer who must settle the statement balance in full or in part by the statement due day. If the consumer pays the statement balance in full by the statement due day, no interest will be charged. However, if only part of the statement balance is paid by the statement due day, interest will be charged on all outstanding transaction amounts starting from the corresponding transaction days. The total unsettled amount is bound by the credit limit such that the card issuer will not facilitate any transaction amount beyond the credit limit. Thus, a credit card is essentially an agreement from a card issuer to lend on a net basis up to the credit limit.

From the card issuer's perspective, a cash outflow occurs each time when a consumer spends with his credit card. A cash inflow occurs when the consumer makes a full or partial payment towards the statement balance. A minimum payment amount, referred to as minpay, is calculated by the card issuer (e.g., 10 percent of the statement balance or USD 100, whichever is larger) so that in case a consumer chooses not to pay the statement balance in full, he must pay at least the minpay. Otherwise, the consumer is taken to be in default.

A consumer is also allowed to borrow cash directly with a credit card through automatic teller machines. Combining the minpay scheme, this indeed encourages a consumer who cannot afford to pay even the minpay on the statement due day to borrow new cash with the credit card and settle the minpay. This process can be repeated until the credit limit is reached. As such, upon default, the EAD of a credit card usually approaches the credit limit.

When even the minpay is unaffordable to the consumer, it is likely that the consumer has been in financial difficulty for some time. As such, upon the default of the consumer, most debt collection efforts will fail. Therefore, the LGD is expected to be very high, at a typical estimate of 100 percent. In addition, once a credit card is issued, regular updates on the credit quality of the consumer will not be provided from the consumer. Thus it is difficult to track the PD. Combining the large LGD and uncertainty of the PD, a credit card is considered to be a credit product of higher risk. Therefore, a card issuer demands a much higher nominal yield, generally from 16 percent up to 30 percent, to compensate the higher credit risk.

Credit card issuers are aggressive investors with spare cash that could be reserved for investment on an on-going basis. This continuous lending to consumers facilitates an on-going higher investment return.

Upon the default of a consumer, which is observed on the statement due day, the credit card issuer starts the debt collection actions to collect the total outstanding amount, covering both the statement balance and any outstanding balance above the statement balance.

2.4   Mortgage

Property price is expensive relative to the annual income of most working employees. It may take ten to twenty years for a person to accumulate sufficient wealth to purchase a property. Thus banks offer mortgages to finance borrowers who intend to buy their properties in the near future.

Under a mortgage arrangement, a borrower sources funds from a lender to pay for the purchase of a property and uses the property afterwards. However, the legal ownership of the property goes to the lender until the mortgage amount and interests are paid in full to the lender.

From a lender's perspective, the only cash outflow occurs on the drawdown day on which the borrower collects the principal to pay for the property. The borrower then pays the lender through monthly payments at a fixed amount. Each monthly payment comprises the interest and a certain amount of principal. Hence, the principal reduces over the lending period. At the beginning of the lending period, the principal payment is small as the majority of the monthly payment goes to the interest payment. When the principal is settled partially, the corresponding interest payment is also reduced. This principal amortization process is repeated on a monthly basis and more of the fixed monthly payment goes to the principal payment subsequently.

Although the monthly payment is fixed, the interest and principal payments vary every month. The total, interest and principal payments for each month can be calculated easily in Microsoft Excel with the functions PMT(…), IPMT(…) and PPMT(…) respectively. In many developed countries, the monthly payment is limited to 50 percent of the monthly pre-tax income of a borrower to ensure that the monthly payment is affordable to the borrower.[6]

The lending period of a mortgage is long, normally ranging from five to thirty years. It becomes difficult to predict the potential deterioration of the PD of a borrower over such a long lending period. The EAD is the outstanding principal plus the monthly interest calculated according to the outstanding principal. Given that the property price is in the order of million dollars, the initial EAD of a mortgage is large relative to most retail credit products.

A mortgage is offered initially with a lending amount up to a certain percentage of the property price, e.g., 70 percent. When a borrower fails to pay the monthly payment, the lender will sell the property in the property market to recover the EAD. Combining the principal amortization scheme, the LGD of a mortgage is expected to be low, in many developed countries, usually approaching zero. The large initial EAD and RM are offset by the principal amortization scheme and lower LGD. Therefore, in general, a mortgage is considered as a credit product of lower risk. It is therefore an appropriate investment for a conservative lender who has a large amount of cash that can be put aside for a very long period of time but prefers stable cash inflows.

Table 2.1 summaries the typical LGD estimates of common retail credit products.

Collateral	Credit product	LGD (%)
No	Term loan	90
	Credit card	100
Excessive	Mortgage	0

Table 2.1   Typical LGD estimates of common retail credit products

---

[6] In some extreme markets, e.g. Hong Kong, where the property prices maintain at a consistently high level, the regulator may mandate banks to offer mortgages only to borrowers who can pass a stress test in which the monthly payment is calculated by incorporating a stress add-on, e.g. 2 percent, to the mortgage interest rate to ensure the payment ability of the borrowers even at a sudden increase in interest rate.

2.5   Corporate bond

A corporate bond facilitates a corporation to raise medium to longer term funds in the debt market. An investor (lender) acquires a corporate bond issued by a corporation (borrower) with an upfront payment to the corporation, which in turn, promises to pay the investor the principal of the corporate bond at maturity and fixed amount of interests on semi-annual or annual basis. A zero coupon bond is a short term corporate bond that does not pay any interim interest. Instead, the zero coupon bond is acquired by an investor at a discount to the principal amount.

Corporate bonds are tradable among investors at a price negotiated between the buyer and seller. The price of a corporate bond is quoted in the market as a percentage of the principal. For example, a corporate bond quoted at 90 percent with the principal USD 1,000 is priced at USD 900. However, the secondary market of a corporate bond is illiquid. Therefore, most corporate bonds are acquired with an intention to be held until maturity.

The EAD of a corporate bond is calculated as the sum of principal and accrued interest. The accrued interest starts to accumulate from zero on the day just after the last interest payment was made up to $\text{Principal} \times \dfrac{\text{Interest rate}}{\text{Interest frequency}}$ on the day just before the next interest payment will be made. As such, the EAD changes on a daily basis. On average, the EAD of a corporate bond with the RM one year or longer is estimated as:

$$\text{Average EAD} = \text{Principal} + \frac{\text{Principal} \times \text{Interest rate}}{\text{Interest frequency} \times 2}$$

A corporation is in default if it fails to pay in full on schedule the interest and/or principal of any one of the corporate bonds issued by the same corporation. Under this cross default provision, the default of a corporate bond issued by a corporation will trigger the default of the corporation and all corporate bonds issued by the same corporation. The cross default prevision prevents a corporation from defaulting selectively certain corporate bonds but maintaining the survival of other corporate bonds, both issued by the same corporation. Upon the default of a corporation, a liquidation process is started by a liquidator who converts the assets of the corporation into cash and distributes the EAD of corporate bonds to investors in accordance with the seniority of a corporate bond.

The seniority of a corporate bond determines the priority of investors who seek to collect the EAD during the liquidation process. Investors of corporate bonds with the highest seniority have the first priority to collect their EADs before any other corporate bond investors. Upon the completion of the EAD collection by investors of corporate bonds with the highest seniority, the investors of corporate bonds with the second highest seniority start a similar EAD collection process. This process is repeated until either all the EADs are collected or the assets of the defaulted corporation are exhausted in the EAD collection process.

Obviously, a corporate bond with a higher seniority has a smaller LGD, and vice versa. The average LGDs of corporate bonds with different seniority are shown in Table 2.2.

Seniority		Average LGD (%)
Senior	Secured	37.4
	Unsecured	51.6
Subordinated		72.0

Table 2.2   Average LGDs of corporate bonds

Some international standards set out explicitly the LGDs of corporate bonds with different seniorities. Under the foundation IRB approach of the Basel III framework, a senior corporate bond is assigned an LGD 45 percent and a subordinated corporate bond is assigned an LGD 75 percent. When valuating credit default swaps ("CDSs"), the International Swaps and Derivatives Association specifies the LGD of a senior corporate bond to be 60 percent and the LGD of a subordinated corporate bond to be 80 percent.

Seniority	Basel III (%)	ISDA (%)
	Foundation IRB	CDS valuation
Senior	45	60
Subordinated	75	80

Table 2.3   LGDs set out in international standards

Corporate bonds are credit products developed primarily for institutional investors. The transaction size is large, in the order of million dollars, and so is the EAD. The creditworthiness of a corporate bond issuer varies from high to moderate quality. The initial RM also varies from one to five years. Combining with different seniorities, there are a wide range of corporate bonds offered to suit a broad range of investors with various risk-return preferences.

2.6 Qualitative credit risk analysis ★★★

The qualitative impacts from the credit risk factors to term loan, credit card, mortgage and corporate bond at their originations are summarized in Table 2.4.

Credit risk factor	Term loan	Credit card	Mortgage	Corporate bond
EAD	Small to medium	Small to medium	Large	Large
LGD	Large	Very large	Very small	Vary
PD	Stable	Vary		Stable
Initial RM	Short to medium	███████	Medium to very long	Medium
Credit risk level	Medium	Higher	Lower	Vary
No. of credit risk factors	4	3	4	4
Credit risk measure	EL	1-year EL	1-year EL	EL

Table 2.4   Qualitative credit risk analysis

Appendix 2.1   Risk-free security ★★★

A risk-free security is a hypothetical financial instrument created by financial economists on paper for the development of financial theories. An investor, who acquires a risk-free security by paying a principal today, will receive for sure the principal at maturity and fixed interests on scheduled days, without any other monetary and/or non-monetary benefits incorporated.

Nevertheless, such financial instrument never exists in the world since financial instruments with very high certainty of cash inflows all carry other monetary and/or non-monetary benefits outside the definition of a risk-free security. Treasuries issued by governments, due to their very high certainty of cash inflows, are demanded by many conservative investors, e.g., insurance companies and pension funds. This results in a liquid secondary treasuries market in which investors can convert treasuries into cash at any time by selling owned treasuries to other investors, giving a liquidity convenience to treasuries investors. Moreover, in many countries, treasuries are preferred collaterals for commercial banks to borrow from central banks and the interest incomes are also tax exempt. These monetary and non-monetary benefits essentially increase the value of treasuries and reduce the corresponding internal rate of return. Therefore, although treasuries are equipped with cash inflows at very high certainty, they do not match the exact definition of risk-free security.

To put the financial theories into practice, practitioners use top quality assets which deliver steady cash inflows at high certainty as proxies of risk-free securities. The choices of top quality assets include, among others: (i) treasuries issued by governments of major developed countries; (ii) the use of interbank lending rates and swap rates to derive a term structure of interest rates as proxies of risk-free rates which are then utilized to synthesis the cash flows of risk-free securities; and (iii) the most senior tranche of collateralized debt obligations (to be discussed in Chapter 14).

In its simplest form, an investor who pays an initial cash outflow today to acquire a zero coupon risk-free security will receive for sure the principal at maturity. The annualized internal rate of return of this zero coupon risk-free security then becomes the risk-free rate.

Appendix 2.2   Accrued interest

The accrued interest is the amount of accumulated interest entitled but not yet paid to a corporate bond investor. It is calculated as:

$$\text{Accrued interest} = \text{Principal} \times \frac{\text{Interest rate}}{\text{Interest frequency}}$$

$$\times \frac{\text{Number of days since last interest payment day}}{\text{Number of days between last and next interest payment days}}$$

Calculations on: (i) the number of days since the last interest payment day; and (ii) the number of days between the last and next interest payment days are governed by different day count conventions:

- A 30/360 day count conversion unifies artificially that there are thirty days in a month and 360 days in a year. This day count convention was introduced in the early days to simplify the calculation of accrued interest when computers did not exist;

- An actual/actual day count convention adopts the actual number of days in a month and a year;

- An actual/360 day count convention adopts the actual number of days in a month but assumes that there are 360 days in a year; and

- An actual/365 day count convention adopts the actual number of days in a month but assumes that there are 365 days in a year.

Homogeneous Debt Portfolios

3

KEY CONCEPTS

- Debt portfolio
- Independent homogeneous portfolio
- Extreme case loss

- Gaussian copula
- Finite homogeneous portfolio
- Infinite homogeneous portfolio

3.1   Debt portfolio

In a real lending business, a professional lender lends to many borrowers. When the number of borrowers grows beyond hundred, the effort of managing the credit risk on an individual debt basis becomes large. In addition, the diversification effect arising from the investments in many debts also changes the risk characteristics of the debt investments as a whole. Therefore, the concept of debt portfolio emerges.

A debt portfolio is a collection of debts lent to many borrowers from the same lender. The default loss of a debt portfolio is essentially a result of the joint defaults of individual debts in the portfolio. Similar to other financial investments, as an effect of diversification, the overall credit risk is reduced if the same total amount is divided and lent to two different borrowers instead of just one borrower. The overall credit risk is further reduced if the same total amount is divided and lent to many different borrowers instead of just two borrowers. As such, for a debt portfolio, the diversification effect, which is characterized by: (i) the concentration of debts; and (ii) the default dependency among borrowers, essentially introduces a third dimension to the characterization of credit risk.

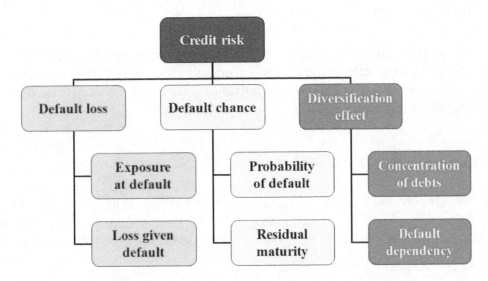

Figure 3.1   Credit risk factors of a debt portfolio

3.2   Portfolio one-year expected loss

The sum of the 1-year ELs of all debts in a portfolio is referred to as the portfolio 1-year EL which is a natural extension of the 1-year EL to a debt portfolio from a single debt.[7] For a debt portfolio comprising NOB debts from NOB different borrowers, the portfolio 1-year EL is:

$$\text{Portfolio 1-year EL} = \sum_{k=1}^{NOB} \text{1-year EL}_k$$

$$= \sum_{k=1}^{NOB} \left\{ \text{EAD}_k \times \text{LGD}_k \times \text{Min}\left[\text{PD}_k, 1 - \left(1 - \text{PD}_k\right)^{RM_k} \right] \right\}$$

$$\approx \sum_{k=1}^{NOB} \left(\text{EAD}_k \times \text{LGD}_k \times \text{PD}_k \times \text{Min}\left[1, RM_k\right] \right)$$

Consider a debt portfolio comprising only one debt with credit risk factors EAD USD 10,000, LGD 90 percent, PD 3 percent and RM one year. The portfolio 1-year EL is simply:

$$10,000 \times 90\% \times 3\% \times 1 = \text{USD } 270$$

Consider another debt portfolio comprising two debts lent to two different borrowers, each with credit risk factors EAD USD 5,000, LGD 90 percent, PD 3 percent and RM one year. Again, the portfolio EAD is:

$$5,000 + 5,000 = \text{USD } 10,000$$

and the portfolio 1-year EL is also:

$$5,000 \times 90\% \times 3\% \times 1 + 5,000 \times 90\% \times 3\% \times 1 = \text{USD } 270$$

Apparently, the portfolio 1-year EL has yet to capture the reduction in credit risk arising from the diversification effect and is not an effective credit risk measure for a debt portfolio. In fact, the formula of the portfolio 1-year EL is constructed without incorporating the diversification effect in any credit risk factors.

3.3   Homogeneous portfolio ★★★

A homogeneous portfolio is a debt portfolio comprising at least thirty debts with identical characteristics in terms of EAD, LGD, PD and default dependency among borrowers. The RMs are unified artificially to one year across all debts, subject to three criteria that:

---

[7] In contrast to the 1-year EL, the concept of the EL cannot be extended to a debt portfolio.

- The lender who invests in debts with maturity longer than one year or without fixed maturity will review and control the credit risk of the debts at the end of the following one year;
- The lender who invests in debts with maturity shorter than one year will re-invest the proceeds at maturity in similar debts up to one year; and
- The debts with maturity shorter than one year accounts for the minority of the homogeneous portfolio, e.g., below 10 percent;

The concentration of debts of a homogeneous portfolio is measured by the number of borrowers ("NOB"). A small NOB indicates that the homogeneous portfolio is highly concentrated. Conversely, a large NOB indicates that the homogeneous portfolio is highly granular.

The default dependency between any two borrowers in a homogeneous portfolio is quantified by a copula correlation coefficient, to be explained later in this chapter. Each debt in the portfolio contributes the same EAD to the homogeneous portfolio and the portfolio EAD is thus equal to the arithmetic product of the EAD and NOB. In summary, the credit risk of a homogeneous portfolio is characterized by five credit risk factors, namely: the portfolio EAD, LGD, PD, NOB and CCC.

The construction of a homogeneous portfolio facilitates the development of the portfolio credit risk theory due to its simplicity and highly analytical tractability.

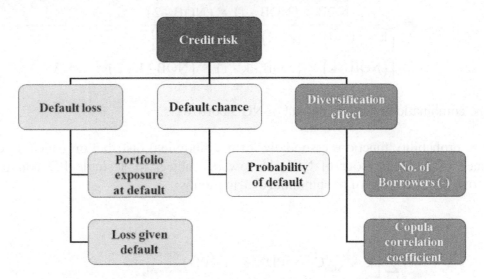

Figure 3.2   Credit risk factors of a homogeneous portfolio

3.4   Independent homogeneous portfolio

In order to introduce an effective portfolio credit risk measure, an independent homogeneous portfolio, being a hypothetical homogeneous portfolio with the default of borrowers totally independent of one another, is proposed. This is an extremity of a homogeneous portfolio in which the default dependency among borrowers is suppressed completely.

With an independent homogeneous portfolio, the probability of experiencing exactly k defaults out of NOB borrowers is:

$$\text{Probability of k defaults out of NOB borrowers} = {}_{NOB}C_k \times PD^k \times (1 - PD)^{NOB-k}$$

and the cumulative probability of up to M defaults out of NOB borrowers is:

$$\text{Cumulative probability of up to M defaults out of NOB borrowers}$$
$$= \sum_{k=1}^{M} \left[{}_{NOB}C_k \times PD^k \times (1 - PD)^{NOB-k} \right]$$

where

$$_{NOB}C_k = \frac{NOB \times (NOB - 1) \times (NOB - 2) \times ... \times 3 \times 2 \times 1}{\left[k \times (k - 1) \times (k - 2) \times ... \times 3 \times 2 \times 1 \right] \times \left[(NOB - k) \times (NOB - k - 1) \times (NOB - k - 2) \times ... \times 3 \times 2 \times 1 \right]}$$

is the combination of k defaults out of NOB borrowers.

These probability functions essentially form a binominal distribution which describes the chance of k defaults out of NOB borrowers, subject to a single PD common to all borrowers. The mean of the binomial distribution is:

$$\text{Mean} = E[k]$$
$$= \sum_{k=0}^{NOB} \left[k \times {}_{NOB}C_k \times PD^k \times (1 - PD)^{NOB-k} \right]$$
$$= PD \times NOB$$

suggesting that the expected default rate is simply equal to the PD.

The extreme case number of defaults is defined as the maximum number of defaults Q out of NOB borrowers with the most severe 0.1 percent situations excluded, i.e., the cumulative probability of up Q defaults out of NOB borrowers is 99.9%. This extreme case number of defaults Q is obtained by solving the equation:

$$\sum_{k=1}^{Q} \left[{}_{NOB}C_k \times PD^k \times \left(1 - PD\right)^{NOB-k} \right] = 99.9\%$$

In Microsoft Excel, the extreme case number of defaults could be obtained easily with the function Critbinom(…).

$$Q = \text{Critbinom(NOB, PD, 99.9\%)}$$

In most situations, as a result of the compounding effect to the joint default probability, the extreme case number of defaults is relatively small when compared to the NOB.

The extreme case default rate ("XCDR") is defined as the ratio between Q and NOB.

$$XCDR = \frac{Q}{NOB}$$

The extreme case loss ("XCL") is defined as the arithmetic product of the portfolio EAD, LGD and XCDR.

$$XCL = \text{Portfolio EAD} \times \text{LGD} \times \text{XCDR}$$

Economically, the XCL represents the maximum potential default loss with the most severe 0.1 percent situations excluded. It is a default loss to be observed under a severe and rare situation. A default loss over the XCL will occur only on average once every one thousand years. The XCL increases with increasing portfolio EAD, LGD and PD, and decreases with increasing NOB, thus serving as a good credit risk measure of an independent homogeneous portfolio.

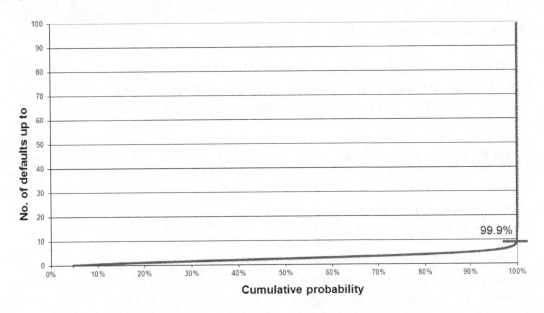

Figure 3.3   Extreme case number of defaults

3.5   Modelling default dependency

The default dependency of two borrowers is modelled by a mathematical framework Gaussian copula which transforms the defaults of many borrowers from a joint Bernoulli distribution where the default dependency among borrowers is not well defined into a joint standard normal distribution where the dependency among random variables is well defined by a correlation coefficient.

3.5.1   Default of a borrower

Modelling the default of a borrower in one year can be accomplished in several ways by different types of random variables, starting from the simplest Bernoulli random variable to the most mathematically convenient standard normal random variable.

Bernoulli random variable

The default of a borrower in one year can be modelled most simply by a Bernoulli random variable characterized by a PD. The Bernoulli random variable returns a value 1 representing the default of a borrower with probability PD and a value 0 representing the survival of a borrower with probability 1 - PD.

Standard uniform random variable

Alternatively, the default of a borrower in one year can be modelled by a standard uniform random variable. Define a standard uniform random variable u with its value ranging from 0 to 1. Given the PD of a borrower, if u is less than or equal to the PD, the borrower is taken to be in default. If u is larger than the PD, the borrower is considered to be in survival.

Standard normal random variable

The default of a borrower in one year can also be modelled by a standard normal random variable. Define a standard normal random variable z as a real number. The value of the cumulative standard normal distribution function corresponding to z is calculated.

$$\Phi(z) = \frac{1}{\sqrt{2\pi}} \int_{-\infty}^{z} \exp(-\frac{\tau^2}{2})d\tau$$

Given the PD of a borrower, if $\Phi(z)$ is less than or equal to the PD, then the borrower is taken to be in default. Otherwise, the borrower is considered to be in survival.

Among the above three types of random variables, the standard normal random variable is the most mathematically convenient for modelling the joint defaults of many borrowers in a debt portfolio since the dependency between any two standard normal random variables is well quantified by a correlation coefficient. This transformation between a

Bernoulli random variable and a standard normal random variable introduces the framework of Gaussian copula.

3.5.2   Gaussian copula

Gaussian copula is essentially a mathematical technique that aims at modelling the dependency of a group of random variables not belonging to the families of normal or student-t distribution since the correlation coefficient is only an effective quantification of dependency between any two normal random variables or two student-t random variables.

Default of a borrower

The default of a borrower in one year can be modelled by two independent standard normal random variables.

Assume that y and z are two independent standard normal random variables. Define a new random variable x such that:

$$x = y\sqrt{\rho} + z\sqrt{1 - \rho}$$
$$0 \le \rho \le 1$$

Then

$$
\begin{aligned}
E[x] &= E\left[y\sqrt{\rho} + z\sqrt{1 - \rho} \right] \\
&= E[y] \times \sqrt{\rho} + E[z] \times \sqrt{1 - \rho} \\
&= 0 \times \sqrt{\rho} + 0 \times \sqrt{1-\rho} \\
&= 0
\end{aligned}
$$

$$
\begin{aligned}
Var[x] &= Var\left[y\sqrt{\rho} + z\sqrt{1 - \rho} \right] \\
&= Var[y] \times \left(\sqrt{\rho} \right)^2 + Var[z] \times \left(\sqrt{1 - \rho} \right)^2 \\
&= 1 \times \rho + 1 \times (1 - \rho) \\
&= 1
\end{aligned}
$$

$$SD[x] = \sqrt{Var[x]} = 1$$

Since x as the sum of two scaled standard normal random variables is also a normal random variable and the mean of x is 0 while the standard deviation of x is 1, the random variable x is also a standard normal random variable and ranges from -∞ to ∞ while the corresponding value of the cumulative standard normal distribution function ranges from 0 to 1.   Thus, if the standard normal random variable x results in a value of the cumulative standard normal distribution function below or equal to the PD, the borrower is taken to be in default.   Otherwise, the borrower is considered to be in survival.

Joint default of two borrowers

Assume that there are two borrowers with the same PD.   The joint default of these two borrowers in one year can be modelled by one common standard normal random variable and two specific standard normal random variables.

Let y be a common standard normal random variable and z_1, z_2 be two specific standard normal random variables.   Define two new random variables x_1 and x_2 such that:

$$x_1 = y\sqrt{\rho} + z_1\sqrt{1-\rho}$$
$$x_2 = y\sqrt{\rho} + z_2\sqrt{1-\rho}$$
$$0 \le \rho \le 1$$

Then

$$\begin{aligned}
\text{Cov}[x_1, x_2] &= \text{Cov}\left[y\sqrt{\rho} + z_1\sqrt{1-\rho}, y\sqrt{\rho} + z_2\sqrt{1-\rho}\right] \\
&= \text{Cov}[y, y] \times \sqrt{\rho} \times \sqrt{\rho} + \text{Cov}[y, z_1] \times \sqrt{\rho} \times \sqrt{1-\rho} \\
&\quad + \text{Cov}[y, z_2] \times \sqrt{\rho} \times \sqrt{1-\rho} + \text{Cov}[z_1, z_2] \times \sqrt{1-\rho} \times \sqrt{1-\rho} \\
&= 1 \times \rho + 0 + 0 + 0 \\
&= \rho
\end{aligned}$$

$$\text{Corr}[x_1, x_2] = \frac{\text{Cov}[x_1, x_2]}{\text{SD}[x_1] \times \text{SD}[x_2]} = \frac{\rho}{1 \times 1} = \rho$$

Following the same argument in the last section, the random variables x_1 and x_2 are also standard normal random variables:

- with correlation coefficient ρ;
- ranging from $-\infty$ to ∞; and
- after substituted into the cumulative standard normal distribution function, will result in two values ranging from 0 to 1.

If the standard normal random variable x_1 results in a value $\Phi(x_1)$ in the cumulative standard normal distribution function below or equal to the PD, the first borrower is taken to be in default.   If the standard normal random variable x_2 results in a value $\Phi(x_2)$ in the cumulative standard normal distribution function below or equal to the PD, the second borrower is taken to be in default. The default dependency between the two borrowers is quantified by ρ, referred to as the copula correlation coefficient ("CCC"). A larger CCC drives more impact to the random variables x_1 and x_2 from the common random variable y. This results in a higher likelihood of joint default of the two borrowers.

Joint default of NOB borrowers

Assume that there are NOB homogeneous borrowers with the same PD and CCC among all borrowers.

The defaults among the NOB homogeneous borrowers in one year can be modelled by one common standard normal random variable and NOB specific standard normal random variables.

Let y be a common standard normal variable and z_1, z_2, z_3, ... z_{NOB} be NOB specific standard normal random variables. Define NOB new random variables x_1, x_2, x_3, ... x_{NOB} such that:

$$x_1 = y\sqrt{\rho} + z_1\sqrt{1 - \rho}$$
$$x_2 = y\sqrt{\rho} + z_2\sqrt{1 - \rho}$$
$$x_3 = y\sqrt{\rho} + z_3\sqrt{1 - \rho}$$

$$.$$
$$.$$
$$.$$

$$x_{NOB} = y\sqrt{\rho} + z_{NOB}\sqrt{1 - \rho}$$
$$0 \leq \rho \leq 1$$

Then, all random variables x_1, x_2, x_3, ... x_{NOB} are standard normal random variables:

- with correlation coefficient ρ between any two of them;
- ranging from $-\infty$ to ∞; and
- after substituted into the cumulative standard normal distribution function, will result in NOB values ranging from 0 to 1.

If a random variable x_k results in a value $\Phi(x_k)$ in the cumulative standard normal distribution function below or equal to the PD, borrower k is taken to be in default. The default dependency between any two borrowers is quantified by a single CCC = ρ. A larger CCC drives more impact to the random variables x_k from the common random variable y. This results in a higher chance of the joint default of the NOB borrowers.

The standard normal random variable y is considered as a systematic risk factor that drives the common credit risk among all borrowers and each of the standard normal random variables z_1, z_2, z_3, ... z_{NOB} is a specific risk factor representing the idiosyncratic credit risk associated with each individual borrowers. The correlation coefficient between y and x_k is simply $\sqrt{CCC}$. The impact from the systematic risk factor y to a standard normal random variable x_k increases with increasing CCC.

3.5.3 Copula correlation coefficient ★★★

The determination of the CCC is critical to modelling the joint default of borrowers in a homogeneous portfolio. Nevertheless, in most practical situations, the CCC is unobservable and cannot be derived from observable parameters. For the regulatory purpose, the Basel Committee on Banking Supervision takes an empirical approach to calibrate a unified set of empirical relationships between the CCC and PD for six types of exposures with historical data from a number of internationally active banks. These relationships suggest a common CCC structure under a bank's regular lending operations on a longer term basis. When there is no alternative, these formulas become a feasible approach to derive the proxies of the CCCs.

Under the Basel III framework, a treatment of the CCCs to six types of exposures with RM one year is proposed.

Residential mortgage

For a homogeneous portfolio of residential mortgages, the CCC is 0.15.

Qualifying revolving retail exposure

For a homogeneous portfolio of qualifying revolving retail exposures, the CCC is 0.04.

Other retail exposure

Any retail exposure other than residential mortgage and qualifying revolving retail exposure is classified as other retail exposure. The CCC for a homogeneous portfolio of other retail exposures is calculated as:

$$CCC = 0.16 - 0.13\left[\frac{1 - \exp(-35PD)}{1 - \exp(-35)}\right] \approx 0.03 + 0.13\exp(-35PD)$$

which ranges from 0.03 when PD = 1 to 0.16 when PD = 0.

Institution exposure

For a homogeneous portfolio of debts issued by institutions, the CCC is calculated as:

$$CCC = 0.24 - 0.12\left[\frac{1 - \exp(-50PD)}{1 - \exp(-50)}\right] \approx 0.12\left[1 + \exp(-50PD)\right]$$

which ranges from 0.12 when PD = 1 to 0.24 when PD = 0.

SME corporate exposure

For a homogeneous portfolio of debts issued by small and medium enterprises, each with annual revenue (S in EUR mn) between EUR 5 mn and EUR 50 mn, the CCC is adjusted downwards to:

$$CCC = 0.24 - 0.12\left[\frac{1 - \exp(-50PD)}{1 - \exp(-50)}\right] + \frac{S - 50}{1125} \approx 0.12\left[1 + \exp(-50PD)\right] + \frac{S - 50}{1125}$$

which ranges from 0.0756 when PD = 1 and S = 0 to 0.24 when PD = 0 and S = 50.

Large financial institution exposure

For a homogeneous portfolio of debts issued by large financial institutions, each with total assets more than USD 100 bn, the CCC is adjusted upwards to:

$$CCC = 1.25\left\{0.24 - 0.12\left[\frac{1 - \exp(-50PD)}{1 - \exp(-50)}\right]\right\} \approx 0.15\left[1 + \exp(-50PD)\right]$$

which ranges from 0.15 when PD = 1 to 0.3 when PD = 0.

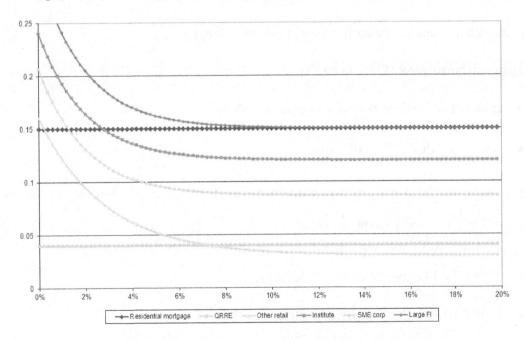

Figure 3.4   CCCs under the Basel III framework

The CCC formulas for instutions suggest two properties of systematic default dependencies:

- The CCC increases with increasing firm size. A larger institution forms part of an economy and in turn has a higher dependency on the overall state of the economy. A smaller institution is more likely to default on its own reasons; and

- The CCC decreases with increasing PD. Intuitively, a larger PD indicates a higher idiosyncratic risk of a borrower whose credit risk depends less on the overall state of the economy but more on a borrower's own financial condition.

3.6   Finite homogeneous portfolio

A finite homogeneous portfolio is a homogeneous portfolio with a unified default dependency existing among a finite number of borrowers.

The extreme case number of defaults of a finite homogeneous portfolio can be derived by Monte Carlo simulation. The number of defaults is simulated directly by a computer programme to form a distribution. The extreme case number of defaults is then set as the maximum number of defaults with the most severe 0.1 percent situations excluded.

The extreme case number of defaults of a finite homogeneous portfolio with NOB borrowers is derived with Monte Carlo simulation by taking the following steps:

- Generate a common standard normal random number y;

- For each borrower k (k = 1 to NOB),

  - generate a standard normal random number z_k;

  - set $x_k = y\sqrt{CCC} + z_k\sqrt{1 - CCC}$;

  - calculate the value of the cumulative standard normal distribution function
    $$\Phi\left(x_k\right) = \frac{1}{\sqrt{2\pi}} \int_{-\infty}^{x_k} \exp(-\frac{\tau^2}{2})d\tau \;;$$

  - if $\Phi(x_k) \leq$ PD, then borrower k defaults;

  - if $\Phi(x_k) >$ PD, then borrower k survives.

- Register the number of defaults; and

- Repeat the above simulation steps for a sufficient large number of times, e.g., one million times.

The extreme case number of defaults of the finite homogeneous portfolio is the maximum number of defaults with the most severe 0.1 percent situations excluded. With the simulated number of defaults registered in a Microsoft Excel worksheet, the extreme case number of defaults can be obtained easily with the function Percentile(…), i.e.:

Extreme case no. of defaults = Percentile(No. of defaults, 99.9%)

Then

$$XCDR = \frac{\text{Extreme case no. of defaults}}{\text{NOB}}$$
$$XCL = \text{Portfolio EAD} \times \text{LGD} \times \text{XCDR}$$

The XCL represents the maximum default loss with the most severe 0.1 percent situations excluded. It increases with increasing portfolio EAD, LGD, PD and CCC, and decreases with increasing NOB, thus serving as a good credit risk measure of a finite homogeneous portfolio.

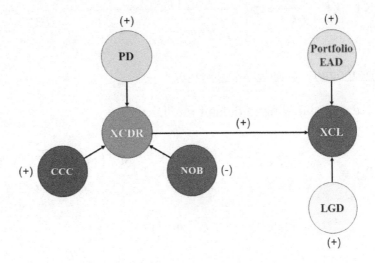

Figure 3.5   XCL of a finite homogeneous portfolio

3.7   Infinite homogeneous portfolio ★★★

An infinite homogeneous portfolio is a hypothetical homogeneous portfolio with an infinite number of homogeneous borrowers. This is an extremity of a homogeneous portfolio in which the concentration of debts approaches zero.

An infinite homogeneous portfolio is utilized to approximate analytically a homogeneous debt portfolio comprising a large number of debts, e.g., three hundred or more, with similar credit risk characteristics. When the NOB in a homogeneous portfolio approaches infinity, the default rate, which is the percentage of borrowers in default, follows a Vasicek default rate ("DR") distribution with the following properties:

Probability density function

The default rate density at default rate DR is:

$$f(DR) = \sqrt{\frac{1 - CCC}{CCC}} \exp\left\{ \frac{\left[\Phi^{-1}(DR)\right]^2}{2} - \frac{\left[\Phi^{-1}(DR)\sqrt{1 - CCC} - \Phi^{-1}(PD)\right]^2}{2CCC} \right\}$$

Cumulative probability distribution function

The cumulative probability up to default rate DR:

$$F(DR) = \int_0^{DR} \sqrt{\frac{1 - CCC}{CCC}} \exp\left\{ \frac{\left[\Phi^{-1}(\tau)\right]^2}{2} - \frac{\left[\Phi^{-1}(\tau)\sqrt{1 - CCC} - \Phi^{-1}(PD)\right]^2}{2CCC} \right\} d\tau$$

$$= \Phi\left[\frac{\Phi^{-1}(DR)\sqrt{1 - CCC} - \Phi^{-1}(PD)}{\sqrt{CCC}} \right]$$

Mean

The mean of the Vasicek default rate distribution is calculated as:

$$E[DR] = \int_0^1 \left[DR \times f(DR) \right] d(DR)$$

$$= \int_0^1 DR \sqrt{\frac{1 - CCC}{CCC}} \exp\left\{ \frac{\left[\Phi^{-1}(DR)\right]^2}{2} - \frac{\left[\Phi^{-1}(DR)\sqrt{1 - CCC} - \Phi^{-1}(PD)\right]^2}{2CCC} \right\} d(DR)$$

$$= PD$$

Extreme case default rate

The XCDR is defined implicitly by the cumulative default rate distribution function as:

$$99.9\% = \Phi\left[\frac{\Phi^{-1}(XCDR)\sqrt{1-CCC}-\Phi^{-1}(PD)}{\sqrt{CCC}}\right]$$

With some simple algebra,

$$XCDR = \Phi\left[\frac{\Phi^{-1}(PD)+\Phi^{-1}(99.9\%)\sqrt{CCC}}{\sqrt{1-CCC}}\right]$$

The XCDR increases with increasing PD and CCC.

Similar to the independent homogeneous portfolio, the XCL of an infinite homogeneous portfolio is defined as the arithmetic product of the portfolio EAD, LGD and XCDR.

$$XCL = \text{Portfolio EAD} \times LGD \times XCDR$$

The XCL represents the maximum default loss with the most severe 0.1 percent situations excluded. It increases with increasing portfolio EAD, LGD, PD and CCC, thus serving as a good credit risk measure of an infinite homogeneous portfolio.

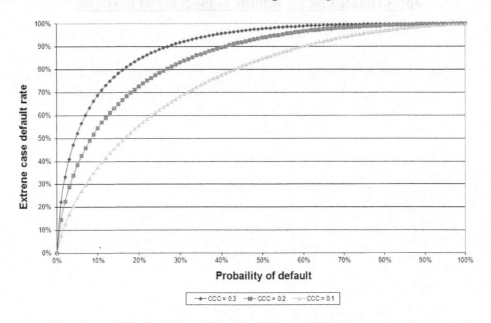

Figure 3.6   Extreme case default rate

3.7.1   Application of infinite homogeneous portfolio   ★★★

Infinite homogeneous portfolio is the most important model in the theory of debt portfolio because the default rate distribution can be well expressed in a simple analytical formula. It is adopted frequently by financial institutions to approximate debt portfolios which comprise many similar but small debts lent to many similar but different borrowers.

Table 3.1 sets out the conditions of the credit risk factors with which a real debt portfolio may be well approximated by an infinite homogeneous portfolio without incurring significant model error. Section 4.5 of Chapter 4 provides further details.

Credit risk factor	Criteria
EAD	Coefficient of variation ≤ 10%
LGD	Coefficient of variation ≤ 10%
PD	Same credit rating or FICO score category
RM	Longer term debts subject to annual review and control Non-fixed term debts subject to annual review and control Short term debts subject to re-investment up to one year Short term debts ≤ 10%
NOB	≥ 300
CCC	Same CCC formula

Table 3.1   Credit risk factors of a debt portfolio well approximated by an infinite homogeneous portfolio

3.8 Diversification effect ★★★

Diversification effectively transforms the default loss of the same debt investment amount to a continue distribution of a debt portfolio with the large default loss occurring only at the extremity, from a jump distribution of a single debt with a sudden default loss. The specific risks of the debts in the portfolio are reduced, leaving only the systematic risk as the dominating factor which exhibits a more favourable risk characteristic to a lender.

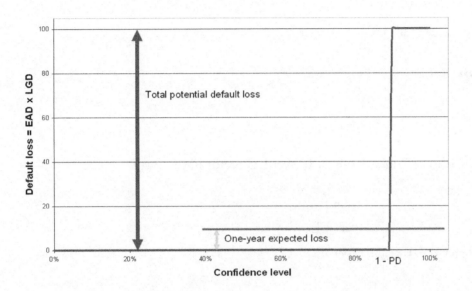

Figure 3.7   Default loss distribution of a single debt

On the other hand, the diversification effect comes at an operational cost of managing many small debts lent to a large number of borrowers. Thus, in practice, a lender must strike a balance between the benefit and cost of diversification.

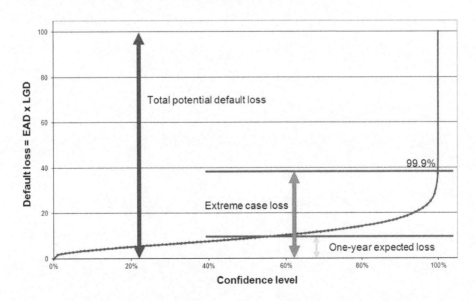

Figure 3.8   Default loss distribution of a debt portfolio

Appendix 3.1   Debt basket

A debt basket is a collection of debts lent to a small number of borrowers from the same lender. Each debt in the basket is equipped with its own EAD, LGD, PD, RM, EL and 1-year EL.

The credit risk of a basket of NOB debts can be represented by an NOB-dimensional basket EL vector in the form:

$$\textbf{Basket EL} = \begin{bmatrix} EL_1 \\ EL_2 \\ EL_3 \\ \vdots \\ EL_{NOB} \end{bmatrix}$$

or an NOB-dimensional one-year basket EL vector in the form:

$$\textbf{Basket 1-year EL} = \begin{bmatrix} \text{1-year } EL_1 \\ \text{1-year } EL_2 \\ \text{1-year } EL_3 \\ \vdots \\ \text{1-year } EL_{NOB} \end{bmatrix}$$

Appendix 3.2   Probability distribution of number of defaults of a finite homogeneous portfolio

The probability distribution of the number of defaults of a finite homogeneous portfolio is subject to a correlated binominal distribution parameterized by both the NOB and CCC, and characterized by the following statistical properties:

Probability mass function

Probability of k defaults out of NOB borrowers

$$
= \frac{{}_{NOB}C_k}{\sqrt{2\pi}} \int_{-\infty}^{\infty} \frac{\exp\left(-\frac{\tau^2}{2}\right)\left\{\Phi\left[\dfrac{\Phi^{-1}(PD) - \tau\sqrt{CCC}}{\sqrt{1 - CCC}}\right]\right\}^k}{\left\{1 - \Phi\left[\dfrac{\Phi^{-1}(PD) - \tau\sqrt{CCC}}{\sqrt{1 - CCC}}\right]\right\}^{NOB-k}} \, d\tau
$$

$$
\approx \frac{{}_{NOB}C_k}{\sqrt{2\pi}} \int_{-5}^{5} \frac{\exp\left(-\frac{\tau^2}{2}\right)\left\{\Phi\left[\dfrac{\Phi^{-1}(PD) - \tau\sqrt{CCC}}{\sqrt{1 - CCC}}\right]\right\}^k}{\left\{1 - \Phi\left[\dfrac{\Phi^{-1}(PD) - \tau\sqrt{CCC}}{\sqrt{1 - CCC}}\right]\right\}^{NOB-k}} \, d\tau
$$

where τ follows a standard normal distribution function. As the improper integral cannot be expressed in simple functions, it is calculated by numerical integration with the lower and upper limits set to -5 and 5 respectively. This range of integration covers over 99.9999 percent occurrences of τ.

Cumulative probability distribution function

Cumulative probability of up to M defaults out of NOB borrowers

$$
= \sum_{k=0}^{M} \left[\frac{{}_{NOB}C_k}{\sqrt{2\pi}} \int_{-\infty}^{\infty} \left(\frac{\exp\left(-\frac{\tau}{2}\right)\left\{\Phi\left[\dfrac{\Phi^{-1}(PD) - \tau\sqrt{CCC}}{\sqrt{1-CCC}}\right]\right\}^k}{\left\{1 - \Phi\left[\dfrac{\Phi^{-1}(PD) - \tau\sqrt{CCC}}{\sqrt{1-CCC}}\right]\right\}^{NOB-k}} \right) d\tau \right]
$$

Mean

$$E[k] = \sum_{k=0}^{NOB} \left[k \times \frac{{}_{NOB}C_k}{\sqrt{2\pi}} \int_{-\infty}^{\infty} \left(\exp\left(-\frac{\tau^2}{2}\right) \left\{ \Phi\left[\frac{\Phi^{-1}(PD) - \tau\sqrt{CCC}}{\sqrt{1-CCC}} \right] \right\}^k \right. \right.$$
$$\left. \left. \left\{ 1 - \Phi\left[\frac{\Phi^{-1}(PD) - \tau\sqrt{CCC}}{\sqrt{1-CCC}} \right] \right\}^{NOB-k} \right) d\tau \right]$$

$$= PD \times NOB$$

Similar to the independent homogeneous portfolio, the extreme case number of defaults of a finite homogeneous portfolio is defined as the maximum number of defaults Q out of NOB borrowers with the most severe 0.1 percent situations excluded, i.e., the cumulative probability of up Q defaults out of NOB borrowers is 99.9%.

$$\sum_{k=0}^{Q} \left[\frac{{}_{NOB}C_k}{\sqrt{2\pi}} \int_{-\infty}^{\infty} \left(\exp\left(-\frac{\tau^2}{2}\right) \left\{ \Phi\left[\frac{\Phi^{-1}(PD) - \tau\sqrt{CCC}}{\sqrt{1-CCC}} \right] \right\}^k \right. \right.$$
$$\left. \left. \left\{ 1 - \Phi\left[\frac{\Phi^{-1}(PD) - \tau\sqrt{CCC}}{\sqrt{1-CCC}} \right] \right\}^{NOB-k} \right) d\tau \right] = 99.9\%$$

The XCDR is the ratio between Q and NOB.

$$XCDR = \frac{Q}{NOB}$$

The XCL is the arithmetic product of the portfolio EAD, LGD and XCDR.

$$XCL = Portfolio\ EAD \times LGD \times XCDR$$

Heterogeneous Debt Portfolios

KEY CONCEPTS

- Moody's binominal expansion technique
- Total heterogeneous portfolio
- Structured heterogeneous portfolio

4.1 Heterogeneous portfolio ★★★

A debt portfolio that is not homogeneous may be modelled as a heterogeneous portfolio which is characterized by the following properties:

- Debts in the portfolio (i) have various EADs and LGDs; and (ii) are lent to many borrowers with various PDs;

- Several debts lent to a single borrower are combined into one consolidated debt with the EAD equal to the sum of all component EADs and the LGD equal to the EAD weighted average of the component LGDs;

- The lender who invests in debts with maturity longer than one year or without fixed maturity will review and control the credit risk of the debts at the end of the following one year;

- The lender who invests in debts with maturity shorter than one year will re-invest the proceeds at maturity in similar debts up to one year;

- The debts with maturity shorter than one year accounts for the minority of the portfolio, e.g., below 10 percent;

- The NOB in the portfolio is sufficiently large, e.g., equal to or more than 30;[8] and

- The default dependency among borrowers is not unified or unknown.

Due to the heterogeneity of the debt portfolio, there is no uniform solution to calculate the credit risk of a heterogeneous portfolio. Instead, partial solutions are developed by relaxing some of the constraints to a homogeneous portfolio. As such, the model error is relatively large since the theory underlying the heterogeneous portfolio is less developed.

---

[8] It is straight forward for a lender to manage his debt investments on an individual debt basis when the total number of debts in a basket is small, e.g., less than 30.

4.2   Moody's binominal expansion technique

Moody's adopted the binominal expansion technique ("BET") in the middle nineties to calculate the credit risk of a corporate debt portfolio by relaxing the assumption of total default independency among borrowers in an independent homogeneous portfolio.

Under the BET, default dependency is assumed to exist only among corporate borrowers in the same industry and no default dependency is assumed for two corporate borrowers in two different industries. Furthermore, the BET recognizes that within the same industry, the diversification effect increases with increasing NOB but decreases with increasing default dependency. Therefore, if the default dependency is suppressed completely, an alternative debt portfolio with the same diversification effect can be constructed by reducing the NOB to a smaller number, referred to as the diversity score.

Despite the lack of a sound theoretical basis, the BET advocates a simple methodology to arrive at a diversity score for the corporate borrowers in the same industry. To derive a diversity score, the NOBs are first arranged into a triangular grid in Table 4.1.

	1	2	3	4	5	6	7	8	9	10
1	1									
2	2	3								
3	4	5	6							
4	7	8	9	10						
5	11	12	13	14	15					
6	16	17	18	19	20	21				
7	22	23	24	25	26	27	28			
8	29	30	31	32	33	34	35	36		
9	37	38	39	40	41	42	43	44	45	
10	46	47	48	49	50	51	52	53	54	55

Table 4.1   Triangular NOB grid

Then for each NOB, a diversity score is calculated with a simple formula:

$$\text{Diversity score} = \text{Row number} - 1 + \frac{\text{Column number}}{\text{Row number}}$$

This procedure arrives at a set of corresponding diversity scores in Table 4.2.

	1	2	3	4	5	6	7	8	9	10
1	1.00									
2	1.50	2.00								
3	2.33	2.67	3.00							
4	3.25	3.50	3.75	4.00						
5	4.20	4.40	4.60	4.80	5.00					
6	5.17	5.33	5.50	5.67	5.83	6.00				
7	6.14	6.29	6.43	6.57	6.71	6.86	7.00			
8	7.13	7.25	7.38	7.50	7.63	7.75	7.88	8.00		
9	8.11	8.22	8.33	8.44	8.56	8.67	8.78	8.89	9.00	
10	9.10	9.20	9.30	9.40	9.50	9.60	9.70	9.80	9.90	10

Table 4.2   Diversity scores

In a debt portfolio, the corporate borrowers are first classified into one of the thirty-five industries defined by Moody's Investors Service in Table 4.3. Then for each industry, a diversity score is calculated. The sum of all diversity scores in individual industries then becomes the diversity score of the debt portfolio. This diversity score is treated as an equivalent NOB in an independent homogeneous portfolio to calculate the XCL.

1.	Aerospace and defence	19.	High technology industries
2.	Automotive	20.	Hotel, gaming and leisure
3.	Banking	21.	Media: advertising, printing and publishing
4.	Beverage, food and tobacco		
5.	Capital equipment	22.	Media: broadcasting and subscription
6.	Chemicals, plastics and rubber	23.	Media: diversified and production
7.	Construction and building	24.	Metals and mining
8.	Consumer goods: durable	25.	Retail
9.	Consumer goods: non-durable	26.	Services: business
10.	Containers, packaging and glass	27.	Services: consumer
11.	Energy: electricity	28.	Government and public finance
12.	Energy: oil and gas	29.	Telecommunications
13.	Environmental industries	30.	Transportation: cargo
14.	Financial institution, retail: finance	31.	Transportation: consumer
15.	Financial institution, retail: insurance	32.	Utilities: electric
16.	Financial institution, retail: real estate	33.	Utilities: oil and gas
17.	Forest products and paper	34.	Utilities: water
18.	Healthcare and pharmaceuticals	35.	Wholesale

Table 4.3   Moody's industry classification scheme

4.3   Structured heterogeneous portfolio ★★★

A structured heterogeneous portfolio is a heterogeneous portfolio with the default dependency following the CCC structure proposed in the Basel III framework, i.e., for each debt k in the heterogeneous portfolio, a CCC_k is calculated according to one of the six CCC formulas set out in the Basel III framework.

The credit risk of a structured heterogeneous portfolio is also measured by the XCL which cannot be expressed in a closed form solution. Monte Carlo simulation thus becomes the dominating approach. The portfolio default loss is simulated directly by a computer programme to form a distribution of portfolio default loss. The XCL is then set as the maximum portfolio default loss with the most severe 0.1 percent situations excluded.

Following the setup of a structured heterogeneous portfolio with NOB borrowers, the XCL is derived with Monte Carlo simulation by taking the following steps:

- Generate a common standard normal random number y;

- For each borrower k (k = 1 to NOB),

    - generate a standard normal random number z_k;

    - set $x_k = y\sqrt{CCC_k} + z_k\sqrt{1 - CCC_k}$;

    - calculate the value of the cumulative standard normal distribution function
      $$\Phi\left(x_k\right) = \frac{1}{\sqrt{2\pi}} \int_{-\infty}^{x_k} \exp(-\frac{\tau^2}{2})d\tau \; ;$$

    - if $\Phi(x_k) \leq PD_k$, then borrower k defaults and a default loss equal to the arithmetic product of EAD_k and LGD_k is registered;

    - if $\Phi(x_k) > PD_k$, then borrower k survives and the default loss is zero.

- Compute the portfolio default loss as the sum of all default losses; and

- Repeat the above simulation steps for a sufficient large number of times, e.g., one million times.

The XCL of the structured heterogeneous portfolio is derived as the maximum portfolio default loss with the most severe 0.1 percent excluded. With the simulated portfolio default losses registered in a Microsoft Excel worksheet, the XCL can be obtained easily with the function Percentile(...), i.e.:

$$XCL = Percentile\left(Portfolio\ default\ loss,\ 99.9\%\right)$$

4.4 Total heterogeneous portfolio

A total heterogeneous portfolio is a heterogeneous portfolio with its default dependency not following the CCC structure proposed in the Basel III framework. This is the realistic situation in which the default dependency among borrowers is neither observable nor quantifiable. Under such situation, a single value of the XCL cannot be derived and Monte Carlo simulation is utilized to arrive at: (i) the lower bound of the XCL by assuming that the defaults of all borrowers are independent; and (ii) the upper bound of the XCL by assuming that the defaults of all borrowers are fully dependent on a single systematic standard normal random variable.

For a total heterogeneous portfolio with NOB borrowers, the lower bound of the XCL is derived with Monte Carlo simulation by taking the following steps:

- For each borrower k (k = 1 to NOB),

    - generate a standard normal random number z_k;

    - calculate the value of the cumulative standard normal distribution function
    $$\Phi\left(z_k\right) = \frac{1}{\sqrt{2\pi}} \int_{-\infty}^{z_k} \exp(-\frac{\tau^2}{2})d\tau \ ;$$

    - if $\Phi\left(z_k\right) \leq PD_k$, then borrower k defaults and a default loss equal to the arithmetic product of EAD_k and LGD_k is registered;

    - if $\Phi\left(z_k\right) > PD_k$, then borrower k survives and the default loss is zero.

- Compute the portfolio default loss as the sum of all default losses; and

- Repeat the above simulation steps for a sufficient large number of times, e.g., one million times.

With the simulated portfolio default losses registered in a Microsoft Excel worksheet, the lower bound of the XCL can be obtained easily as:

Lower bound of the XCL = Percentile(Portfolio default loss, 99.9%)

For a total heterogeneous portfolio with NOB borrowers, the upper bound of the XCL is derived with Monte Carlo simulation by taking the following steps:

- Generate a standard normal random number y;

- Calculate the value of the cumulative standard normal distribution function

$$\Phi(y) = \frac{1}{\sqrt{2\pi}} \int_{-\infty}^{y} \exp(-\frac{\tau^2}{2}) d\tau ;$$

- For each borrower k (k = 1 to NOB),

  - if $\Phi(y) \le PD_k$, then borrower k defaults and a default loss equal to the arithmetic product of EAD_k and LGD_k is registered;

  - if $\Phi(y) < PD_k$, then borrower k survives and the default loss is zero;

- Compute the portfolio default loss as the sum of all default losses; and

- Repeat the above simulation steps for a sufficient large number of times, e.g., one million times.

With the simulated portfolio default losses registered in a Microsoft Excel worksheet, the upper bound of the XCL can be obtained easily as:

$$\text{Upper bound of the XCL} = \text{Percentile}\left(\text{Portfolio default loss, } 99.9\%\right)$$

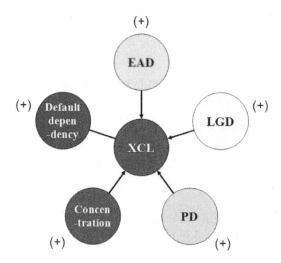

Figure 4.1   The XCL vs five credit risk factors

4.5 The XCL calculation in practice

So far, six different parametric approaches have been introduced for the calculation of the XCL. Table 4.4 summarises these parametric approaches. Practitioners may select the most appropriate approaches to calculate the credit risk of their debt portfolios, having considered the trade off between the computational simplicity and reality. The more assumptions made on a debt portfolio, the easier the calculation of the XCL is, but at a cost of higher model error.

In practice, the XCL can best be calculated by approximating a debt portfolio with either an infinite homogeneous portfolio or a structured heterogeneous portfolio.

For a debt portfolio comprising debts:

- with similar EADs with coefficient of variation[9] $\leq$ 10%;
- with similar LGDs with coefficient of variation $\leq$ 10%;
- with same credit rating or within same FICO score category;
- with maturity longer than one year or without fixed maturity will be subject to annual credit risk review and control;
- with maturity shorter than one year will be subject to re-investment of the proceeds at maturity in similar debts up to one year; and
- with the no. of RMs below one year less than 10%;
- lent to at least three hundred borrowers; and
- subject to the same CCC formula set out in the Basel III framework,

the debt portfolio is well approximated by an infinite homogeneous portfolio and the XCL is calculated in a closed form solution with the Vasicek default rate distribution.

Otherwise, the debt portfolio is approximated by a structured heterogeneous portfolio and the XCL is calculated with Monte Carlo simulation where the CCCs follow the structure proposed in the Basel III framework.

---

[9] The coefficient of variation is the ratio between the standard deviation and the mean of a group of samples.

	Homogeneous debt portfolio		
	Independent	**Finite**	**Infinite***
XCL	Simple closed form solution with binominal distribution	XCDR with Monte Carlo simulation	Closed form solution with Vasicek default rate distribution
EAD **LGD**	Coefficient of variation ≤ 10%		
PD	Same credit rating or FICO score category		
RM	• Debts with maturity longer than one year or without fixed maturity will be subject to annual credit risk review and control; • Debts with maturity shorter than one year will be subject to re-investment of the proceeds at maturity in similar debts up to one year; and • No. of RMs below one year ≤ 10%		
NOB	≥ 30[#]		≥ 300
CCC		Subject to the same CCC formula	

	Heterogeneous debt portfolio		
	BET	**Structured***	**Total**
XCL	Simple closed form solution with binominal distribution and diversity score	Single XCL with Monte Carlo simulation	Lower and upper bounds of the XCL with Monte Carlo simulation
EAD **LGD**	Coefficient of variation ≤ 10%		
PD	Same credit rating or FICO score category		
RM	• Debts with maturity longer than one year or without fixed maturity will be subject to annual credit risk review and control; • Debts with maturity shorter than one year will be subject to re-investment of the proceeds at maturity in similar debts up to one year; and • No. of RMs below one year ≤ 10%		
NOB	Diversity score ≥ 30	≥ 30[#]	
CCC	Captured through diversity score	CCC formulas in the Basel III framework	

* The choice of industry practices.

[#] The XCL is not an economically meaningful credit risk measure for a debt basket with less than 30 different borrowers. Under such situation, credit risk of the debts in a small basket could be well measured by the ELs and/or 1-year ELs on an individual debt basis.

Table 4.4 Summary of the XCL calculations ★★★

Appendix 4.1   Historical simulation

Historical simulation is a convenient non-parametric alternative to derive the XCL of a debt portfolio which comprises corporate bonds with their seniority and credit quality well characterized by a credit rating agency's seniority and credit rating scales respectively. Moreover, a sufficiently long and relevant history of LGDs and DRs must be available from the publication of the credit rating agency.

Assuming that a credit rating agency has published N years of LGDs for different seniorities and DRs for different credit ratings. For a homogeneous portfolio of corporate bonds characterized by a portfolio EAD, a seniority and a credit rating, the portfolio EAD is multiplied by the corresponding LGD and DR in each year. This arrives at N years of portfolio default losses. With the assumption that "history will repeat itself," the XCL is assigned as the maximum among these N portfolio default losses.

For a heterogeneous portfolio comprising many corporate bonds with different seniorities and credit ratings, the heterogeneous portfolio is divided into several homogeneous sub-portfolios, each with its own seniority and credit rating. Each sub-portfolio EAD is multiplied by the corresponding LGD and DR in each year to result in a sub-portfolio default loss. This results in several sub-portfolio losses. The total of sub-portfolio losses becomes the portfolio default loss. This arrives at N years of portfolio default losses. The XCL is then assigned as the maximum among these N portfolio default losses.

Credit Quality Monitoring 5

KEY CONCEPTS

- Individual borrowers monitoring
- Financial markets monitoring
- Large borrowers monitoring
- CapLogic SiFi credit index

5.1 Credit risk monitoring

Ideally, credit risk monitoring means tracking the credit risk by updating regularly the EL in case of a single debt and the XCL in case of a debt portfolio. If the credit risk is above his tolerance level, a lender then takes appropriate actions to bring the credit risk back to or below his tolerance level. This involves the frequent estimation of the credit risk with the six underlying credit risk factors: EAD, LGD, PD, RM, concentration of debts and default dependency.

Nevertheless, among these six credit risk factors, five of them are relatively stable and/or predictable, leaving only the PD which may vary in a broader range during the lending period as a result of the change in financial condition of a borrower. As such, in practice, most of the efforts are concentrated on credit quality monitoring which tracks the credit quality of borrowers.

5.2 Risk tolerance level

The risk tolerance level of a lender on a single debt is the maximum EL which the lender can accept. Since the EL cannot be observed directly in the real world (only the default loss is observable), the risk tolerance level of a lender is determined through an experiment in which a lender is provided a large number of debts with different EADs, LGDs, PDs and RMs to the lender. During the experiment, the lender agrees to invest in a debt when the EAD, LGD, PD, RM, default loss, default chance and EL are all admissible but refuses to invest a debt when any one of the EAD, LGD, PD, RM, default loss, default chance and EL is too large. The maximum of the ELs of the debts invested by the lender then becomes the risk tolerance level of the lender on a single debt.

The risk tolerance level of a lender on a debt portfolio is the maximum XCL which the lender can accept. Although the XCL cannot be observed in the real world, it can be well approximated by the maximum portfolio default loss within a period of one year. Therefore, a lender can easily determine his tolerance level on a debt portfolio by suggesting the maximum portfolio default loss which the lender can accept in one year.

Every lender is equipped with his own subjective risk tolerance level. A lender with limited funds has a tolerance level lower than that of a lender with abundant funds. Also a lender with more experience in credit risk management has a tolerance level higher than a lender with less experience. As such, there is no single framework to derive the risk tolerance level of a lender.

5.3   Individual borrowers monitoring

The credit quality of a borrower can be monitored conveniently by its updated credit quality indicators, e.g., credit rating for an institutional borrower and FICO score for a retail borrower.[10] By tabulating the credit quality indicators in a time series, the improvement or deterioration in credit quality of a borrower is observed.

However, credit ratings and FICO scores are updated usually on an annual basis or when there is a major credit event. This makes the monthly and/or quarterly credit monitoring less effective. Also, some borrowers have neither credit ratings nor FICO scores if they are not covered by credit rating agencies and retail credit bureaus. Therefore, internal credit assessment by a lender himself is necessary to supplement the external credit assessment.

Theoretically, any method used for internal credit assessment by a lender at debt origination can be utilized to monitor the credit quality by re-assessing the credit quality of a borrower, riding on the assumption that the most recent status of the explanatory variables of a borrower could be collected at any time similar to the moment when a debt is originated. Nevertheless, this assumption is far from reality since most borrowers will not provide updates of their financial information to their lenders except for the situation where contractual benefits are exchanged if updates are provided and/or contractual penalties are applied if updates are not provided.

In practice, a default event starts to emerge on the payment day when a borrower fails to pay the interest and/or principal in full. As such, a delay in interim interest payment demonstrates empirically the deterioration in credit quality of a borrower. Professional lenders thus design debts with regular interest payments, usually monthly for retail lending and monthly/quarterly/semi-annually/annually for corporate debts.

Some banks request their borrowers to open a regular savings account for monthly payroll collection purpose. The income, a critical explanatory variable of an individual borrower, is recorded by the lender through this payroll account. Taking it one step further, banks may request their borrowers to open an operating account which is utilized for all incoming and out-going cash transactions. In addition, all major financial investments are deposited into this operating account. Thus, the complete financial picture of a borrower is well displayed in front of the lender. A large amount of cash outflows over cash inflows will trigger the attention from a lender.

Typically, a bank may lend to a large number of different borrowers. Therefore, even though individual credit assessments can be conducted on an on-going basis by the lender,

---

[10] Details about credit rating and FICO will be discussed in detail in Chapter 7.

the abundant amount of credit assessment results make this micro approach of individual borrowers monitoring less efficient. In addition, individual credit assessments are not direct profit making activities but expensive in terms of resources. Therefore, regular individual borrowers monitoring is conducted on a less frequent basis, e.g., once a year for corporate borrower and once every three years for individual borrowers.

5.4   Financial markets monitoring   ★★★

Financial markets monitoring is an efficient macro approach to catch up the latest status of systematic credit risk facing a lender. Under the assumption that the debt portfolio of a professional lender is largely granular, the majority of the specific credit risk is diversified away, leaving the systematic credit risk as the dominating component.

Instead of assessing the credit quality of many individual borrowers, financial markets monitoring seeks to track a manageable number of major systematic market monitoring factors, e.g., thirty to one hundred, falling within the lending universe of a lender. If the systematic market monitoring factors exhibit a confirmed trend of deterioration, a lender then takes immediate actions to mitigate the credit risk of his debt portfolio.

The major systematic market monitoring factors include, among others:

- major currency rates, e.g., USD, EUR, GBP, JPY and CNY;

- major interest rates, e.g., zero treasury rates with maturities one year for short term, five years for medium term and ten years for longer term;

- major equity market indices, e.g., United States Standard and Poor's 500 index, German DAX index, French CAC 40 index, United Kingdom FTSE 100 index, Japan Nikkei 225 index and China Shanghai Stock Exchange composite index;

- major volatility indices, e.g., the corresponding volatility of the above equity market indices, if available;

- major commodity prices, e.g., gold and oil prices; and

- major credit indices, e.g., CapLogic's SiFi credit indices.

During a financial crisis, the systematic market monitoring factors always exhibit rapid transitions. As such, in tracking the systematic market monitoring factors, the latest weekly percentage change is compared with the weekly percentage change of the same systematic market monitoring factor over the most recent business cycle, i.e. 260 weeks where the weekly percentage change is defined as:

Weekly percentage change

$$= \left(\frac{\text{Market value of monitoring factor current week}}{\text{Market value of monitoring factor previous week}} - 1 \right) \times 100\%$$

In case the latest weekly percentage change exhibits itself to be an outlier consecutively for a few weeks, the lender should look into the corresponding reasons behind the signal which may suggest a potential credit deterioration of a group of borrowers. A lender then re-calculates the ELs and/or XCLs of the corresponding debts to assess whether the credit risks remain within his tolerance level. If not, the lender then takes appropriate actions to mitigate the credit risk of his debt portfolio.

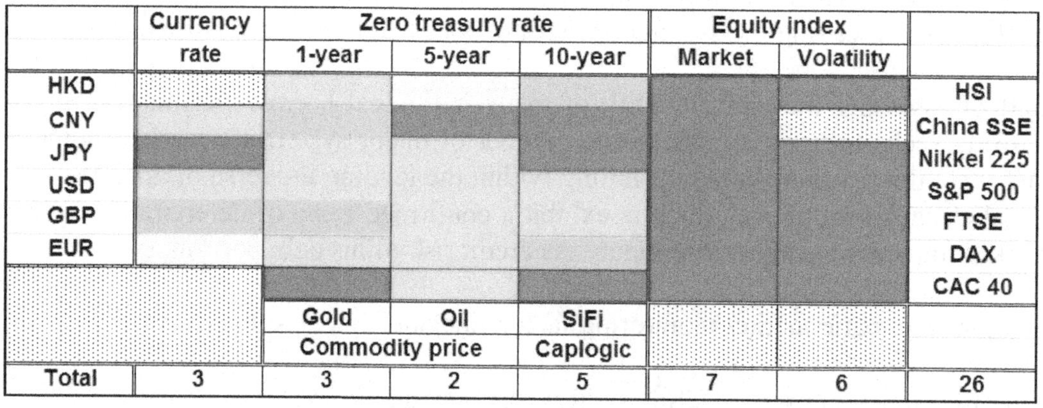

	Currency rate	Zero treasury rate			Equity index		
		1-year	5-year	10-year	Market	Volatility	
HKD							HSI
CNY							China SSE
JPY							Nikkei 225
USD							S&P 500
GBP							FTSE
EUR							DAX
							CAC 40
		Gold	Oil	SiFi			
		Commodity price		Caplogic			
Total	3	3	2	5	7	6	26

Figure 5.1   Major systematic market monitoring factors

With a distribution of weekly percentage changes over 260 weeks, a simple outlier scheme is proposed:

• If the latest weekly percentage change of a systematic market monitoring factor falls in 1 percent of two extremities, a red emergency signal is registered;

• If the latest weekly percentage change of a systematic market monitoring factor falls between 1 percent and 5 percent in two wing regions, an amber warning signal is registered;

• If the latest weekly percentage change of a systematic market monitoring factor falls between 5 percent and 10 percent in two wing regions, a yellow attention signal is registered; and

• If the latest weekly percentage change of a systematic market monitoring factor falls within the middle 80 percent, a green normal signal is registered.

In accordance with the level of severity, a lender takes corresponding actions to review the credit risk of his debts. In general, a higher level of severity triggers a more frequent and comprehensive review and a lower level of severity exhibits the need of review only at regular frequency and coverage. This essentially reserves most of the lender's resources to business operations under a regular market condition and shifts the lender's resources to risk management under a critical market situation, subject to some objective rules exhibited in historical data. In addition, the entire financial markets monitoring process could be automated with computer programmes that prompt a lender pro-actively when a potential crisis emerges.

Figure 5.2   A simple outlier scheme

Finally, by arranging the major systematic market monitoring factors in a time series, a trend analysis is conducted to indicate the corresponding improvement or deterioration over a recent period. This may serve as a set of early warning signals to detect the potential credit deterioration of a particular market and/or the global markets.

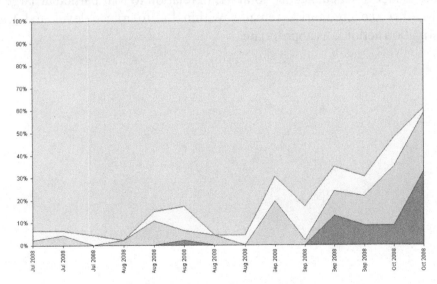

Figure 5.3   Trend analysis

5.5   Large borrowers monitoring ★★★

Financial markets monitoring is by far the most convenient method for credit quality monitoring. Nevertheless, this approach ignores the specific credit quality of individual borrowers, in particular, the debts with larger EL. While the impact from specific credit quality varies from lender to lender, it is suggests that a certain level of specific credit quality monitoring should be put in place as a minimum compensation.

Major specific credit risk arises from debts with larger EL. Therefore, the credit quality of those borrowers with the largest ELs should be monitored on an individual borrower basis. While this involves the calculations of all EADs, LGDs, PDs and RMs before the determination of borrowers with the largest ELs, practitioners adopt simply the outstanding debt amount as a proxy of the EL to determine the borrowers with the largest credit exposure since the outstanding debt amounts are available readily from lending records.

The granularity of a debt portfolio determines the number of large borrowers to be monitored.   For a well diversified debt portfolio, large borrowers may include ten financial industry borrowers with the largest outstanding debt amount and ten non-financial industry borrowers with the largest outstanding debt amount.

For these large borrowers, the credit ratings, FICO scores and/or CDS spreads[11] are registered on a weekly basis to form some time series to facilitate trend analysis. In addition, the news in relation to these large borrowers from financial information providers is also recorded. In case a potential deterioration of a large borrower is observed, the lender re-calculates the total EL in relation to that particular large borrower to assess whether the credit risk remains within his tolerance level and triggers the relevant mitigation actions, as appropriate.

---

[11] Details of the CDS and CDS spread are described in Chapter 11.

5.6   Practical monitoring ★★★

The financial markets monitoring and large borrowers monitoring together form an efficient and effective monitoring framework to track the credit quality of a large debt portfolio with many borrowers at a minimum effort. The systematic credit quality and specific credit quality arising from large borrowers account for the majority of the portfolio credit quality, leaving the immaterial specific credit quality attributed to smaller borrowers.

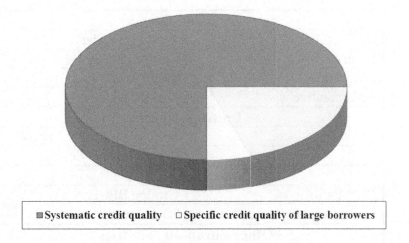

■ Systematic credit quality   □ Specific credit quality of large borrowers

Figure 5.4   Practical monitoring

5.7   CapLogic SiFi credit index

CDX indices and iTraxx indices published by Mark-it are credit indices representing the credit quality of a group of reference institutions within the same region (North America, Europe or Asia), same institution category (corporation or country), similar credit quality (investment grade or high yield grade) and/or same standard maturity. They are constructed as the arithmetic average of the CDS spreads of the CDSs referencing a selected group of institutions and are primarily designed for systematic credit trading purpose.

Although very popular, when used as market monitoring factors, these credit indices are subject to the deficiencies of default effect, discontinuity and selection bias.

CapLogic SiFi index is designed to redress the above deficiencies by focusing the construction of credit index only on those systematically important reference entities that impact specifically the systematic credit quality facing most professional lenders. Moreover, every systematically important reference institution is registered with a long history of CDS spreads to ensure the continuity and compatibility.

CapLogic SiFi credit index is constructed as an arithmetic average of the five-year CDS spreads of the major members of the 30 systematically important financial institutions

("SiFis") designated by the Financial Stability Board. A SiFi is a financial institution whose distress or disorderly failure would cause significant disruption to the wider financial system and economic activity because of its size, complexity and systemic inter-connectedness. The list of SiFis is reviewed and published in November every year.

The credit quality of these 30 SiFis plays the most critical role in monitoring and analyzing the global credit markets. Among these 30 SiFis, there are eight North American, fifteen European and seven Asian financial institutions.

United States	
Bank of America	JP Morgan Chase
Bank of New York Mellon	Morgan Stanley
Citigroup	State Street
Goldman Sachs	Wells Fargo
United Kingdom	
Barclays	Standard Chartered Bank
HSBC	Royal Bank of Scotland
France	
BNP Paribas	Groupe BPCE
Groupe Credit Agricole	Societe Generale
Other European countries	
Credit Suisse	Nordea
UBS	Santander
Deutsche Bank	Unicredit
ING Bank	
Asia	
Bank of China	Mitsubishi UFJ FG
ICBC	Mizuho FG
Agricultural Bank of China	Sumitomo Mitsui FG
China Construction Bank	

Table 5.1   Systematically important financial institutions

Credit Risk Controls

6

KEY CONCEPTS

- Bilateral netting
- Collateral
- Credit guarantee

- Downgrade trigger
- Diversification
- Credit limit

6.1   Credit risk mitigation

In order to gain an excess return over the risk-free rate, a lender takes credit risk consciously to originate a debt. Through credit risk mitigation, the credit risk is reduced with an effect of reducing the excess return. At a first glance, credit risk mitigation seems to act against the initiative of a lending business.

However, along the horizon of a debt investment, a lender may desire to lock in the unrealized profit when his debts have registered a significant reduction in the EL and/or XCL. Conversely, a lender must limit the unrealized loss when his debts have recorded a significant increase in the EL and/or XCL. Moreover, due to the deterioration on a systematic or specific basis, the credit risk of the debts may have increased beyond the tolerance level of a lender. Finally, a lender may become conservative and prefer to take less credit risk. All these reasons drive a lender to hedge his credit risk through credit risk mitigation.

Credit risk mitigation is triggered by credit risk monitoring through which a lender detects that the credit risk of a single debt or debt portfolio has exceeded his tolerance level.

In most cases, a lender cannot terminate unilaterally a debt during the middle of the lending period, i.e., he must hold the debt until maturity. Therefore, credit risk controls, which are tools for mitigating credit risk, serve as indirect substitutions. With the EL and XCL as the credit risk measures of a single debt and debt portfolio respectively, credit risk is an increasing function of the EAD, LGD, PD, RM, concentration of debts and default dependency. Therefore, by implementing adequate controls to alter these six credit risk factors, the credit risk to a lender can be well mitigated.

The following sections illustrate some common controls to mitigate credit risk through the reduction of these six credit risk factors. Most credit risk controls have to be implemented at the origination as pre-lending contractual controls, except credit default swap and credit securitization.

6.2   EAD reduction

6.2.1   Bilateral netting ★★★

It is a common situation in a real business operation that two lenders are also borrowers to each other. For example: (i) bank A and bank B lend to each other on different loan products; and (ii) corporation A and corporation B purchase different goods from each other on a credit basis. In such case, if party A defaults, upon the liquidation process, party B must first surrender the EAD, including principal and interest owed by party B to party A, before party B can start the debt collection process to claim the EAD owned by party A to party B. The process is reversed in case party B defaults. This results in a paradox that a lender must first pay a borrower upon the default of the borrower.

To rectify this paradox, the two parties may enter a bilateral netting agreement to offset the EAD common to each other upon the default of either party. Under a bilateral netting agreement, if party A defaults, before the liquidation process, party B is allowed to use the EAD owed by party B to party A to offset fully or partially the EAD owed by party A to party B. In case the EAD owed by party B to party A is less than the EAD owed by party A to party B, party B continues the debt collection process to claim the residual EAD owned by party A to party B. In case the EAD owed by party B to party A is more than the EAD owed by party A to party B, party B must surrender the residual EAD to the liquidator of party A upon liquidation. As such, the bilateral netting agreement reduces effectively the EAD to the larger of: (i) the difference between the lending EAD and borrowing EAD; and (ii) zero, i.e.:

$$\text{Net EAD} = \text{Max[Lending EAD - Borrowing EAD, 0]}$$

6.2.2   Principal amortization

For a debt with a very long lending period, it is difficult for a lender to forecast accurately the credit quality of a borrower throughout the entire lending period. To compensate for the risk arising from this long initial RM, the borrower is required to return on a regular basis a small part of the principal. This process of principal amortization allows the potential deterioration in credit quality of a borrower over a long period of time to be offset by the scheduled reduction in the EAD of a debt.

Principal amortization is often applied to a residential mortgage with a longer initial RM, from five up to thirty years. Each month a fixed amount comprising the interest and part of the principal is paid to the lender.

6.3   LGD reduction

6.3.1   Collateral ★★★

In many lending businesses, a lender requests a borrower to provide some collaterals to secure against the debts. The lender then owns legally the collaterals which will continue to be used by the borrower. This contractual transfer of ownership is reversed when the debt is paid fully to the lender. In case the borrower defaults, the lender sells the collaterals to compensate part of the EAD. If the collaterals are sold at a price below the EAD, the lender will take further debt collection actions to recovery the residual EAD from the borrower. With collaterals, the LGD of a debt is reduced in a controlled manner.

When a debt is supported by collaterals, the LGD is driven primarily by the value of collaterals at default and is calculated as:

$$
\begin{aligned}
LGD &= \frac{\text{Default loss}}{\text{EAD}} \times 100\% \\
&= \frac{\text{Max}\left[\text{EAD - Collaterals, 0}\right]}{\text{EAD}} \times 100\% \\
&= \text{Max}\left[1 - \frac{\text{Collaterals}}{\text{EAD}}, 0\right] \times 100\%
\end{aligned}
$$

A lender prefers collaterals with: (i) high liquidity, so that they can be converted into cash quickly, like common financial instruments; and (ii) low mobility, in case the collaterals are not deposited to the lender, like properties and lands. Other common collaterals include, among others, cars, machineries and red wine recently.

Typically, a lender mandates the value of collaterals to be well above the EAD so that the LGD remains zero throughout the entire lending period even if the value of collaterals decreases. Many banks offer mortgages to borrowers at 70 percent of the property value. Then, even in a severe property market downturn when the price of a property drops by 30 percent, the LGD will still be maintained at zero.

6.3.2   Margining

When a lending business uses liquid financial instruments as collaterals, there is a risk that the value of collaterals may fall below the EAD within a short period of time. Thus a lender requests the borrower to top up the collaterals with some cash, referred to as margin, up to a certain threshold in order to absorb the potential decrease in collateral value in a few days. As such, a higher volatility of collateral value demands a larger margin amount. The borrower is also welcomed to withdraw the excess margin as long as the total value of collaterals and margin deposited remains above the threshold. In case the total value of collaterals and margin deposited falls below the threshold, the borrower must take an action within a short period of time to deposit additional margin to bring the total value up to the threshold. Otherwise, the lender will declare the default of the borrower and conduct a fire sale immediately on the collaterals.

Margin lending is very common in foreign currency trading.[12] A trader borrows an amount of local currency to purchase foreign currency which, in turn, is deposited to the lender as collaterals together with a cash margin in local currency, totalling up to 105 percent of the EAD. If the total value of the foreign currency and cash margin falls below 103 percent of the EAD, the borrower must take an immediate action to deposit additional cash margin to bring the total value back to 105 percent of the EAD again within one business day. If the total value of the foreign currency and the cash margin falls below 101 percent of the EAD, the lender will conduct a fire sale immediately on the collaterals.

6.4   PD reduction

6.4.1   Credit guarantee   ★★★

Most lenders are hesitant to lend to a borrower of lower credit quality due to his larger PD or a lack of understanding on the financial condition of a borrower. Through credit guarantee, a borrower sources a credit guarantor who agrees to pay the EAD to the lender upon the default of the borrower. The credit guarantor must be considered as high credit quality by the lender and have a positive view on the credit quality of the borrower.

The lender then assesses the joint credit quality of both the borrower and credit guarantor instead of just the borrower to arrive at a lending decision. In case the loan is granted and the borrower defaults, the lender will collect the EAD from the credit guarantor. Nevertheless, the lender will still suffer from default loss if both the borrower and credit guarantor default together. The arrangement of credit guarantee essentially replaces the larger PD of a borrower with a smaller joint PD of the borrower and credit guarantor.

6.4.2   Credit default swap

A credit default swap ("CDS") is a financial instrument that offers default insurance on a debt to a lender. With a CDS, a lender will receive an amount largely equal to the default loss from an insurer upon the default of the debt.

In order to acquire this insurance benefit, the lender must pay the insurer a premium in the form of a series of deterministic cash flow on a regular basis during the insurance period until the CDS expires or a default event occurs. Thus a CDS works similar to a credit guarantee except that the insurer, acting as a paid credit guarantor, is sourced at a fee by the lender instead of the borrower. Similar to credit guarantee, the lender will still suffer from default loss if both the borrower and insurer default together. The PD of a borrower is replaced by the joint PD of the borrower and insurer.

---

[12] Historical currency rates can be downloaded with the URL "http://stooq.com".

The CDS can be entered at any time during the life of a debt as long as there is an insurer willing to take over the credit risk. Therefore, a lender may acquire a CDS as a credit risk control when he observes that there is a potential deterioration in the credit quality of a particular borrower. This essentially offers the greatest flexibility to the lender. In fact, the CDS is by far the most popular post-origination credit risk control in the financial market. Further details about the CDSs will be described in Chapter 11.

6.5   RM reduction

6.5.1   Downgrade trigger ★★★

Many banks lend only to corporate borrowers with credit quality of investment grade. This requirement can be enforced easily at the origination of a debt. Nevertheless, throughout the lending period, there is a chance that the borrower will be downgraded by a credit rating agency and fall into the high yield grade.

To mitigate such potential deterioration, a lender may incorporate in the lending agreement that a borrower must maintain his credit rating at investment grade by major global credit rating agencies. In case the borrower deteriorates to a high yield grade, the borrower is obligated to return the EAD to the lender immediately and terminate the debt.

6.5.2   Call provision

Call provision is essentially a tightened form of downgrade trigger. At the origination of a debt, a list of positive conditions is set out in the lending agreement, e.g., the borrower must:

- maintain its credit rating at investment grade by major global credit rating agencies;
- deposit sufficient collaterals to the lender;
- meet certain sales and/or profit targets every quarter;
- complete a project following a scheduled timeline; and/or
- demonstrate a significant improvement in financial condition within a certain period of time.

If any of these positive conditions are breached, the borrower is obligated to return the EAD to the lender immediately and terminate the debt.

Both downgrade trigger and call provision are indeed an early debt collection action before the default of a borrower. They seek to collect the EAD ahead of other lenders of the same borrower. The borrower is likely to be placed in an even worse financial situation after the early return of the EAD as a result of a downgrade trigger or call provision. This essentially accelerates the default of a borrower.

6.6   Concentration reduction

Concentration of debts in a debt portfolio is measured by the Herfindahl-Hirschman index ("HHI") which is defined as:

$$EL_k = EAD_k \times LGD_k \times \left[1 - \left(1 - PD_k \right)^{RM_k} \right]$$

$$\approx EAD_k \times LGD_k \times PD_k \times RM_k$$

$$HHI = \frac{\sum_{k=1}^{NOB} EL_k^2}{\left(\sum_{k=1}^{NOB} EL_k \right)^2}$$

The HHI approaches:

- 1 when the debt portfolio is dominated by a few debts with larger EL; and
- 0 when the debt portfolio is distributed over a large number of debts with smaller EL.

The HHI suggests a very simple method to reduce the portfolio credit risk: the lender should lend to many borrowers with smaller EL instead of just a few borrowers with larger EL. Nevertheless, in practice, a lender must also take into account the operating cost of managing a large number of smaller debts of many borrowers.

Many lenders simply adopt the outstanding debt amount, which is readily available, as a proxy of the EL to avoid the excessive computation of the EAD, LGD, PD and RM in order to arrive at an EL. This results in an alternative form of the HHI.

$$HHI = \frac{\sum_{k=1}^{NOB} \text{Outstnding debt amount}_k^2}{\left(\sum_{k=1}^{NOB} \text{Outstnding debt amount}_k \right)^2}$$

6.7   Dependency reduction

Default dependency, driven by some systematic factors, e.g., economy of a country, prospect of an industry, demand of a profession, causes the systematic credit risk of a debt portfolio. A closer relationship between the borrowers and common systematic factors results in a higher systematic credit risk. Such a close relationship is usually observed in borrowers in the same country, industry and/or profession. Indeed, for a closely related group of borrowers, the credit risk is primarily driven by the common systematic factors instead of by individual borrowers. Thus a high default dependency is equivalent to a high concentration in common systematic factors.

Applying the same argument as that of concentration reduction, the systematic credit risk can be reduced by lending to a group of borrowers with exposures to many systematic factors instead of just a few systematic factors.

To reduce the impacts from these systematic factors, a lender should adopt a strategy to lend to borrowers in a broad list of lending segments, e.g., in different countries, industries and professions, noting that the lender must also take into account the operating cost of managing debts in many lending segments.

The HHI can be modified to indicate the level of default dependency. Assuming that the index (h, k) represents the hth borrower in the kth lending segment (country, industry, profession or their combination), there are M_k borrowers in the kth lending segment and there are N lending segments, then the HHI based on lending segment can be computed as:

$$EL_k = \sum_{h=1}^{M_k} \left\{ EAD_{h,k} \times LGD_{h,k} \times \left[1 - \left(1 - PD_{h,k} \right)^{RM_{h,k}} \right] \right\}$$

$$\approx \sum_{h=1}^{M_k} \left(EAD_{h,k} \times LGD_{h,k} \times PD_{h,k} \times RM_{h,k} \right) \qquad \text{for lending segment k}$$

$$HHI = \frac{\sum_{k=1}^{N} EL_k^2}{\left(\sum_{k=1}^{N} EL_k \right)^2}$$

or in a convenient alternative form:

$$\text{Outstanding debt amount}_k = \sum_{h=1}^{M_k} \text{Outstanding debt amount}_{h,k}$$

$$\text{for lending segment k}$$

$$HHI = \frac{\sum_{k=1}^{N} \text{Outstanding debt amount}_k^2}{\left(\sum_{k=1}^{N} \text{Outstanding debt amount}_k \right)^2}$$

6.8 Portfolio reduction

Portfolio reduction seeks to reduce the portfolio credit risk by selling some debts in a portfolio to other debt investors. It is accomplished through credit securitization.

Debts, in particular loans, have an illiquid secondary market. There are very few investors interested in buying individual credit risky debts from the secondary market as a result of: (i) the mis-match between demand and supply of debts; and (ii) the information asymmetry between investors.

Through credit securitization, the cash flows generated from a pool of debts are packaged into different tranches with varies risk-return characteristics in order to match the investment objectives of different investors. This essentially offers a product line with comprehensive varieties to reach a much broader range of investors, thus establishing a new credit market. Further details about credit securitization will be described in Chapter 14.

6.9 Credit limit ★★★

A credit limit is the upper bound of the total EAD of all outstanding debts lent to the same borrower from a lender. It is by far the most popular integrated credit risk control to restrict the EAD, LGD, PD, concentration of debts and default dependency in a debt portfolio. A lender sets a credit limit for each borrower to cap the default loss of the lender in case many borrowers default together in one year under an extreme situation.

For a lender investing in a homogeneous portfolio, if the maximum portfolio default loss ("MPDL") in one year that the lender can afford is a fixed amount[13] and the maximum number of borrowers in the homogeneous portfolio is NOB, then the portfolio and borrower credit limits can be calculated simply by setting the XCL of a homogeneous portfolio to the MPDL:

$$\text{Portfolio EAD} \times \text{LGD} \times \text{XCDR} = \text{XCL}$$
$$\text{Portfolio credit limit} \times \text{LGD} \times \text{XCDR} = \text{MPDL}$$

$$\text{Portfolio credit limit} = \frac{\text{MPDL}}{\text{LGD} \times \text{XCDR}}$$

$$\text{Borrower credit limit} = \frac{\text{Portfolio credit limit}}{\text{NOB}} = \frac{\text{MPDL}}{\text{NOB} \times \text{LGD} \times \text{XCDR}}$$

---

[13] In the case of a bank lender, the MDPL could be determined by the annual profit of plus long term investment funding to the bank. Further details will be described in Chapter 17.

Obviously, the credit limit of a borrower, which is essentially the maximum EAD for each borrower, decreases with: (i) increasing LGD and PD due to the deterioration in credit quality of the homogeneous portfolio and (ii) increasing CCC due to the increasing default dependency among the borrowers in the homogeneous portfolio.

The calculation of credit limit can be easily extended to borrowers of debts in a heterogeneous portfolio subject to a MPDL and a maximum of NOB borrowers. For a borrower k, the existing and potential debts of the borrower are first consolidated with an LGD_k estimated. Then the credit limit of borrower k in a heterogeneous portfolio is calculated as:

$$\text{Borrower credit limit}_k = \frac{\text{MPDL}}{\text{NOB} \times \text{LGD}_k \times \text{WCDR}_k}$$

6.10 Summary of credit risk controls ★★★

Table 6.1 summarizes the major properties of various credit risk controls. In practice, several credit risk controls may be combined to make the credit risk mitigation be more effective.

Credit risk factor	Control	Implement-ation	Limitation
EAD	Netting	At debt origination	
EAD	Principal amortization	At debt origination	
LGD	Collateral	At debt origination	
LGD	Margining	At debt origination	
PD	Credit guarantee	At debt origination	
PD	Credit default swap	Any time	Existence of an insurer
RM	Downgrade trigger	At debt origination	Availability of credit rating
RM	Call provision	At debt origination	
Concentration of debts	Smaller EAD to more borrowers	At debt origination	Higher operating cost
Default dependency	Smaller segmental EAD to more lending segments	At debt origination	Higher operating cost
All	Credit securitization	Any time	Existence of a liquid credit securitization market
All	Credit limit	At debt origination	

Table 6.1 Summary of credit risk controls

Appendix 6.1   Average LGD of a debt supported by a liquid collateral

(A)   Instant LGD

For a debt supported by a liquid collateral with transparent market value, the instant LGD can be estimated by the Black-Scholes framework.

Define q_t as the collateral ratio between the collateral value and the EAD at time t. The the LGD can be expressed in the form of payoff of a put option:

$$\text{Max}\left[1 - \frac{\text{Collateral value at time t}}{\text{EAD at time t}}, 0\right] = \text{Max}\left[1 - q_t, 0\right]$$

Then the LGD at time t can be characterized as the payoff of a European put option. Following the Black-Scholes framework,

$$\text{LGD}(t) = \Phi(-d_2) - q_0 \exp(\mu t)\Phi(-d_1)$$

$$d_1 = \frac{\ln(q_0) + \left(\mu + \frac{\sigma^2}{2}\right)t}{\sigma\sqrt{t}}$$

$$d_2 = d_1 - \sigma\sqrt{t}$$

where q_0 is the current collateral-EAD ratio, μ is the drift of the collateral-EAD ratio and σ is the volatility of the collateral-EAD ratio.

(B)   Hazard rate

The hazard rate λ of a PD is defined as:

$$\lambda = -\ln(1 - PD)$$

Conversely, given a hazard rate, the PD is calculated as:

$$PD = 1 - \exp(-\lambda)$$

The hazard rate is essentially the default rate per year expressed in continuous time convention, similar to the treatment of interest rate. A hazard rate may range from 0 to ∞.

For a large number of identical borrowers with the same PD, the expected number of survival borrowers after T years is calculated as:

Expected no. of survival borrowers after T years

= Initial no. of borrowers $\times (1 - PD)^T$

= Initial no. of borrowers $\times \exp(-\lambda T)$

(C)   Average LGD

Combining the instant LGD and the hazard rate, a formula can be derived to estimate the average LGD between times 0 and T.

At time t,

- the LGD is $\Phi(-d_2) - q_0 \exp(\mu t) \Phi(-d_1)$;
- the survival probability of a borrower is $\exp(-\lambda t)$; and
- the default chance within an infinitesimal small time interval is λdt.

In addition, the default chance between times 0 and T is $1 - \exp(-\lambda T)$.

Putting everything together, the average LGD between times 0 and T becomes:

$$\frac{\int_0^T \left[\Phi(-d_2) - q_0 \exp(\mu t) \Phi(-d_1) \right] \times \exp(-\lambda t) \times \lambda dt}{1 - \exp(-\lambda T)}$$

This definite integral can be evaluated using common numerical methods.

PART TWO

CREDIT ASSESSMENTS
The Discovery of Credit Quality

Credit Ratings and FICO Scores

KEY CONCEPTS

- Credit rating agency
- Credit rating
- Default rate

- ECAI Plus rating scale
- Credit bureau
- FICO score

7.1   Credit assessment ★★★

In Chapter 2, the credit risk factors of and their impacts to four common credit products are examined. A lender can design a credit product that matches his risk-return characteristic and investment horizon by selecting the right mix of the EAD, LGD and initial RM. In addition, the lender chooses to lend only to a borrower with credit quality conforming to his preference, having considered the objective evidences provided by the borrower. This process of discovering the credit quality of a borrower with some objective evidences is referred to as credit assessment.

Credit assessment seeks to answer the following two strategic questions:

- Is the borrower a good borrower (e.g., likely to survive during the lending period) or a bad borrower (e.g., likely to default during the lending period)? If the lender will review and control the credit risk of the debt at the end of the following one year, the latest, a unified hypothetical lending period of one year may be assumed; and

- What is the PD of the borrower?

In real lending practices, huge amounts of resources are spent on credit assessments, having regard to various types of borrowers, the lender's technical expertise and the availability of relevant information. The prevailing credit assessment techniques are summarized in Figure 7.1 and will be explained in detail in Chapters 7 through 9.

For economic and practical reasons, many lenders leverage on credit assessments conducted by independent experts to eliminate the repeated assessment efforts by individual lenders. This arrives at credit ratings for corporate borrowers and FICO scores for retail borrowers.

In accordance with the credit assessment techniques and available information, borrowers are classified into:

- corporate borrowers, which cover listed companies and private firms; and
- retail borrowers, which cover individual persons and small businesses.

These two groups of borrowers take very different positions in the lending market, thus driving the separate developments of credit rating agencies and retail credit bureaus.

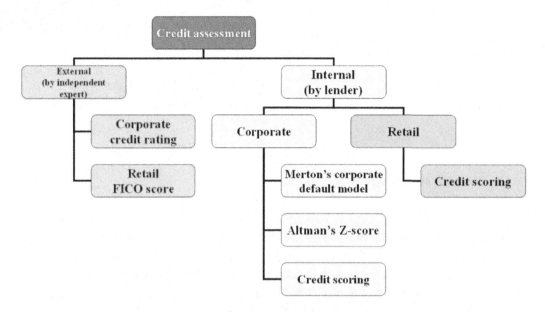

Figure 7.1   Credit assessment techniques

7.2   Credit rating agency

A credit rating agency is an independent expert that assesses the credit quality of a corporation with standardized procedures and presents the assessment result in the form of a rank, referred to as a credit rating. This credit rating is shared among many lenders who are interested in conducting lending businesses directly or indirectly with the rated corporation.

Credit assessment for corporations is highly technical and relatively difficult to be mastered by lenders without sufficient expertise and experience. A lender thus relies invariably on a credit rating from a credit rating agency as one of the major inputs to determine the credit quality of a borrower, leaving the lender's resources to focus on business functions in which he finds more important and/or competent.

The market of credit rating is dominated by three major global credit rating agencies, namely:

- Moody's Investors Service;
- Standard & Poor's; and
- Fitch Ratings.

Some credit rating agencies specialize in certain particular industries or geographic areas, e.g., A.M. Best is famous for its specialist credit ratings of insurance companies and Dagong Global Credit Rating concentrates its efforts on credit ratings in mainland China.

A credit rating agency may operate its business in a solicited or an unsolicited model. Under the solicited model, a corporation pays a service charge and provides its confidential information to a credit rating agency for the purpose of credit assessment in order to obtain a credit rating. The major revenue of a credit rating agency providing solicited ratings is generated from the service charges collected from the rated corporations.

The three major global credit rating agencies are operated in the solicited model by charging the rated corporations and distributing free of charge the credit ratings on the websites of the credit rating agencies. This essentially creates certain conflicts of interest where a credit rating agency is encouraged to provide a more favourable credit rating to a corporation in order to attract the service contract against the competing credit rating agencies. To minimize the effect arising from these conflicts of interest, credit rating agencies in major developed countries are now under the supervision of financial authorities to ensure their professional integrity.

Conversely, some smaller credit rating agencies are operated under the unsolicited model in which a credit rating agency takes an initiative to assess the credit quality of a corporation based on publicly available information. The major revenue is then generated from the lenders who subscribe the credit ratings. Listed companies with updated financial statements published in their annual reports are the primary candidates under the unsolicited model.

7.3   Credit rating scale

Credit rating agencies express credit assessment results in the form of credit ratings. Standard & Poor's and Fitch Ratings share the same credit rating scale while Moody's Investors Service follows a similar but different credit rating scale, as illustrated in Table 7.1.

Due to the simplicity, many practitioners use the credit rating symbols shared by Standard & Poor's and Fitch Ratings even when referring to the credit ratings published by Moody's Investors Service, e.g., BBB also means Baa. Credit ratings are defined qualitatively, detailed in Table 7.2.

A corporation rated BBB or above is regarded as investment grade which is appropriate for conservative lenders who invest to seek stable cash inflows. In contrast, corporation rated BB or below is classified as high yield grade which is the candidate of aggressive lenders who seek to speculate on the survival of a corporation in order to arrive at a higher return.

Many banks restrict their lending to corporations with credit ratings at investment grade. Under such lending mandates, investment grade corporations are classified as good borrowers while high yield grade corporations are classified as bad borrowers.

Grade	Standard & Poor's, Fitch[14]	Moody's[15]
Investment	AAA	Aaa
	AA	Aa
	A	A
	BBB	Baa
High yield	BB	Ba
	B	B
	CCC	Caa
	CC	Ca
	C	C

Table 7.1   Credit rating scales

Rating	Description
AAA	A corporation rated AAA has an extremely strong capacity to meet its debt obligations. AAA is the highest borrower credit rating.
AA	A corporation rated AA has a very strong capacity to meet its debt obligations. It differs from a highest rated borrower only to a small degree.
A	A corporation rated A has a strong capacity to meet its debt obligations but is somewhat more susceptible to the adverse effects of changes in circumstances and economic conditions than a borrower in higher rating categories.
BBB	A corporation rated BBB has an adequate capacity to meet its debt obligations. However, adverse economic conditions or changing circumstances are more likely to lead to a weakened capacity of the borrower to meet its debt obligations.
BB	A corporation rated BB is judged to have speculative elements and subject to substantial credit risk.
B	A corporation rated B is more vulnerable than a borrower rated BB but the borrower currently has the capacity to meet its financial obligations. Adverse business, financial or economic conditions will likely impair the borrower's capacity and/or willingness to meet its debt obligations.
CCC	A corporation rated CCC starts to experience financial distress and is dependent upon favourable business, financial and economic conditions to meet its debt obligations.
CC	A corporation rated CC is currently in financial distress.
C	A corporation rated C is in deep financial distress with very little prospect to meet its debt obligations.

Table 7.2   Qualitative definition of credit ratings

[14] For the credit ratings between AA and B, modifiers "+" and "-" are supplemented to further differentiate the credit quality at a higher granularity, with "+" being the best in the same group and "-" being the worst in the same group.

[15] For the credit ratings between Aa and Caa, modifiers "1," "2," and "3" are supplemented to further differentiate the credit quality at a higher granularity, with "1" being the best in the same group and "3" being the worst in the same group.

7.4   Default rates vs credit ratings

Credit rating agencies publish regularly the annual default rates of their rated corporations for individual credit ratings. The average annual default rates over a long period published by the three major global credit rating agencies are listed in Table 7.3.

Credit quality	Credit rating	Moody's (%) 1983 - 2016	S&P's (%) 1981 - 2016	Fitch (%) 1990 - 2016
Excellent	AAA	0.00	0.00	0.13
Good	AA	0.02	0.02	0.05
	A	0.06	0.06	0.06
	BBB	0.19	0.18	0.15
Moderate	BB	0.94	0.72	0.73
	B	3.56	3.76	2.12
Bad	CCC to C	10.54	26.78	21.24

Table 7.3   Average historical corporate annual default rates

With the long history and large number of rated corporations, these annual default rates may serve as proxies of the PDs of corporations with various credit ratings.

As at 2018, there are only two corporations with AAA rating, namely: Johnson & Johnson and Microsoft Corporation.

7.5   ECAI Plus rating scale ★★★

The Basel III framework proposes a unified credit rating scale for an external credit assessment institution ("ECAI") as an alternative to the credit rating agencies' qualitative definition of credit rating scale by associating the credit ratings with the average default rates over a period of three years, as depicted in Table 7.4.

Credit rating	Average 3-year default rate (%)
AAA and AA	0.10
A	0.25
BBB	1.00
BB	7.50
B	20.00

Table 7.4   ECAI rating scale

The AAA and AA ratings are combined into one group due to the very small number of AAA rated corporations. Also the average three-year default rates for CCC, CC and C are not exhibited. This creates certain operational difficulties to credit analysis. Therefore, an ECAI Plus rating scale is proposed with the average three-year default rates assigned artificially to the ratings AAA, CCC, CC and C in accordance with the pattern demonstrated systematically in the generic ECAI rating scale. This ECAI Plus rating scale is exhibited in Table 7.5.

Credit quality	Credit rating	3-year DR (%)	PD (%)
Excellent	AAA	0.03	0.0100
Good	AA	0.10	0.0333
	A	0.25	0.0834
	BBB	1.00	0.3345
Moderate	BB	7.50	2.5652
	B	20.00	7.1682
Bad	CCC	40.00	15.6567
	CC	65.00	29.5270
	C	95.00	63.1597

Table 7.5   ECAI Plus rating scale

In accordance with the ECAI Plus rating scale, a corporation rated:

- AAA is almost equivalent to a default free entity in one year;

- between AA and BBB is considered as a borrower of good credit quality with PD below 1 percent;

- either BB or B is considered as a borrower of moderate credit quality with a single digit PD; and

- between CCC and C is considered as a borrower of bad credit quality with a double digit PD.

7.6   Other credit ratings

In addition to credit ratings for corporations, some credit rating agencies also provide credit assessment services specifically for:

- financial institutions: including banks, securities firms and insurance companies; and
- governments: including country governments, super nations and municipal governments.

The credit assessment of a financial institution is generally difficult due to its complexity and the regulations imposed. Therefore, credit rating serves as a dominating method for assessing the credit quality of a financial institution. Virtually all major international financial institutions are assessed on an annual basis and assigned a credit rating by at least one of the three major global credit rating agencies.

Credit rating is also important for assessing the credit quality of a country since the political situations must be factored in and the default experience on countries is extremely rare. Most of the quantitative methods will fail in such situation. In addition, the default rates of countries are consistently below the ECAI scale. Therefore, it is preferred to follow the empirical statistics from credit rating agencies.

Credit quality	Credit rating	Moody's (%) 1983 - 2016	S&P's (%) 1975 - 2016	Fitch (%) 1995 - 2016
Excellent	AAA			
Good	AA		0	
	A			
	BBB			
Moderate	BB	0.55	0.5	0.29
	B	2.76	2.6	1.30
Bad	CCC to C	12.18	37.2	24.14

<u>**Table 7.6   Average historical annual default rates for countries**</u>

In terms of annual default rates, credit ratings do not provide any differentiation among the investment grade countries. As such, it is more appropriate to look at the ten-year default rates and derive a prudent estimate of the PD as:

$$PD = 1 - (1 - \text{Maximum of 10-year default rates from Moody's, S\&P's, Fitch})^{\frac{1}{10}}$$

Some credit rating agencies also provide credit assessment services directly on financial instruments instead of their issuers. These include credit ratings on corporate bonds, government bonds, collateralized debt obligations and investment funds.

It is interesting to observe that the default rates of A-rated countries are larger than those of BBB-rated countries.[16] These figures suggest that credit rating is never an absolutely correct credit assessment approach.

Credit quality	Credit rating	Moody's (%) 1983 - 2016	S&P's (%) 1975 – 2016	Fitch (%) 1995 – 2016	Prudent PD (%)
Excellent	AAA	0			
Good	AA	1.053	0.0	0.00	0.11
	A	4.004	5.8	4.00	0.60
	BBB	1.628	3.6	3.85	0.39
Moderate	BB	10.928	8.6	4.88	1.15
	B	21.367	26.6	8.33	3.05
Bad	CCC to C	50.579	79.3	25.00	14.57

Table 7.7   Average historical ten-year default rates for countries

7.7   Retail credit bureaus

A retail credit bureau is an independent credit assessment expert specializing in conducting credit assessments on individual persons and/or small businesses. Major retail credit bureaus include, among others:

- TransUnion, Equifax and Experian, which conduct credit assessments on individual persons; and

- Dun & Bradstreet, which conducts credit assessments on small businesses.

Retail credit bureaus are operated in the unsolicited model of credit assessment. They collect borrowers' information from banks that provide lending services and public records, like company registries and courts. Each time when a borrower applies for a lending service from a bank, the application form essentially includes a statement that seeks the borrower's consent for the bank to contribute the borrower's information to retail credit bureaus.

The data privacy laws limit the extent to which a borrower's information can be contributed by a bank. Banks are only permitted to contribute selected negative data (e.g., overdue and late payment records) and selected positive data (e.g., numbers of mortgages and credit cards).

---

[16] The increases in default rates of A-rated countries were caused by the default of Greece government bonds during the European debt crisis in 2010.

7.8   FICO score

A retail credit bureau consolidates the credit information of an individual person or small business in the form of a numerical FICO score ranging from 350 to 850. The FICO score was developed initially by the Fair Issac Corporation in the 1950s to facilitate the quantification of retail credit quality. A higher FICO score indicates a better credit quality.

The FICO score is calculated by a secret FICO formula that has never been released to the general public. The retail credit bureaus claim that they maintain the confidentiality of the FICO formula to avoid individual persons and/or small businesses to massage their credit information in order to boost artificially their FICO scores.

A FICO score is derived from five major factors:

- Payment history (35%): The historical records of default, bankruptcy, lawsuit, court order and delayed payment will reduce the FICO score. The more recent, frequent and severe the negative payment history, the lower the FICO score will be;

- Credit utilization (30%): A large ratio of outstanding debt amount to total credit limit will reduce the FICO score;

- Credit history (15%): Credit history is represented by the age of the oldest loan account and the average age of all loan accounts. A longer credit history will increase the FICO score;

- Credit experience (10%): Credit experience means the history of using different types of credit products. A more diversified credit experience will increase the FICO score; and

- Recent enquiry (10%): The recent enquiries from a large number of loan applications will decrease the FICO score.

7.9   Annual default rates vs FICO scores   ★★★

The full range of FICO score is divided broadly into five categories, namely: super prime, prime, Alt-A, subprime and deep subprime, as depicted in Table 7.8.

Most banks' retail lending services will be provided only to borrowers in the super prime and prime categories. Some non-bank financial institutions focus on borrowers of Alt-A and subprime categories in order to avoid competition with banks and seek a higher return by taking a higher risk.

The association between annual default rates and FICO scores is also shown in Table 7.8. With the large number of individual persons and small businesses assessed by retail credit bureaus, these annual default rates may serve as proxies of the PDs.

Credit quality	From	To	Annual default rate (%)
Super prime	740	850	0.4
Prime	680	739	2.8
Alt-A	620	679	7.5
Subprime	550	619	17.0
Deep subprime	350	549	33.8

Table 7.8   FICO score classification

Appendix 7.1   Credit ratings of major countries in 2016

Country	GDP (USD billion)	Moody's	S&P	Fitch
United States	18,569	Aaa	AA+	AAA
China	11,218	A1	AA-	A+
Japan	4,939	A1	A+	A
Germany	3,467	Aaa	AAA	AAA
United Kingdom	2,629	Aa1	AA	AA
France	2,463	Aa2	AA	AA
India	2,256	Baa3	BBB-	BBB-
Italy	1,851	Baa2	BBB-	BBB+
Brazil	1,799	Ba2	BB	BB
Canada	1,529	Aaa	AAA	AAA
South Korea	1,411	Aa2	AA	AA-
Russia	1,281	Ba1	BB+	BBB-
Australia	1,259	Aaa	AAA	AAA
Spain	1,233	Baa2	BBB+	BBB+
Mexico	1,046	A3	BBB+	BBB+
Indonesia	932	Baa3	BBB-	BBB-
Turkey	857	Ba1	BB	BB+
Netherlands	771	Aaa	AAA	AAA
Switzerland	660	Aaa	AAA	AAA
Saudi Arabia	640	A1	A-	AA
Argentina	545	B3	B	B
Taiwan	529	Aa3	AA-	A+
Sweden	511	Aaa	AAA	AAA
Poland	468	A2	BBB+	A-
Belgium	467	Aa3	■■■■■	AA
Thailand	407	Baa1	BBB+	BBB+
Nigeria	406	■■■■■	B	BB-
Austria	387	Aa1	AA+	AA+
Egypt	332	B3	B-	B
Hong Kong	321	Aa2	AAA	AA+

Table 7.9   Credit ratings of major countries in 2016

Appendix 7.2   Credit Research Initiative

The Credit Research Initiative ("CRI") is a non-profit undertaking by the Risk Management Institute ("RMI") of the National University of Singapore.   This undertaking seeks to promote research and development in credit risk management.

The foundation of the CRI is the PD model that has been developed using a database of about 65,000 listed companies in Asia Pacific, North America, Europe, Latin America, Middle East and Africa. The CRI web portal presents the outputs from the CRI's PD model, including daily updated PDs for individual listed companies in the aforementioned regions and aggregate PDs for different economies and sectors.

This non-profit initiative was conceptualized by Professor Jin-chuan Duan in March 2009. It takes a "public good" approach to credit rating with the goal of keeping the PD model current, evolutionary and organic, and functions like a "selective Wikipedia." The RMI announced the CRI in July 2009 and started releasing results from its PD model in July 2010 at its fourth Annual Risk Management Conference.

Registered users can access the PDs, research results and publications for free from the CRI website with the following URL:

http://rmicri.org/en

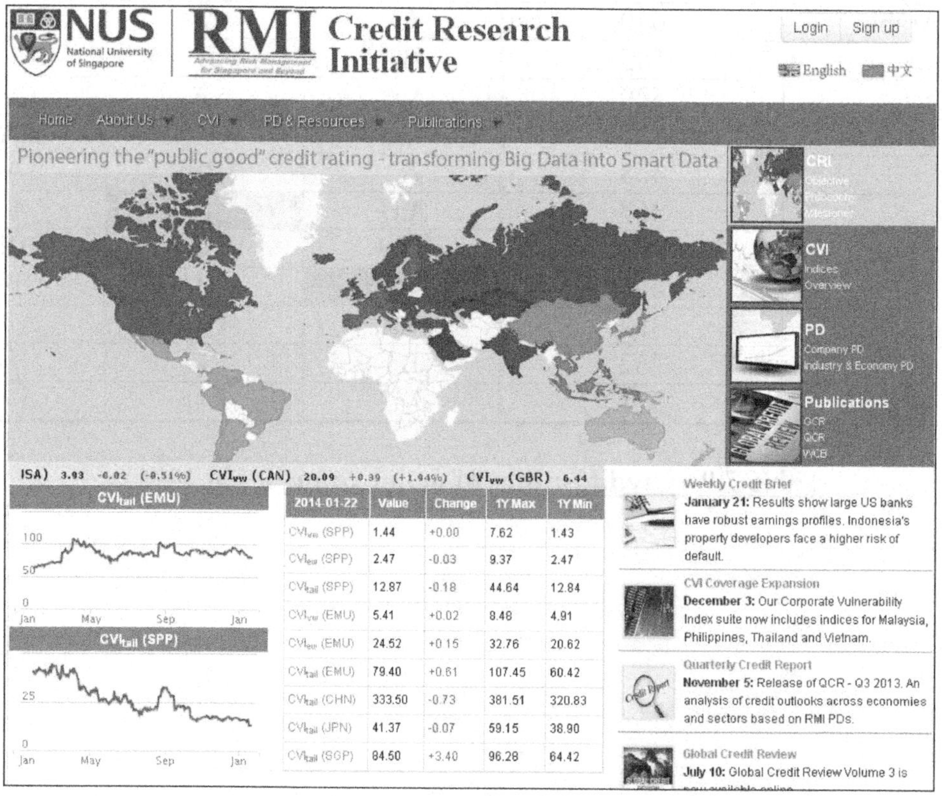

Figure 7.2   Credit Research Initiative, RMI

Appendix 7.3   Rating migration

In addition to default rates, the major global credit rating agencies also publish annually the migration rates of their rated corporations. A one-year migration rate from rating X to rating Y is the percentage of corporations that were rated X one year ago and are rated Y one year later.

To facilitate the ease of presentation of migration rates, "default" and "no rating" are also treated as two ratings. When all migration rates are tabulated in a table, a rating migration matrix is formed. According to the rating migration matrix from the three major credit rating agencies, over a period of one year, most corporations will stay in the same rating. Moreover, the credit ratings of investment grade corporations are more stable than those of the high yield grade corporations.

From/To (%)	AAA	AA	A	BBB	BB	B	CCC to C	Default	No rating
AAA	87.05	9.03	0.53	0.05	0.08	0.03	0.05	0.00	3.17
AA	0.52	86.82	8.00	0.51	0.05	0.07	0.02	0.02	3.99
A	0.03	1.77	87.79	5.33	0.32	0.13	0.02	0.06	4.55
BBB	0.01	0.10	3.51	85.56	3.79	0.51	0.12	0.18	6.23
BB	0.01	0.03	0.12	4.97	76.98	6.92	0.61	0.72	9.63
B	0.00	0.03	0.09	0.19	5.15	74.26	4.46	3.76	12.06
CCC to C	0.00	0.00	0.13	0.19	0.63	12.91	43.97	26.78	15.39

Table 7.10   One-year rating migration matrix

If the migration rates are accumulated starting from the column AAA, an aggregated rating migration matrix is constructed. The aggregated rating migration matrix demonstrates an important characteristic that over a period of one year, at least 90 percent of the time an investment grade corporation will be upgraded, maintained at the same rating or downgraded by one rating.

From/To (%)	AAA	AA	A	BBB	BB	B	CCC to C	Default	No rating
AAA	87.05	96.08	96.61	96.66	96.74	96.77	96.82	96.82	100
AA	0.52	87.34	95.34	95.85	95.90	95.97	95.99	96.01	100
A	0.03	1.80	89.59	94.92	95.24	95.37	95.39	95.45	100
BBB	0.01	0.11	3.62	89.18	92.97	93.48	93.60	93.78	100
BB	0.01	0.04	0.16	5.13	82.11	89.03	89.64	90.36	100
B	0.00	0.03	0.12	0.31	5.46	79.72	84.18	87.94	100
CCC to C	0.00	0.00	0.13	0.32	0.95	13.86	57.83	84.61	100

Table 7.11   One-year aggregated rating migration matrix

Appendix 7.4   PDs corresponding to credit ratings with modifier and specific FICO scores

To differentiate the credit quality of a corporation at a higher granularity, a modifier may be appended at the end of the credit ratings between AA and B. Obviously, within the same credit rating, a corporation with a modifier "+" is entitled to a lower PD while a corporation with a modifier "-" is subject to a higher PD. Applying linear and cubic interpolations to the Probit of the three-year default rates in the ECAI Plus rating scale, the PDs of the ECAI Plus rating scale with modifiers are derived in Table 7.12.

Credit quality	Credit rating	3-year DR (%)	PD (%)
Excellent	AAA	0.0300	0.0100
Good	AA+	0.0678	0.0226
	AA	0.1000	0.0333
	AA-	0.1341	0.0447
	A+	0.1803	0.0601
	A	0.2500	0.0834
	A-	0.3692	0.1232
Moderate	BBB+	0.5844	0.1952
	BBB	1.0000	0.3345
	BBB-	2.0598	0.6914
	BB+	4.1162	1.3913
	BB	7.5000	2.5652
	BB-	11.0869	3.8413
Bad	CCC	40.00	15.6567
	CC	65.00	29.5270
	C	95.00	63.1597

Table 7.12   ECAI Plus rating scale with rating modifiers using linear and cubic interpolations

With similar interpolation techniques, the PDs corresponding to some specific FICO scores are derived in Table 7.13.

FICO score	PD (%)	FICO score	PD (%)
Super prime			
825	0.1786	780	0.5846
820	0.2052	775	0.6611
815	0.2353	770	0.7464
810	0.2694	765	0.8412
805	0.3079	760	0.9464
800	0.3512	755	1.0630
795	0.4000	750	1.1918
790	0.4547	745	1.3340
785	0.5160	740	1.4906
Prime		Alt-A	
735	1.6628	675	5.1318
730	1.8517	670	5.5548
725	2.0585	665	6.0024
720	2.2847	660	6.4753
715	2.5314	655	6.9743
710	2.8000	650	7.5000
705	3.0711	645	8.0730
700	3.3616	640	8.6755
695	3.6722	635	9.3072
690	4.0038	630	9.9676
685	4.3571	625	10.6560
680	4.7329	620	11.3713

Table 7.13   FICO scores interpolated with liner and cubic interpolations

Corporate Credit Analysis

KEY CONCEPTS

- Black-Scholes option valuation model
- Merton's corporate default model

- Financial ratios
- Altman's Z-score

8.1 Internal credit assessment

Chapter 7 introduced the idea of leveraging on a credit rating issued by credit rating agencies to assess the credit quality of corporations. There, the credit quality of a corporation was assumed to have been reflected fairly by its credit rating. The exact methodology adopted by a credit rating agency in conducting the credit assessment is behind the scenes and remains a trade secret.

However, many corporations do not invite credit rating agencies to assess their credit quality for various reasons. For example, a corporation in national security business may have a strong hesitation to disclose its information to an external party. In addition, banking regulations demand that a bank put in place appropriate procedures to ensure the adequacy of credit assessment results provided by a third party. As such, there is a need for a lender to develop its own techniques to facilitate the credit analysis on a corporation regardless of whether the corporation is assigned with a credit rating.

Traditional corporate credit analysis covers:

- the macro analysis on the risks of: (i) the country where a corporation resides; and (ii) the industry to which a corporation belongs;

- the qualitative analysis on management, business and operation of a corporation;

- the quantitative analysis of financial statements that exhibit directly the financial healthiness of a corporation; and

- the projection of cash flows of a corporation in the near future.

This comprehensive framework is conceptually sound since major direct and indirect factors that may impact the credit quality of a corporation are examined. The credit assessment results are well ascertained by sufficient reasoning. Nevertheless, the success of this comprehensive framework is at a huge cost for covering many dimensions. Regular assessment to retrieve the up-to-date credit quality of a corporation becomes time consuming and expensive. Moreover, the interpretation of qualitative information is subject to experience and certain subjective views of a credit analyst. Thus the assessment results may be prone to inconsistency among credit analysts.

Modern financial economists take an alternative approach to identify a few observable and quantifiable factors that explain directly the credit quality of a corporation and derive a mathematical relationship between the credit quality of a corporation and these explanatory variables. The most representative academic works include Merton's corporate default model and Altman's family of Z-scores.

8.2   Black-Scholes option valuation model

In this section, the theory of option valuation is introduced since Merton's corporate default model essentially rides on this theory.

A call option is a financial contract between an acquirer and a writer. The acquirer of a call option has the right but not the obligation to buy the underlying equity from the writer at a strike price K at maturity T. The writer of a call option, in turn, is obligated to sell the underlying equity to the acquirer at the strike price K upon the acquirer's request at maturity T. The acquirer of a call option is benefited if, at maturity, the market price of underlying equity S_T is above the strike price so that he can buy the underlying equity at a cost lower than the market price.

Mathematically, the payoff of a call option with strike price K at maturity T is expressed as:

$$\text{Payoff}[\text{Call}] = \text{Max}[\text{Equity price at maturity - Strike price, 0}]$$

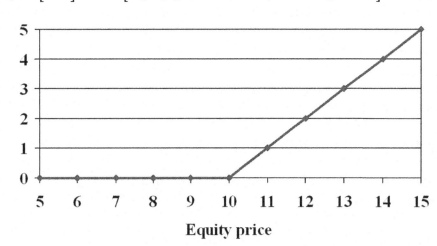

Figure 8.1   Payoff of a call option

In order to acquire a call option that will provide a monetary benefit, the acquirer must pay a premium to the option writer who is obligated to deliver the monetary benefit at maturity. To determine the fair value of this premium, which is essentially the value of a call option, a methodology is required. This triggers a large amount of researches on option valuation.

The Black-Scholes model is by far the most popular valuation methodology being used by practitioners in option trading. The model was first proposed in 1973 by Professor Fisher Black and Professor Myron Scholes and further extended by Professor Robert Merton, all from Massachusetts Institute of Technology. This seminal work facilitated Scholes and Merton to become the laureates of the Nobel Prize in Economics in 1997.[17]

Starting with the following assumptions:

- the call option can only be exercise at maturity;
- the underlying equity does not pay any dividend up to maturity;
- the volatility and risk-free rate are constant;
- the equity market is efficient;
- there are no transaction cost and tax; and
- the evolution of the price of underlying equity follows a geometric Brownian motion,

let S_0 be the current equity price;
σ be the volatility;
r be the risk-free rate;
K be the strike price; and
T be the time to maturity,

the Black-Scholes option valuation model states that the value of a call option (c) can be calculated with the following set of formulas:

$$c = S_0 \Phi(d_1) - K\exp(-rT)\Phi(d_2)$$

where

$$d_1 = \frac{\ln\left(\frac{S_0}{K}\right) + \left(r + \frac{\sigma^2}{2}\right)T}{\sigma\sqrt{T}}$$

$$d_2 = d_1 - \sigma\sqrt{T}$$

$$\Phi(d_1) = \int_{-\infty}^{d_1} \frac{1}{\sqrt{2\pi}}\exp\left(-\frac{\tau^2}{2}\right)d\tau$$

$$\Phi(d_2) = \int_{-\infty}^{d_2} \frac{1}{\sqrt{2\pi}}\exp\left(-\frac{\tau^2}{2}\right)dt\tau$$

---

[17] Professor Fisher Black passed away in 1995.

At maturity, the probability that the equity price will be lower than the strike price is $1 - \Phi(d_2)$. This Black-Scholes framework lays the foundation of modern option valuation theory and become the standard language in the market of option trading.

In the Black-Scholes formula, the option value is driven by five parameters: the current equity price, volatility, risk-free rate, strike price and time to maturity. The strike price and time to maturity are specified in the call option contract. The current equity price is observed directly from the stock exchange. The volatility is implied from those liquidly traded options with similar characteristics in terms of underlying equity, strike price and time to maturity. In case such liquidly traded options are not available, the historical volatility may be used as a proxy, subject to some adjustments in accordance with the market outlook. The interbank rate is used as a proxy of the short term risk-free rate with maturity up to one year.

8.3   Merton's corporate default model ★★★

Riding on the Black-Scholes framework, in 1974, Professor Robert Merton derived a corporate default model for listed companies. The model recognizes that the assets of a listed company comprise both equity and liabilities. While the economic value of equity (E) can be observed from the market, the value of liabilities (L) is registered in book value in accordance with the accounting rules. Therefore, the economic value of assets (A) as the sum of value of equity and value of liabilities is unobservable directly.

Merton's corporate default model assumes that all liabilities will mature in one year. At maturity, the listed company converts its assets into cash in order to pay off the liabilities. If the value of assets is above the value of liabilities, after the liabilities are paid off, the residual of the assets goes to the shareholders' equity. If the value of assets is below the value of liabilities, the cash amount will be insufficient to pay off the liabilities. Then the listed company defaults and no equity will be left to shareholders.

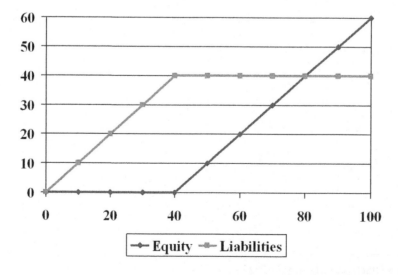

Figure 8.2   Simplified asset structure of a listed company

Therefore, the value of equity at maturity forms a payoff function similar to that of a call option:

Value of equity in one year

$= \text{Max}\left[\text{Value of assets in one year - Value of liabilities in one year, } 0\right]$

and the current value of assets must satisfy the Black-Scholes formula in the form:

$$E_0 = A_0\Phi(d_1) - L\exp(-rT)\Phi(d_2)$$

$$d_1 = \frac{\ln\left(\dfrac{A_0}{L}\right) + \left(r + \dfrac{\sigma_A^2}{2}\right)T}{\sigma_A\sqrt{T}}$$

$$d_2 = d_1 - \sigma_A\sqrt{T}$$

where the current value of equity is calculated as the arithmetic product of equity price and number of shares[18].

$$E_0 = \text{Equity price} \times \text{No. of shares}$$

Since the value of assets is the sum of values of equity and liabilities, the volatility of assets (σ_A) and volatility of equity (σ_E) are linked by the following gear ratio formula:[19]

$$\sigma_A = \sigma_E \times \frac{E_0}{E_0 + (1 - LGD)L} = \frac{E_0\sigma_E}{E_0 + 0.5L}$$

where the average LGD is set to 50%.

When the current value of equity, value of liabilities, asset volatility, risk-free rate and time to maturity are readily available, the current value of assets can be backed out from the Black-Scholes formula by some numerical methods,[20] i.e., a value of assets, when substituted into the Black-Scholes formula, will result in a value of equity that matches the observed from the market.

Once the current value of assets is derived, the PD of a listed company is then calculated as:

$$PD = 1 - \Phi(d_2)$$

---

[18] Please refer to Annex 8.3 for the procedure to obtain the number of shares from Morningstar Financial.
[19] According to JPMorgan's CreditGrades, 2002.
[20] In case this relationship is set up in Microsoft Excel, the Goal Seek menu option can be utilized conveniently to back out the current value of assets.

with the assumption that the value of assets grows at the risk-free rate.

Inline with the ECAI credit rating scale, a listed company with its PD:

- below 1 percent is subject to a good credit quality;
- between 1 percent and 10 percent is subject to a moderate credit quality; and
- above 10 percent is subject to a poor credit quality.[21]

Merton's corporate default model suggests that the credit quality of a listed company is driven by three observable parameters:

- market value of equity;
- book value of liabilities; and
- volatility of equity.

Empirically, the model was found to be less accurate in estimating the PD of a listed company, primarily due to the following unrealistic model specifications:

- All liabilities are unified to mature in one year;
- The value of assets follows a geometric Brownian motion; and
- The value of assets grows at the risk-free rate.

In other words, the PD derived from the Merton's corporate default model could never be used directly in credit assessment. Nevertheless, the model remains useful in determining the credit quality of a list company when combining with other corporate credit assessment approaches. Please see section 8.6 for further details of the consolidated corporate credit assessment.

8.4   Financial ratios

Traditional corporate credit analysis is conducted by accountants who are trained to analyze the position of a corporation with financial ratios derived from financial statements which consist of balance sheet, income statement and cash flow statement.[22] These financial statements consolidate numerous financial transactions conducted by a corporation into a manageable set of items which ease the analysis, comparison and decision making.

From the financial statements, many financial ratios are created for various types of analysis, for example:

---

[21] This classification scheme is highly asymmetric due to the effect of mis-classification cost, to be discussed in Chapter 9.

[22] Nasdaq provides over the Internet the most recent years of financial statements for companies listed in United States. These financial statements can be accessed with the URL https://www.nasdaq.com/quotes/company-financials.aspx.

- Liquidity ratios indicate the ability of a corporation to fulfil its short term liabilities. The three major liquidity ratios are:

$$\text{Current ratio} = \frac{\text{Current assets}}{\text{Current liabilities}}$$

$$\text{Quick ratio} = \frac{\text{Cash} + \text{Marketable securities} + \text{Account receivables}}{\text{Current liabilities}}$$

$$\text{Cash ratio} = \frac{\text{Cash} + \text{Marketable securities}}{\text{Current liabilities}}$$

- Leverage ratios indicate the level of liabilities within the capital structure of a corporation. The three major leverage ratios are:

$$\text{Liabilities to equity ratio} = \frac{\text{Total liabilities}}{\text{Total equity}}$$

$$\text{Liabilities to assets ratio} = \frac{\text{Total liabilities}}{\text{Total assets}}$$

$$\text{Equity to assets ratio} = \frac{\text{Total equity}}{\text{Total assets}}$$

- Return on investment ratios indicate the earnings ability of a corporation. The three major return on investment ratios are:

$$\text{Return on total assets} = \frac{\text{Earnings before interest and taxes}}{\text{Total assets}}$$

$$\text{Return on total equity} = \frac{\text{Earnings before interest and taxes}}{\text{Total equity}}$$

$$\text{Return on common equity} = \frac{\text{Earnings before interest and taxes}}{\text{Common equity}}$$

Liquidity ratios, leverage ratios and return on investment ratios relate directly to the credit quality of a corporation. Other financial ratios related less directly to the credit quality of a corporation include, among others, turnover ratios, operating profitability ratios, operating efficiency ratios, coverage ratios and growth ratios.

Obviously, a standalone group of financial ratios will not portray clearly the credit quality of a corporation. To analyze the credit quality of a corporation, financial ratios are compared with: (i) those of peer group to indicate the relative position within the industry; and (ii) their history to indicate the potential improvement and/or deterioration.

Financial ratios suffer from the following major limitations:

- The combination of a useful set of financial ratios is highly industry specific. In other words, there is no single set of financial ratios that can serve as a universal rule to explain the credit quality of a large number of corporations in many industries;

- Through the years, many financial ratios are created for different purposes and industries. This results in a large number of financial ratios carrying overlapping information;

- Inconsistency may be observed among several less related financial ratios;

- Financial statements are prepared in book values which may deviate materially from the economic values;

- Financial statements are subject to accounting cosmetics within the scope of the generally accepted accounting principles. This results in a further deviation from the economic values; and

- It is difficult to obtain for comparison the corresponding financial ratios of the peer group of private firms and/or in emerging industries.

In summary, although financial ratios are the most direct indicators of the financial healthiness of a corporation, they are never conclusive when applied to the corporate credit analysis in a straight forward setup.

8.5   Altman's family of Z-scores

Recognizing both the advantages and limitations of financial ratios, in 1968, Professor Edward Altman of New York University applied linear discriminant analysis to determine:

- a minimum set of financial ratios that explain the majority of the credit quality of a corporation;

- a simple linear formula to summarize the credit quality of a corporation into a single number; and

- two cutoff values to classify the credit quality of a corporation into good, moderate or bad.

8.5.1 Listed manufacturing company ★★★

In his pioneer research in 1968, Professor Altman selected thirty-three listed US manufacturing companies defaulted between 1946 and 1965 and thirty-three listed US manufacturing companies that survived until or after 1966, and investigated the relationship between financial ratios of a corporation and the survival status within one year after the financial ratios were published.

The research suggests that the credit quality of a listed manufacturing company could be well explained by the following five financial ratios:

$$X_1 = \frac{\text{Market value of equity}}{\text{Total liabilities}}$$

$$X_2 = \frac{\text{Current assets - Current liabilities}}{\text{Total assets}}$$

$$X_3 = \frac{\text{Retained earnings}}{\text{Total assets}}$$

$$X_4 = \frac{\text{Earnings before interest and taxes}}{\text{Total assets}}$$

$$X_5 = \frac{\text{Total revenue}}{\text{Total assets}}$$

These five explanatory financial ratios are then combined linearly to form a Z-score formula:

$$Z = 0.6X_1 + 1.2X_2 + 1.4X_3 + 3.3X_4 + 0.999X_5$$

The research further demonstrates that for a manufacturing company listed in the United States, a Z-score:

- above 2.99 suggests that the company is subject to a good credit quality;

- between 1.81 and 2.99 suggests that the company is subject to a moderate credit quality; and

- below 1.81 suggests that the company is subject to a bad credit quality.

8.5.2   Private manufacturing company ★★★

Following the success of the Z-score for listed manufacturing companies, Professor Altman extended the Z-score to private manufacturing companies by replacing the market value of equity for listed manufacturing companies with the book value of equity for private manufacturing companies.   This resulted in the Z'-score for private manufacturing companies.

The explanatory variables and the Z'-score formula are:

$$X_1 = \frac{\text{Book value of equity}}{\text{Total liabilities}}$$

$$X_2 = \frac{\text{Current assets - Current liabilities}}{\text{Total assets}}$$

$$X_3 = \frac{\text{Retained earnings}}{\text{Total assets}}$$

$$X_4 = \frac{\text{Earnings before interest and taxes}}{\text{Total assets}}$$

$$X_5 = \frac{\text{Total revenue}}{\text{Total assets}}$$

$$Z' = 0.420X_1 + 0.717X_2 + 0.847X_3 + 3.107X_4 + 0.998X_5$$

The research demonstrates that for a private manufacturing company, a Z'-score:

- above 2.90 suggests that the company is subject to a good credit quality;

- between 1.23 and 2.90 suggests that the company is subject to a moderate credit quality; and

- below 1.23 suggests that the company is subject to a bad credit quality.

8.5.3   Non-manufacturing company ★★★

A similar research on non-manufacturing companies covering both listed and private corporations, also conducted by Professor Altman, suggests that the credit quality of a non-manufacturing company could be well explained by four financial ratios and resulted in the Z"-score formula.

These four explanatory variables and the Z"-score formula are:

$$X_1 = \frac{\text{Book value of equity}}{\text{Total liabilities}}$$

$$X_2 = \frac{\text{Current assets - Current liabilities}}{\text{Total assets}}$$

$$X_3 = \frac{\text{Retained earnings}}{\text{Total assets}}$$

$$X_4 = \frac{\text{Earnings before interest and taxes}}{\text{Total assets}}$$

$$Z'' = 1.05X_1 + 6.56X_2 + 3.26X_3 + 6.72X_4$$

The research demonstrates that for a non-manufacturing company, a Z"-score:

- above 2.60 suggests that the company is subject to a good credit quality;

- between 1.10 and 2.60 suggests that the company is subject to a moderate credit quality; and

- below 1.10 suggests that the company is subject to a bad credit quality.

The three formulas for the Altman's family of Z-scores also exhibit clearly that the credit quality of a corporation is most sensitive to the earnings ability demonstrated by the coefficient of X_4.

8.5.4   Limitations and contributions

Altman's family of Z-scores were developed with the historical records of US corporations in the middle of the twentieth century. As other econometric models, without re-calibration, it becomes less relevant when the three Z-score formulas are applied to corporations outside the United States and/or in the twenty-first century.

Due to its simplicity, since the introduction of the Altman's family of Z-scores, the linear discriminant analysis applied by Professor Altman to derive the Z-score formulas become the most popular approach for conducting quantitative credit assessment for corporations. Many financial institutions utilize similar methodology to derive their own credit scoring formulas subject to their own customer base and re-calibrate these credit scoring formulas on a regular basis.

8.6   Consolidated corporate credit assessment   ★★★

So far, three different credit assessment techniques, namely: credit rating, Merton's corporate default model and Altman's Z-score, have been introduced to assess the credit quality of corporations. They are connected to the credit quality of a corporation with the relationship exhibited in the Table 8.1.

Credit quality	Credit rating	Merton's PD	Altman's Z-score
Good	BBB or above	Below 1%	Above upper cutoff
Moderate	BB and B	Between 1% and 10%	Between upper and lower cutoffs
Bad	CCC or below	Above 10%	Below lower cutoff

Table 8.1   Credit quality vs credit assessments

Inconsistencies may be observed from the results derived from different credit assessment techniques due to the differences among the theories underlying the credit assessment techniques. A credit analyst must finalize the credit quality from these credit assessment results based on his judgement.

A more comprehensive corporate credit assessment framework is formed by applying these credit assessment techniques along a sufficient long but relevant history of a corporation and summarizing the overall credit quality, credit rating and PD. This approach results in a more representative consolidated corporate credit assessment.

Table 8.2 suggests a simple consolidated corporate credit assessment template which lays out a procedure to take the advantage of the three credit assessment techniques. While the three credit assessment techniques are effective in determining the credit quality of a corporation and the relative position of the credit quality in the same range (good, moderate or bad), the PD can be looked up from the ECAI Plus rating scale once a credit rating is determined. Therefore, in this template, the overall credit quality, credit rating and PD can be determined by the following procedure:

- The credit ratings, Merton's PDs and Altman's Z-scores for a period of three years are tabulated in the green cells;

- The changes to the credit ratings, Merton's PDs and Altman's Z-scores are entered in the yellow cells;

- The credit qualities (good, moderate, bad) implied by the credit ratings, Merton's PDs and Altman's Z-scores are entered in the orange cells;

- The overall credit quality is concluded from the nine individual credit qualities;

- The overall credit rating is determined by the relative position of the corporation within the range of credit quality. For example, for a corporation classified as good credit quality, if the credit ratings, Merton's PDs and Altman's Z-scores exhibit in general that the corporation is at the higher end, than a AA rating may be assigned to the corporation. In contrast, if the credit ratings, Merton's PDs and Altman's Z-scores exhibit in general that the corporation is at the lower end, than a BBB rating may be assigned to the corporation;

- The overall PD is then assigned in accordance with the ECAI Plus rating scale; and

- A final adjustment to PD may be applied as appropriate.

	Date	Credit quality	Credit rating	PD	Altman's Z-score
Credit assessment result					
	Change				
	Change				
Credit quality					
	Overall				

Table 8.2   Consolidated corporate credit assessment template

Appendix 8.1   Historical volatilities ★★★

The historical volatility of equity can be estimated from a time series of equity prices that are collected from Nasdaq, Bloomberg and/or Thomson Reuters.

For a time series of equity prices on N + 1 consecutive trading day, N daily returns are calculated as:

$$\text{Return on day k} = \ln\left(\frac{\text{Price on day k}}{\text{Price on day k - 1}}\right) \quad k = 1 \text{ to } N$$

The average of the N daily returns is:

$$\text{Average return} = \frac{\sum_{k=1}^{N}\text{Return on day k}}{N} = \frac{1}{N}\ln\left(\frac{\text{Price on day N}}{\text{Price on day 0}}\right)$$

The standard deviation of the N daily returns is:

$$\text{Standard deviation} = \sqrt{\frac{\sum_{k=1}^{N}\left(\text{Return on day k - Average return}\right)^2}{N - 1}}$$

If the N daily returns are registered in Microsoft Excel, the standard deviation can be calculated conveniently with the function Stdev(…).

This standard deviation multiplied by the square root of 250 then becomes the historical volatility of an equity.

$$\text{Volatlity} = \text{Standard deviation} \times \sqrt{250}$$

There is no simple rule that specifies the length of the time series of equity prices, i.e., what value of N should be used. As a rule of thumb, if the historical volatility is adopted as a proxy for valuating a financial instrument that will mature in M trading days, the time series should contain the historical equity prices of M + 1 or thirty consecutive trading days, whichever is longer.

Appendix 8.2   Interbank rates ★★★

Interbank rates are interest rates for short term lending from one bank to another bank of top credit quality, with maturity from one day to one year. In practice, interbank rates are adopted by practitioners as proxy of short term risk-free rates for valuation purposes.

Historical interbank rates for major international currencies can be downloaded free of charge from:

1.   Federal Reserve Bank of St. Louis

        https://research.stlouisfed.org/fred2/release?rid=253

2.   Free financial market data website

        https://stooq.com

The interbank rates downloaded from these websites are annualized, in percentage numeric and discrete compounding.   They can be converted into continuous compounding with the following formula:

$$\text{Interbank rate in continuous compounding}$$
$$= \frac{\ln\left(1 + \dfrac{\text{Figure of interbank rate downloaded}}{100} \times \text{Maturity in year}\right)}{\text{Maturity in year}}$$

Appendix 8.3   Morningstar Financials ★★★

Morningstar Financials is a website which consolidates the financial statements and related reports of the companies listed in the United States.   In particular, the number of shares on the financial year end of a company can be observed with the following steps:

1.   Go to the Morningstar Financials website:

        http://financials.morningstar.com

2.   Enter the ticker of a listed company, e.g. "F".

3.   Select "Balance Sheet" and then "Key Ratios".

4.   The numbers of shares on the financial year ends, in million, are tabulated at the middle of the table.

Appendix 8.4   Relationship between asset and equity volatilities

Jones, Mason and Rosenfeld (1984) proposed an alternative approach to link the asset and equity volatilities.

This alternative approach starts with the assumptions that both the asset value (A) and equity value (E) follow their own geometric Brownian motions, i.e.:

$$dA = \mu_A A dt + \sigma_A A dW_{A,t}$$
$$dE = \mu_E E dt + \sigma_E E dW_{E,t}$$

Since the equity value is a function of the asset value, by applying Ito's lemma to the first stochastic differential equation, the following relationship is resulted:

$$\sigma_E E_0 = \sigma_A A_0 \frac{\partial E}{\partial A} = \sigma_A A_0 \Phi(d_1)$$

This relationship and the Black-Scholes formula for equity value:

$$E_0 = A_0 \exp(-rT) \Phi(d_1) - L \exp(-rT) \Phi(d_2)$$

where

$$d_1 = \frac{\ln\left(\frac{A_0}{L}\right) + \left(r + \frac{\sigma_A^2}{2}\right)T}{\sigma_A \sqrt{T}}$$
$$d_2 = d_1 - \sigma_A \sqrt{T}$$

form a set of simultaneous equations with two unknowns: A_0 and σ_A. Once these two unknowns are solved from the simultaneous equations, the PD of a corporation can be calculated as:

$$PD = 1 - \Phi(d_2)$$

There are two major issues with the Jones, Mason and Rosenfeld approach. First the approach involves solving a set of non-linear simultaneous equations, thus requiring a more complicated implementation to obtain the solution. Second, the approach in general produces a lower volatility and a higher asset value, thus pushing the PD unrealistically high. Therefore, although the Jones, Mason and Rosenfeld approach is theoretically more rigorous than JPMorgan's CreditGrades approach, this book adopts the simpler JPMorgan's CreditMetrics approach in which the relationship between asset and equity volatilities are described by a simple algebraic formula.

Appendix 8.5   Moody's KMV model

Moody's KMV model addresses the issues of Merton's corporate default model by relaxing the model assumptions that:

- liabilities are divided into short and longer terms;
- default occurs at a default point somewhere between the values of short and longer term liabilities;
- the value of assets follows an empirical distribution;
- the value of assets grows at an estimated drift; and
- the PD is an empirically increasing function of distance to default which is defined as:

$$\text{Distance to default} = \frac{\text{Market value of assets - Default point}}{\text{Market value of assets} \times \text{Volatility of assets}}$$

With a proprietary methodology to estimate the default point, growth rate of value of assets and volatility of assets, and a large historical database of listed companies, Moody's KMV model becomes one of the major providers to deliver PD estimates of listed companies to financial institutions in the world. The actual methodology remains a trade secret and has never been released to the general public.

Credit Scoring

9

KEY CONCEPTS

- Explanatory variable
- Statistical distance

- Linear discriminant analysis
- Probit transformation

9.1   Quantitative credit assessment

Credit scoring is a collection of quantitative techniques that aim to:

- use a set of historical lending records to identify a few variables that can explain effectively the credit quality of a borrower;

- discover a quantitative relationship between the credit quality of a borrower and the few explanatory variables in numerical format; and

- use this quantitative relationship to assess the credit quality of a potential borrower outside the set of historical lending records.

With credit scoring, credit assessment is guided by some empirical rules exhibited from historical lending records. Through automation of credit scoring, credit assessments on a large number of borrowers can be conducted within a shorter period of time. This makes credit scoring the most popular and efficient credit assessment technique. In fact, Altman's Z-score formulas are classical deliverables of credit scoring.

The underlying principle of credit scoring is essentially very intuitive. Over the years, a professional lender has accumulated a sufficient number of approved lending applications, with borrowers' characteristics well registered in the application material. Most borrowers survive in the following year while some borrowers default in the following year. These two groups of borrowers form two clusters with respect to their characteristics. For example, the group of survival borrowers, in general, concentrate around the region of higher income, less outstanding loan amount, etc., while the group of defaulted borrowers, in general, concentrate around the region of lower income, more outstanding loan amount, etc.. This phenomenon suggests that there is an empirical relationship between the credit quality of a borrower and some explanatory variables.

From the historical lending records, if such empirical relationship between the credit quality of borrowers and relevant explanatory variables is recovered, this empirical relationship can be utilized to predict the credit quality of a potential borrower outside the set of historical lending records and answer the two strategic questions:

- Is the potential borrower a good borrower or a bad borrower? and

- What is the PD of the borrower?

A well structured credit scoring process comprises three major building blocks:

- A set of historical lending records with a sufficient number of good borrowers and a sufficient number of bad borrowers;

- A set of numerical explanatory variables that explain effectively the credit quality of most borrowers; and

- A scoring formula that describes the quantitative relationship between the credit quality of a borrower and the set of numerical explanatory variables.

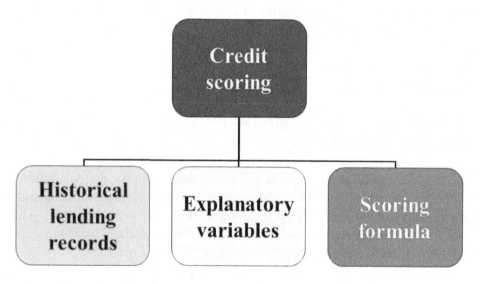

Figure 9.1   Credit scoring

9.2   Historical lending records ★★★

The empirical relationship between the credit quality of borrowers and explanatory variables is recovered from a set of recent and relevant historical lending records that consist of a sufficient and equal number of records of good and bad borrowers. At least thirty records and preferably sixty records in each group are required. In a typical bank lending operation with conservative lending practices, there are usually a large number of good borrowers but only a small number of bad borrowers. Thus, in practical credit scoring, most of the relevant records of bad borrowers are used and the same number of records of good borrowers are selected through stratified sampling which aims at matching, for each bad borrower record, a randomly selected record from a subgroup of good borrowers with similar characteristics in terms of, for example, country, industry and firm size.

9.3   Explanatory variables

Under a credit scoring framework, the credit quality of a borrower is driven by a few explanatory variables. Therefore, the choice of explanatory variables is fundamental to the effectiveness of credit scoring.

9.3.1   Properties of good explanatory variables ★★★

Although a lot of data can be collected from a borrower, to serve the purpose of credit scoring, an explanatory variable must satisfy the following criteria:

- An explanatory variable must be numerical in order to fit into the credit scoring process. Some explanatory variables exist as numeric in their generic format, e.g., income and outstanding loan amount while some explanatory variables are in a qualitative description as their generic format.

  Qualitative data that comprise only two possible values can be converted into a numerical explanatory variable by assigning "0" to represent one value and "1" to represent another value. For example, a male borrower can be represented by a "0" while a female borrower can be represented by a "1."

  Qualitative data that comprises several possible values in rank order can be converted into a numerical explanatory variable by assigning an integer value from "1" to "5" to represent the relationship with credit quality. For example, if it is believed that the industry will impact directly the credit quality of a corporation, then an industry classification scheme can be developed to categorize all industries into five levels, with level 1 assigned to industries facing difficulties and level 5 assigned to industries facing excellent prospects. The most frequently used number of levels is three and five, and seldom more than seven. An odd number of levels is preferred over an even number of levels.

- An explanatory variable must be economically intuitive to explain the credit quality of a borrower. Income and outstanding loan amount are good candidates of explanatory variables while the height of a borrower does not serve the purpose of explaining his credit quality.

- The credit quality of a borrower must have a monotonic relationship with an explanatory variable when other explanatory variables are fixed. For example, when other explanatory variables are constants, a borrower with more income always implies a higher credit quality and a borrower with more outstanding loan amount always implies a lower credit quality. Any financial ratio with a denominator that may range from negative to positive should never be used as an explanatory variable because the economic meaning of the financial ratio is different with different signs.

- Without going into the technical details of the statistical significance of an explanatory variable, the appropriateness of an explanatory variable could be verified simply by comparing the average of the explanatory variable for the group of good borrowers with that for the group of bad borrowers. If the difference between these two averages is obvious and the relative levels are in line with the economic intuition, then this explanatory variable serves as a good candidate.

- The explanatory variables must have low inter-dependency. This avoids a large set of explanatory variables carrying redundant information to be included in the same credit scoring process.

In most practical situations, the number of explanatory variables ranges from four to eight. It is a rare case to find in an efficient credit scoring model with more than ten explanatory variables.

9.3.2   Explanatory variables identification ★★★

Explanatory variables are identified using statistical techniques on a set of selected variables in numerical format. These selected variables are expected to be good for explaining the credit quality of borrowers.

To identify a set of explanatory variables, the set of historical lending records are retrieved to derive a linear regression formula in the form:

$$\text{Default status} = \beta_0 + \beta_1 x_1 + \beta_2 x_2 + \beta_3 x_3 + ... + \beta_N x_N$$

where x_1, x_2, x_3, ... to x_N are the explanatory variables, β_1, β_2, β_3, ... to β_N are the corresponding coefficients to be determined and the default status is coded as 0 for a borrower survives after one year and 1 for a borrower defaults in one year, after a loan has been granted to the borrower one year ago.

A set of explanatory variables are considered as effective if the linear regression results:

- an large F-static or a small significance of F, suggesting that at least one of the explanatory variable is significant;

- a large R-squared, suggesting that the variance of the default status can be well explained by the variances of the explanatory variables; and

- for each coefficient β_k of the explanatory variable x_k, a large t-statistic and a small p-value, suggesting that x_k is a significant explanatory variable.

The large number of computer programmes, including the Analysis ToolPak in Microsoft Excel, developed for linear regression allow the identification of explanatory variables to be conducted conveniently.

9.3.3 Corporate credit scoring ★★★

Financial ratios are by far the most efficient and effective information that concludes the financial healthiness of a corporation in a manageable number of figures. Thus they serve as a set of good candidates of explanatory variables for corporate credit scoring. Nevertheless, through the years, many financial ratios have been created for various specific analyses. This results in a large number of financial ratios carrying overlapping information due to their similarity. Thus a simple adoption of all major financial ratios in corporate credit scoring is less appropriate.

Since the introduction of Altman's Z-score, a great amount of researches have been conducted to identify the most effective set of financial ratios that can explain the credit quality of a corporation. The simplest set of explanatory variables is the few financial ratios adopted in Altman's Z-score formulas.

Category	Financial ratio	Formula	Proportion (%)
Profitability (23%)	Return on assets ("ROA")	$\dfrac{\text{Net income}}{\text{Total assets}}$	9
	Growth of ROA	ROA current year - ROA previous year	7
	Interest coverage	$\dfrac{\text{EBIT}}{\text{Total interest}}$	7
Capital structure (21%)	War chest	$\dfrac{\text{Retained earnings}}{\text{Total assets}}$	12
	Leverage	$\dfrac{\text{Total liabilities}}{\text{Total assets}}$	9
Liquidity (19%)	Cash position	$\dfrac{\text{Cash}}{\text{Total assets}}$	12
	Quick ratio	$\dfrac{\text{Cash} + \text{Marketable securities} + \text{Account receivables}}{\text{Current liabilities}}$	7
Others (38%)	Total assets to consumer price index ("CPI")	$\dfrac{\text{Total assets}}{\text{CPI}}$	14
	Growth of sales	$\dfrac{\text{Sales current year}}{\text{Sales previous year}} - 1$	12
	Stock return	$\dfrac{\text{Inventory}}{\text{Cost of goods sold}}$	12

Table 9.1   Explanatory variables for corporate credit scoring

Falkenstein (2000) analyzed Moody's credit research database and suggested that there were ten low inter-dependency explanatory variables that can explain effectively the credit quality of a corporation. These financial ratios are listed in Table 9.1.

9.3.4 Retail credit scoring

Retail borrowers include individual persons and small businesses with their financial healthiness primarily driven by shareholders. For a retail borrower, his financial statements are either unavailable or less relevant to his financial healthiness. Therefore, the application form and retail credit bureau serve as two effective sources of explanatory variables.

9.3.4.1 Application form ★★★

The application form is the primary tool for collecting financial and operational data from a retail borrower. Due to the competition among banks, modern application forms tend to be user friendly, with only a few most critical and independent data to be collected. Currently, most of the data on an application form can serve as explanatory variables. Some qualitative information is required to be converted into numerical format before it can be applied to retail credit scoring. The major information collected by an application form is listed in Table 9.2.

9.3.4.2 Retail credit bureau ★★★

A retail credit bureau supplements an application form with information publicly available and/or previously collected by other lenders, thus delivering the data that a borrower is reluctant to provide or required to be provided repeatedly.

Since most data provided by a retail credit bureau are descriptive, it is impractical to adopt those data directly from a retail credit bureau report as explanatory variables. In practice, instead of using individual data items, the five major assessment areas (payment history, credit utilization, credit history, credit experience and recent credit enquiry) of a FICO score are adopted as explanatory variables. Each assessment area is analyzed by an expert who then assigns a rank order from 1 to 5 to that particular assessment area. For those lenders without sufficient resources or expertise to analyze credit bureau reports, the FICO score may be adopted directly as a single explanatory variable.

Category	Explanatory variable	Data type
Employment	Income	Numeric
	Job position	Rank order
	Industry of current employer	Rank order
	Duration with current employer	Numeric
	Duration with previous employer	Numeric
Residence	Current residential area	Rank order
	Ownership of residence	Binary
	Duration with current residential address	Numeric
	Duration with previous residential address	Numeric
Financial	Assets	Numeric
	Liabilities	Numeric
	Number of mortgages	Numeric
	Outstanding mortgage amounts	Numeric
	Number of credit cards	Numeric
	Total limit of credit lines	Numeric
Personal	Age group	Rank order
	Gender	Binary
	Marital status	Binary
	Education level	Rank order
	Number of dependants	Numeric

Table 9.2   Explanatory variables for retail credit scoring

9.3.5   Behavioural scoring variables   ★★★

So far, most of the data adopted in credit scoring are submitted during the application of a loan. The data remain static and are seldom updated on a regular basis, unless a lender mandates a borrower to provide regular updates as a requirement in the lending agreement. This makes the monitoring of credit quality and revision to the PD for a loan with longer RM or revolving loan without a fixed maturity difficult due to the change in a borrower's financial condition and operational status over time.

Therefore, instead of using solely the application data for the PD revision, the payment behaviours exhibited by a borrower are also included as explanatory variables to incorporate the updated information of the credit quality of a borrower in credit scoring.

Large drawdown, partial payments and/or late payments are observed frequently before a default event. Thus the major behavioural explanatory variables include, among others, the ratio between drawdown amount and credit limit, overdue amount, overdue period and age of overdue record.

9.4   Cluster analysis

Cluster analysis is the most institutive credit scoring method. Assume that the credit quality of a borrower is explained by N numerical explanatory variables:

$$\begin{bmatrix} x_1 \\ x_2 \\ x_3 \\ \vdots \\ x_N \end{bmatrix}$$

For a set of historical lending records of good borrowers, the averages of these explanatory variables are calculated. This forms the centre of the group of good borrowers.

$$\overline{X^{Good}} = \begin{bmatrix} \overline{x_1^{Good}} \\ \overline{x_2^{Good}} \\ \overline{x_3^{Good}} \\ \vdots \\ \overline{x_N^{Good}} \end{bmatrix}$$

Similarly, for a set of historical lending records of bad borrowers, the averages of these explanatory variables are calculated. This forms the centre of the group of bad borrowers.

$$\overline{X^{Bad}} = \begin{bmatrix} \overline{x_1^{Bad}} \\ \overline{x_2^{Bad}} \\ \overline{x_3^{Bad}} \\ \vdots \\ \overline{x_N^{Bad}} \end{bmatrix}$$

For a potential borrower who reports his explanatory variables in his loan application, the lender compares the potential borrower's position with the two groups of historical lending records.[23] The potential borrower is considered as a good borrower if his position is closer to the centre of the group of good borrowers. In contrast, the potential borrower is considered as a bad borrower if his position is closer to the centre of the group of bad borrowers.

---

[23] Outliers should be excluded from the historical records. An outlier is a good borrower with his position very close to the centre of the group of bad borrowers, a bad borrower with his position very close to the centre of the group of good borrowers or a borrower far away from the two groups.

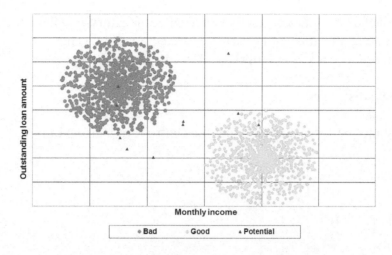

Figure 9.2   Two groups of borrowers

9.4.1   Euclidean distance

On the face of it, the Euclidean distance appears to be the natural choice for measuring the distance between a potential borrower and the centre of a group of borrowers. For any two points P and Q in an N-dimensional space,

$$\mathbf{P} = \begin{bmatrix} p_1 \\ p_2 \\ p_3 \\ \vdots \\ p_N \end{bmatrix} \qquad \mathbf{Q} = \begin{bmatrix} q_1 \\ q_2 \\ q_3 \\ \vdots \\ q_N \end{bmatrix}$$

the Euclidean distance is defined as:

$$\sqrt{\left(p_1 - q_1\right)^2 + \left(p_2 - q_2\right)^2 + \left(p_3 - q_3\right)^2 + ... + \left(p_N - q_N\right)^2}$$

Thus the distance from a potential borrower to the centre of a group of good borrowers is calculated as:

$$\sqrt{\left(x_1^{Po} - \overline{x_1^{Good}}\right)^2 + \left(x_2^{Po} - \overline{x_2^{Good}}\right)^2 + \left(x_3^{Po} - \overline{x_3^{Good}}\right)^2 + ... + \left(x_N^{Po} - \overline{x_N^{Good}}\right)^2}$$

and the distance from a potential borrower to the centre of a group of bad borrowers is calculated as:

$$\sqrt{\left(x_1^{Po} - \overline{x_1^{Bad}}\right)^2 + \left(x_2^{Po} - \overline{x_2^{Bad}}\right)^2 + \left(x_3^{Po} - \overline{x_3^{Bad}}\right)^2 + ... + \left(x_N^{Po} - \overline{x_N^{Bad}}\right)^2}$$

However, the Euclidean distance assumes that all explanatory variables are independent and the scales among all explanatory variables are compatible. These strong assumptions make Euclidean distance a less appropriate choice of distance measure.

9.4.2 Statistical distance

A statistical distance between a point P and the centre R of a group of points

$$\mathbf{P} = \begin{bmatrix} p_1 \\ p_2 \\ p_3 \\ \vdots \\ p_N \end{bmatrix} \quad \mathbf{R} = \begin{bmatrix} r_1 \\ r_2 \\ r_3 \\ \vdots \\ r_N \end{bmatrix}$$

is defined as:

$$\sqrt{\begin{bmatrix} p_1 - r_1 \\ p_2 - r_2 \\ p_3 - r_3 \\ \vdots \\ p_N - r_N \end{bmatrix}^T CovMat(\mathbf{R})^{-1} \begin{bmatrix} p_1 - r_1 \\ p_2 - r_2 \\ p_3 - r_3 \\ \vdots \\ p_N - r_N \end{bmatrix}}$$

where CovMat($\mathbf{R}$) is the covariance matrix of all points in the group with centre R and CovMat($\mathbf{R}$)$^{-1}$ is the inverse of the covariance matrix. Through the covariance matrix, the interdependency among the N explanatory variables is eliminated and the scales among the N explanatory variables are normalized by their standard deviations. Thus the statistical distance serves as an appropriate alternative to measure:

- the distance between a potential borrower and the centre of a group of good borrowers; and

$$\sqrt{\begin{bmatrix} x_1^{Po} - \overline{x_1^{Good}} \\ x_2^{Po} - \overline{x_2^{Good}} \\ x_3^{Po} - \overline{x_3^{Good}} \\ \vdots \\ x_N^{Po} - \overline{x_N^{Good}} \end{bmatrix}^T CovMat(\mathbf{X})^{-1} \begin{bmatrix} x_1^{Po} - \overline{x_1^{Good}} \\ x_2^{Po} - \overline{x_2^{Good}} \\ x_3^{Po} - \overline{x_3^{Good}} \\ \vdots \\ x_N^{Po} - \overline{x_N^{Good}} \end{bmatrix}}$$

- the distance between a potential borrower and the centre of a group of bad borrowers.

$$
\begin{bmatrix} x_1^{Po} - \overline{x_1^{Bad}} \\ x_2^{Po} - \overline{x_2^{Bad}} \\ x_3^{Po} - \overline{x_3^{Bad}} \\ \vdots \\ x_N^{Po} - \overline{x_N^{Bad}} \end{bmatrix}^T \; CovMat\left(\mathbf{X}\right)^{-1} \begin{bmatrix} x_1^{Po} - \overline{x_1^{Bad}} \\ x_2^{Po} - \overline{x_2^{Bad}} \\ x_3^{Po} - \overline{x_3^{Bad}} \\ \vdots \\ x_N^{Po} - \overline{x_N^{Bad}} \end{bmatrix}
$$

Ideally, with statistical distance, any good borrower in the historical lending records should be closer to the centre of good borrowers and any bad borrower in the historical lending records should be closer to the centre of bad borrowers. In a real situation, a small number of good borrowers in the historical lending records may be closer to the centre of bad borrowers and a small number of bad borrowers in the historical lending records may be closer to the centre of good borrowers. The number of such discrepancies measures the quality of the explanatory variables. A set of high quality explanatory variables will result in a small number of discrepancies.

9.4.3 Three-group classification

The application of statistical distance can be extended to the differentiation of borrowers among three groups. The historical lending records are divided into three groups instead of two. The centres of these three groups are then calculated. For a potential borrower, the three distances between the potential borrower and the three centres are calculated. This potential borrower is then assigned to the closest group of borrowers.

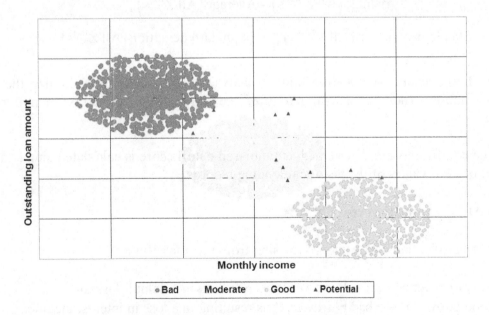

Figure 9.3   Three groups of borrowers

For the purpose of credit assessment, an intermediate group of borrowers that has exhibited material late payments due to financial difficulties may be classified as "moderate." By the same token, the number of groups can be extended to four or five, as long as there is a clear definition for and sufficient number of historical lending records in each group.

9.5   Linear discriminant analysis   ★★★

The linear discriminant analysis seeks to identify:

- a set of coefficients α_1, α_2, α_3, ... α_N to form a linear discriminant formula for N independent explanatory variables x_1, x_2, x_3, ... x_N in the form:

$$Z = \alpha_1 x_1 + \alpha_2 x_2 + \alpha_3 x_3 + ... + \alpha_N x_N \text{ and}$$

- a cutoff score,

both from the historical lending records, such that when the N independent explanatory variables of a borrower are substituted into the linear discriminant formula, a Z value above the cutoff score suggests that the borrower is a good borrower and a Z value below the cutoff score suggests that the borrower is a bad borrower.

For each historical record, a Z value can be calculated. The set of coefficients α_1, α_2, α_3, ... α_N are chosen to maximize the objective function:[24]

$$\frac{\left[\text{Average}\left(\text{All } Z^{\text{Good}}s \right) - \text{Average}\left(\text{All } Z^{\text{Bad}}s \right) \right]^2}{\left[\text{Standard deviation}\left(\text{All } Z^{\text{Good}}s \right) \right]^2 + \left[\text{Standard deviation}\left(\text{All } Z^{\text{Bad}}s \right) \right]^2}$$

This is the seminal Fisher's discriminant analysis which seeks to maximize the inter group variability (nominator) but minimize the intra group variability (denominator) together.

Once the coefficients are determined, an unbiased cutoff score is calculated simply as the average of all Z values of the historical lending records.

9.5.1   Mis-classification cost   ★★★

The mis-classification cost is the loss arising from mis-classifying:

- a bad borrower as a good borrower, thus resulting in a default loss; or
- a good borrower as a bad borrower, thus resulting in a loss in interest income.

---

[24] This maximization can be set up and solved in Microsoft Excel with the Solver add-in.

Under normal circumstances, for a period of one year, the magnitude of a default loss is several times greater than that of interest income. This essentially encourages a bank to be more conservative by lending only to a borrower with a credit score well above the unbiased cutoff score. As such, taking into account the mis-classification cost, a biased prudent cutoff score is determined as follows.

If the ratio between the two mis-classification costs is:

$$\frac{\text{Loss of classifying a good borrower as bad borrower}}{\text{Loss of classifying a bad borrower as good borrower}} = \frac{a}{b}$$

then a prudent cutoff score is calculated as:

$$\frac{b \times \text{Average}\left(\text{All Z}^{\text{Good}}\text{s}\right) + a \times \text{Average}\left(\text{All Z}^{\text{Bad}}\text{s}\right)}{a + b}$$

When the N independent explanatory variables of a potential borrower are substituted into the linear discriminant formula, a potential borrower with his credit score above the prudent cutoff score is considered as a good borrower, below the unbiased cutoff score is considered as a bad borrower, and between the prudent and unbiased cutoff scores is considered as a moderate borrower. For a moderate borrower, a lender may look into the additional information, e.g., the relationship with the lender, not incorporated in the linear discriminant function in order to decide whether to accept or reject the borrower.

9.6   PD modelling

9.6.1   Linear PD regression ★★★

The linear regression formula derived in the explanatory variables identification with a set of effective explanatory variables can be used to form a linear unbounded PD formula:

$$\text{Unbounded PD} = \beta_0 + \beta_1 x_1 + \beta_2 x_2 + \beta_3 x_3 + ... + \beta_N x_N$$

However, such a linear unbounded PD formula may deliver an unbounded PD below 0 percent or above 100 percent, contradicting to the definition of a PD which ranges only between 0 percent and 100 percent. As such, the linear PD regression in its generic format appears to be a less appropriate method for deriving a PD between 0 percent and 100 percent.

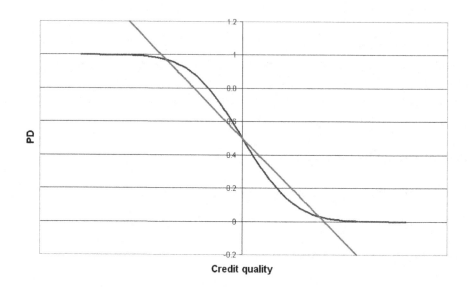

Figure 9.4   PD modelling

9.6.2   Probit transformation   ★★★

The issue of linear PD regression can be resolved by the Probit transformation which seeks to convert the unbounded PD estimated by a linear PD regression to a bound PD between 0 percent and 100 percent.

The transformation starts with setting a Probit coefficient[25] and then derive a Probit from the unbound PD estimated by the linear PD formula. The total number of records refers to the complete historical data set from which equal numbers of good and bad borrowers are sampled.

$$\text{Probit coefficient} = \Phi^{-1}\left(\frac{\text{Total no. of records}}{\text{Total no. of records} + 1}\right)$$

$$= \text{Normsinv}\left(\frac{\text{Total no. of records}}{\text{Total no. of records} + 1}\right)$$

$$\text{Probit} = \text{Probit coefficient} \times \left(2 \times \text{Unbounded PD} - 1\right)$$

This Probit is then substituted into the cumulative standard normal distribution function and results in a bounded PD which always falls between 0 percent and 100 percent. Given a Probit, the bounded PD can be calculated in Microsoft Excel with the function Normsdist(…).

$$\text{Bounded PD} = \Phi\left(\text{Probit}\right) = \text{Normsdist}\left(\text{Probit}\right)$$

---

[25] In case the exact total number of records is unavailable but more than ten thousand, the Probit coefficient may be set artificially to $\Phi^{-1}(99.99\%) = 3.719$.

This bounded PD estimation process, referred to as Probit transformation, combines the simplicity of linear regression and the boundary characteristics of PD.

The Probit transformation is a convenient but less rigorous PD modelling technique due to the highly non-linear relationship between the PD and explanation variables. It suffers from many common issues of linear to non-linear transformation. Nevertheless, its theoretical deficiency is compensated by the popularity of computer programmes well developed for linear regression. Therefore, the Probit transformation serves as a very convenient approach to derive a simple PD formula from a set of historical lending records.

9.7   Credit assessment with credit scoring ★★★

Table 9.3 summarizes the procedures of credit assessment with credit scoring. These procedures deliver:

- a linear discriminant formula with unbiased and prudent cutoff scores to determine whether a borrower is good, moderate or bad; and

- a PD formula to estimate the PD of a borrower.

Since the linear PD regression is practical in identifying the effective explanatory variables, it is adopted as the first step to derive a set of variables which explain effectively the credit quality of borrower.

Step	Input	Objective/output
Explanatory variables identification	A total of at least 30 good and 30 bad records of borrowers	To identify a set of effective explanatory variables
Discriminant analysis	At least 30 good and 30 bad records of borrowers with effective explanatory variables only	To calibrate a linear discriminant formula and an unbiased cutoff score
	Mis-classification cost	To calibrate a prudent cutoff score
Linear PD regression	Effective explanatory variables	To derive an unbound PD formula
Probit transformation	Unbound PD formula	To derive the bound PD

Table 9.3   Practical credit scoring

Appendix 9.1   Key explanatory variables proposed in 2014 the revision to the Basel III proposal

In December 2014, the BCBS proposed for consultation in the revision to the Basel III framework, a set of key explanatory variables for various types of debt exposures. This set of key explanatory variables are exhibited in Table 9.4.

	Exposure	Key explanatory variables
1.	Corporation	• Annual income • Leverage ratio
2.	Bank	• Common equity ratio • Asset quality ratio
3.	Residential mortgage	• Loan-to-value ratio • Debt-service coverage ratio
4.	Commercial mortgage	• Loan-to-value ratio

Table 9.4   Key explanatory variables proposed

where

$$\text{Leverage ratio} = \frac{\text{Total assets}}{\text{Total equity}}$$

$$\text{Common equity ratio} = \frac{\text{Common equity}}{\text{Capital charge}}$$

$$\text{Asset quality ratio} = \frac{\text{Non-performing debts}}{\text{Total debts}}$$

$$\text{Loan-to-value ratio} = \frac{\text{Outstanding loan amount}}{\text{Market value of the property}}$$

$$\text{Debt-service coverage ratio} = \frac{\text{Monthly interest payment} + \text{Monthly principal payment}}{\text{Monthly income}}$$

Although this set of key explanatory variables were not adopted eventually in the revision to the Basel III framework, the proposal demonstrates essentially the importance of these key explanatory variables among the BCBS's consideration.

Appendix 9.2 Probit regression

The Probit regression seeks to identify a set of coefficients for the explanatory variables which best fit a non-linear PD model directly in the following form:

$$\text{Probit} = \beta_0 + \beta_1 x_1 + \beta_2 x_2 + \beta_3 x_3 + \dots + \beta_N x_N$$

$$\text{PD} = \frac{1}{\sqrt{2\pi}} \int_{-\infty}^{\text{Probit}} \exp\left(-\frac{\tau^2}{2}\right) d\tau$$

For a bad borrower h, its PD^{Bad} is considered to be predictive if a set of coefficients have been chosen such that the PD^{Bad} approaches 1.

For a good borrower k, its PD^{Good} is considered to be predictive if a set of coefficients have been chosen such that the PD^{Good} approaches 0. This is equivalent to the situation where the probability of survival $1 - \text{PD}^{\text{Good}}$ approaches 1.

For a set of recent and relevant historical lending records that consist of U good borrowers and V bad borrowers, a likelihood function is formed:

$$L = \text{PD}_1^{\text{Bad}} \times \text{PD}_2^{\text{Bad}} \times \text{PD}_3^{\text{Bad}} \times \cdots \times \text{PD}_U^{\text{Bad}}$$
$$\times \left(1 - \text{PD}_1^{\text{Good}}\right) \times \left(1 - \text{PD}_2^{\text{Good}}\right) \times \left(1 - \text{PD}_3^{\text{Good}}\right) \times \cdots \times \left(1 - \text{PD}_V^{\text{Good}}\right)$$

The best fitted PD model is constructed if a set of coefficients $\beta_0, \beta_1, \beta_2, \beta_3, \dots \beta_N$ for the explanatory variables can be identified such that that L approaches 1 as much as possible. This is equivalent to maximize the natural logarithm of the likelihood function L:

$$\ln(L) = \ln\left(\text{PD}_1^{\text{Bad}}\right) + \ln\left(\text{PD}_2^{\text{Bad}}\right) + \ln\left(\text{PD}_3^{\text{Bad}}\right) + \cdots + \ln\left(\text{PD}_U^{\text{Bad}}\right)$$
$$+ \ln\left(1 - \text{PD}_1^{\text{Bad}}\right) + \ln\left(1 - \text{PD}_2^{\text{Bad}}\right) + \ln\left(1 - \text{PD}_3^{\text{Bad}}\right) + \cdots + \ln\left(1 - \text{PD}_V^{\text{Bad}}\right)$$

The search of this set of coefficients can be performed by specialist Probit regression programmes, e.g. SAS.

Practical Issues In Credit Assessments

10

KEY CONCEPTS

- Domestic credit rating agency
- Financial distress
- Altman's Z_{China}-score
- Earnings manipulation

10.1 Practical issues

Invariably, many less experienced lenders set up their corporate credit analysis framework with some underlying assumptions:

- The default of a borrower is triggered on the due day when the full payment of interest and/or principal is not on schedule;

- The major global credit rating agencies deliver credit ratings of most corporations in the world under a similar standard;

- Historical default records are available for the development of credit scoring models;

- The credit qualities of corporations are explained by a universal set of financial ratios; and

- Financial statements provided by corporations are reliable in characterizing their financial healthiness.

However, these assumptions are at times less realistic: a lender may classify a borrower as in default before the next due day if the borrower has already exhibited significant weaknesses in his financial condition; the major global credit rating agencies issue a total of fewer than twenty thousand corporate credit ratings every year; historical default records are rare and difficult to collect; the credit qualities of corporations in different countries and industries are explained by very different sets of financial ratios; and all financial statements are subject to a certain degree of accounting cosmetics.

This chapter demonstrates how to overcome these issues. An example is illustrated to assess the credit qualities of listed companies in mainland China.

10.2   Definition of default ★★★

Although it is straight forward and objective to classify a borrower to be in default when he fails to pay the interest and/or principal in full on schedule, such definition of default is far from practice. In case a borrower fails to pay the interest and/or principal in full on a due day, in practice, the borrower is classified as overdue instead of default. An overdue period from several days to several months may be granted to the borrower at a small penalty. During this overdue period, the lender will remind continuously the borrower to pay the overdue amount immediately. If the borrower pays the overdue amount during the overdue period, the borrower is resumed to survival from overdue. However, if the borrower eventually fails to pay the overdue amount, the borrower is classified as in default technically after the overdue period. This arrangement essentially helps maintain a good relationship with the customer.

On the other hand, in a situation where a corporation has declared bankruptcy, even though the next interest payment will not take place until next year, a lender must classify the borrower as in default and take immediate action to recover part of the principal and interest.

Therefore, in practice, a more flexible definition of default must be imposed. Under the Basel III framework, a borrower is considered in default when any one of the following conditions emerges:

* A borrower has an outstanding debt overdue for over ninety days;

* A borrower's outstanding debt amount, after incorporating the interest, has exceeded the prevailing credit limit;

* A lender unilaterally reduces a borrower's credit limit to an amount below the current outstanding debt amount; and

* A lender is unlikely to recoup the interest and/or principal from a borrower in full without taking recovery actions such as selling collaterals pledged by a borrower.

10.3   Domestic credit rating agencies ★★★

Although the major global credit rating agencies set the *de facto* standard of credit ratings, their coverage is largely confined only to developed countries. Other countries, especially developing countries, limit the local operations of these credit rating agencies for fear of potential economic intervention from other countries through credit ratings. Instead, these countries encourage the establishment of their own domestic credit rating agencies.

A domestic credit rating agency is a credit rating agency established with a primary mission to provide credit assessment services to corporations in its home country. It competes with the major global credit rating agencies by specializing in local corporations which the domestic credit rating agency has more understanding on and a closer relationship with. Some major domestic credit rating agencies are listed in Table 10.1.

Country	Credit rating agency
United States	Egan-Jones Rating Company
Canada	DBRS
Mexico	HR Ratings
Brazil	Liberum Ratings
United Kingdom	First Report
Germany	Scope Credit Rating
Italy	Cerved Group
Russia	RusRating
Japan	Japan Credit Rating Agency Limited Rating and Investment Information, Inc.
China	Dagong Global Credit Rating Co., Ltd. Pengyuan Credit Rating Co., Ltd. China Chengxin (Asia Pacific) Credit Ratings Company Limited China Lianhe Credit Rating Co., Ltd. Shanghai Brilliance Credit Rating & Investors Service Co., Ltd.
India	Brickwork Ratings India Private Limited Credit Analysis and Research Limited CRISIL ICRA Limited SMEEA Ratings Limited

Table 10.1   Major domestic credit rating agencies

A domestic credit rating agency customizes its credit assessment methodology to incorporate the local laws, regulations, accounting standards, industry practices and political situations. Normally, a domestic credit rating agency conducts a more tailor-made credit assessment and delivers a more accurate result due to the local competitive advantages.

However, this localization may also result in a credit rating scale and rating definition different from those of major global credit rating agencies. A corporation labelled "A" by a domestic credit rating agency may not have a credit quality similar to a corporation rated A by Moody's Investors Service. Therefore, although domestic credit rating agencies serve as a good supplementary source to those major global credit rating agencies, before using the credit ratings from a domestic credit rating agency, the credit rating scale and definition must be well understood.

Recognizing these discrepancies, the Basel Committee on Banking Supervision sets out in the Basel III framework the ECAI rating scale with which the credit ratings issued by a credit rating agency must comply if this credit rating agency is registered under the label

"ECAI" by a national bank regulator. This standard unifies the credit rating scales from many different credit rating agencies through the average three-year default rates.

If a credit rating agency delivers credit ratings with three-year default rates consistently above those specified in the ECAI rating scale, the credit rating agency will be considered by the national bank regulator to be too aggressive. Under such situation, the national bank regulator will revoke the credit rating agency from the list of the ECAIs. Conversely, if a credit rating agency delivers credit ratings with three-year default rates consistently below those specified in the ECAI rating scale, the credit rating agency will be considered by lenders and borrowers to be overly conservative. This essentially encourages both lenders and borrowers to switch to another credit rating agency, if available.

10.4   Differentiation of credit quality

So far, the credit quality of a borrower has been assessed against the likelihood of default in one year. In accordance with this principle, credit scoring models like Altman's Z-score, statistical distance, linear discriminant function and linear PD regression are all developed and validated primarily with one-year default records. However, in many situations, one-year default records are difficult to obtain.

According to the statistics from Moody's Investors Service, the average annual default rate for investment grade corporations is 0.0578 percent which is translated into one default out of 1,729 corporations. In other words, a conservative lender, e.g., a bank, must have on average 51,873 corporate borrowers in its portfolio during the previous year in order to arrive at thirty default records in one year for the development and/or validation of a credit assessment model. Nevertheless, in 2016, Moody's Investors Service issued fewer than seven thousand corporate credit ratings. This phenomenon essentially triggers a second thought on whether it is practical to classify borrowers as good or bad solely according to their potential survival/default status over a period of one year.

10.4.1 Three-year assessment horizon ★★★

The assessment over a period of one year against default is not the only criterion to differentiate good and bad borrowers. The assessment horizon can be extended to three years from one year. This allows more default records to be accumulated over a longer period with only a small loss of relevance.[26]

---

[26] By the same token, the assessment horizon may be extended to five years at a cost of more loss of relevance.

10.4.2 Financial distress ★★★

Additionally, taking into account the actual conservative practices of most banks that only lend to borrowers of high credit quality, it is unlikely that a bank will lend to a corporate borrower that is expected to experience financial distress, if not default, in the following three years.

The potential of financial distress in the following three years thus provides a practical alternative to classify borrowers into either good or bad, i.e., a financially healthy corporation that remains financially healthy in the following three years is classified as a good borrower while a financially healthy corporation that becomes financially distressed/default in the following three years is classified as a bad borrower. This allows more historical lending records, which consist of both financial distress and default records, to be available for the development and/or validation of credit scoring models.

Under this revised approach, the credit assessment framework now takes these steps:

- Classify a borrower as good or bad in accordance with his financial healthiness (in financial distress/default or not) over a period of three years;

- Find the probability of financial distress/default ("PFD") of a corporation over a period of three years; and

- Convert the three-year PFD into a PD.

In contrast to default, there is no universal definition of financial distress. Nevertheless, based on the qualitative definition of credit ratings, a corporation could be classified as in financial distress if it is rated by a credit rating agency as CCC or below. Similarly, a retail borrower may be considered as in financial distress if he has a FICO score below 620. In addition, a listed company delisted for any reason other than privatization may also be classified as in financial distress.

Major securities regulators and stock exchanges publish their regulatory definition of a problematic corporation. For example, the China Securities Regulatory Commission sets out guidelines to classify a listed company as "special treatment" if a listed company satisfies any one of the few criteria, including among others:

- A listed company has registered negative cumulative earnings over the last two consecutive years;

- A listed company's financial audit report highlights that the value of shareholders' equity last year was below the registered capital;

- A listed company is likely to be dissolved;

- A listed company is approved by the count for its application of re-organization, settlement or bankruptcy liquidation;

- A listed company's financial audit report is commented by its auditor with a disclaimer of opinion or adverse opinion; and

- Other circumstances as determined by the China Securities Regulatory Commission.

As such, a listed company in China classified as special treatment is indeed in financial distress. With a much broader definition of financial distress, credit scoring models could be modified easily to distinguish a borrower as either a good borrower who will remain financially healthy or a bad borrower who will be in financial distress/default in the following three years. Following the similar methodologies described in Chapter 9, a three-year PFD can be calculated.

Based on a bank's historical records, a default ratio κ between the number of defaults and the number of migrations to financial distress plus defaults in the most recent several three-year periods is calculated. The three-year PFD is then converted into a PD with the following relationship:

$$\kappa = \frac{\text{No. of defaults in 3 years}}{\text{No. of migrations to financial distress in 3 years} + \text{No. of defaults in 3 years}}$$

$$\text{3-year default rate} = \text{3-year PFD} \times \kappa$$

$$PD = 1 - \left(1 - \text{3-year default rate}\right)^{\frac{1}{3}}$$

$$= 1 - \left(1 - \text{3-year PFD} \times \kappa\right)^{\frac{1}{3}}$$

10.4.3 High yield grade

Some lenders may find that due to their extremely conservative lending policy, even the number of financial distress records over a period of three years is still too small to work with. Their corporate borrowers are expected to be in investment grade for a sufficiently long period of time. In this case, the differentiation between investment grade and high yield grade could be considered as a criterion to separate good borrowers from bad borrowers, i.e., an investment grade corporation that remains as investment grade in the following three years is classified as a good borrower while an investment grade corporation that deteriorates to high yield grade or defaults in the following three years is classified as a bad borrower.

Based on a bank's historical records, a default ratio κ between the number of defaults and the number of migrations to high yield grade plus defaults in the most recent several three-year periods is calculated. The PD is then derived with the following relationship:

$$\kappa = \frac{\text{No. of defaults in 3 years}}{\text{No. of migrations to high yield grade in 3 years} + \text{No. of defaults in 3 years}}$$

$$\text{3-year default rate} = \text{Probabilty of migration to high yield grade or default in 3 year} \times \kappa$$

$$PD = 1 - \left(1 - \text{3-year default rate}\right)^{\frac{1}{3}}$$

$$= 1 - \left(\begin{array}{c}1 - \text{Probabilty of migration to} \\ \text{high yield grade or default in 3 year} \times \kappa\end{array}\right)^{\frac{1}{3}}$$

10.5   Practical credit scoring   ★★★

Step	Input	Objective/output
Definition	No. of relevant default /financial distress /high yield grade records in recent years	To define what is a bad borrower
Collection of bad borrower records	A lending period of three years	To collect at least 30 records of clustered[27] bad borrowers
Stratified sampling	At least 30 records of clustered bad borrowers	To match with at least 30 records of clustered good borrowers
Explanatory variable identification	A total of at least 30 good and 30 bad records of borrowers	To identify a set of significant explanatory variables
Discriminant analysis	At least 30 good and 30 bad records of borrowers with significant explanatory variables	To calibrate a linear discriminant function and an unbiased cutoff score
	Mis-classification cost	To calibrate a prudent cutoff score
Historical statistics	No. of good borrowers became bad borrowers in three years and no. of good borrowers defaulted in three years	To calculate the default ratio (κ) among bad borrowers
Linear PFD regression	Statistically significant explanatory variables	To derive an unbounded PFD formula
Probit transformation	Unbounded PFD formula	To derive the bounded PFD
From PFD to PD	Bounded PFD and κ	To derive the PD

Table 10.2   Practical credit scoring

---

[27] Outliers deviating substantially from the centre of the group should be excluded.

Table 10.2 summarizes the credit scoring procedures in a real bank lending operation. These procedures deliver:

- a linear discriminant function with unbiased and prudent cutoff scores to determine whether a borrower is good, moderate or bad; and

- a PD formula to estimate the PD of a borrower.

10.6   Low default borrowers ★★★

A group of similar and extremely high credit quality borrowers who will experience almost no default, no financial distress and no credit downgrade within a medium period of time is referred to as low default borrowers. This is justified by an almost zero historical rates of default, financial distress and credit downgrade within this group of borrowers and the economic reasons behind, e.g., the debt issued by a low default borrower is supported by some collaterals with value much higher than the EAD. In case the borrower cannot meet any interest and/or principal payment, he must choose to convert the collaterals into cash and pay the interest and/or principal in a controlled manner. This avoids the fire sale by the lender to result in a substantial loss that will be suffered by the borrower.

Since the number of negative historical lending records is extremely small, a low default borrower must be classified as a good borrower and credit scoring becomes a less effective approach for deriving the PD of a low default borrower. Therefore, an alternative approach has to be adopted in order to arrive at a PD of a low default borrower.

Assume that in the recent three years, the complete data set of low default borrowers comprises totally M defaults out of N historical lending records where M is much smaller than N and a new borrower is added to this group of low default borrowers. In the worst situation, the new borrower defaults and becomes one of the historical default records. Thus, the default rate becomes $\frac{M+1}{N+1}$. The PD of a low default borrower is then derived from this hypothetical but prudent default rate.

This simple but institutive approach exhibits two advantages:

- In an extreme situation where there is totally no historical default record for a group of low default borrowers, this argument still results in a non-zero PD; and

- A smaller PD is justified by a larger total number of historical records of low default borrowers (denominator), subject to a fixed number of historical default records (numerator).

10.7   Credit assessment for a new lending operation

In the case of a newly formed lending operation, there is a total lack of historical records. Credit scoring thus cannot be conducted. This issue is overcome with a set of compatible historical records of listed companies whose data are readily available from stock exchanges and/or major financial information providers.

For a particular lending segment, a corresponding subset of listed companies are selected as a proxy group in accordance with the country, industry and firm size, subject to the condition that there must be a sufficient number of bad listed companies (e.g., thirty) during the last three years. Credit scoring is then conducted on the proxy group to derive the linear discriminant function and PD formula. The cutoff scores of the linear discriminant function and the PD formula are then scaled up for the stake of prudency to incorporate the loss of transparency.

There is no simple rule to dictate what degree of up scaling should be applied to the cutoff scores and PDs. It is indeed subject to the lender's understanding on and experience with the lending segment. The less the lender's knowledge on the borrowers, the larger up scaling to the cutoff scores and PDs should be applied.

10.8   Summary of credit assessment techniques

Table 10.3 summarizes the applicability, advantages and limitations of the credit assessment techniques introduced in Chapters 7, 8 and 9. There is no single technique that dominates the rest.

In some situations, a credit assessment technique may be inapplicable, e.g., credit rating is not available for some corporations and credit scoring cannot be conducted for countries. In other situations, a credit assessment technique may break down when it fails to differentiate the credit quality of many borrowers who indeed have exhibited a strong differentiation among their survival capacity. The breakdown of a credit assessment technique arises primarily from its foundation limitations, e.g., the Altman's Z-score may fail to differentiate the credit quality of contemporary Internet technology companies since there was no Internet technology company when the Altman's Z-score was developed in 1960s.

In practice, several applicable techniques will be applied simultaneously to the same borrower to assess his credit quality. A consistent result demonstrated by several different credit assessment techniques will facilitate a bank to decide directly whether it should lend to the borrower. Conversely, in case inconsistent results are exhibited by several different credit assessment techniques, a bank must look into the reasons behind the discrepancies and make certain judgments.

		Borrower	Deliverable	Advantages	Limitations
External assessment	**Credit rating**	Corporation, financial institution, country	Credit quality /PD	• Lower technical expertise • Lower cost • Industry standard • Stable due to the longer term nature of assessment	• Many corporations do not have credit rating • Updated only annually or when triggered by credit events
	FICO score	Individual person, small business	Credit quality /PD		• Many less developed countries do not have retail credit bureau • Not available for a borrower without prior borrowing record • Updated only annually
Classical academic model	**Merton's corporate default model**	Listed companies	Credit quality	• Equity price, equity volatility and value of liabilities as the only input parameters • Sensitive to financial market	• Underlying assumptions over simplified • Unstable results due to continuous changes in equity price and volatility
	Altman's Z-score	Corporation	Credit quality	• Easy to compute • Financial statements and value of equity as input parameters • Audited financial statements provide a direct presentation of financial healthiness	• Delayed financial statements information due to month/quarter end closing • Audited financial statements published quarterly at most • Financial statements subject to accounting cosmetics • Z-scores were developed initially for corporations in the United States in the 1960s and 1970s

Table 10.3 Summary of credit assessment techniques (to be continued on the next page) ★★★

	Borrower	Deliverable	Advantages	Limitations
Statistical distance	Corporation, individual person, small and medium enterprise	Credit quality	• Easy to understand • Customized to particular lending segment • Highly automated • Allow dependent explanatory variables	• Technical • Sufficient and relevant historical data required • Equal numbers of borrowers in each group required
Linear discriminant analysis			• Customized to particular lending segment • Highly automated • Required samples less than statistical distance to produce multiple group classification	• Highly technical • Limit to independent explanatory variables • Sufficient and relevant historical data required • Equal numbers of borrowers in each group required • Specialist optimization computer software required
Linear PD regression and Probit transformation		PD	• Customized to particular lending segment • Highly automated	• Highly technical • Limit to independent explanatory variables • Sufficient and relevant historical data required • Equal numbers of borrowers in each group required

Econometric model (spans the three rows above)

Table 10.3   Summary of credit assessment techniques (continued from the last page) ★★★

10.9   Altman's Z_{China}-score ★★★

Based on the definition of "special treatment" set out by the China Securities Regulatory Commission, Professor Jerome Yen of Hong Kong University of Science and Technology and Professor Edward Altman conducted a joint research in 2007 on Altman's Z-score for listed companies in mainland China, referred to as Z_{China}-score.

The research suggests that the credit quality of a listed company in mainland China can be well explained by the following four financial ratios:

$$X_6 = \frac{\text{Total liabilities}}{\text{Total assets}}$$

$$X_7 = \frac{\text{Net profit}}{\text{Total assets}}$$

$$X_8 = \frac{\text{Currrent assets - Current liabilities}}{\text{Total assets}}$$

$$X_9 = \frac{\text{Retained earnings}}{\text{Total assets}}$$

These four financial ratios are then combined linearly to form a Z_{China}-score formula:

$$Z_{China} = 0.517 - 0.460X_6 + 9.320X_7 + 0.388X_8 + 1.158X_9$$

The research further demonstrates that for a company listed in mainland China, a Z_{China}-score:

- above 0.9 suggests that the company is subject to a lower chance of special treatment;

- between 0.5 and 0.9 suggests that the company is subject to a moderate chance of special treatment; and

- below 0.5 suggests that the company is subject to a higher chance of special treatment.

Similar to the three Z-score formulas, the Z_{China}-score also exhibits that the net profit is the single most important factor in determining the credit quality of a corporation in China.

It is surprised to observe that the ratio between the market value of equity and total assets is not included as a financial ratio to explain the credit quality of a listed company in China. This observation can be justified by the fact that the China government remains as the major shareholder of the largest listed companies in the country. This virtually guarantees the credit quality of the listed companies, regardless of the market value of equity. The result also suggests that a direct adoption of a discriminant function for other countries may result in a less discriminatory power.

10.10 Earnings manipulation ★★★

So far, corporate credit analysis is conducted on the premises that financial statements provided by corporations are reliable in characterizing their financial healthiness, with the assumption that those accounting cosmetics applied to financial statements have not distorted materially the financial positions.

When these accounting cosmetics are beyond the tolerance of generally accepted accounting principles, accounting frauds are resulted. According to the report in 2008 from the Securities and Exchange Commission, a large portion of financial statement frauds are resulted in some forms of earnings manipulation which is essentially the most efficient and effective way to boost the financial position of a corporation.

Financial statement fraud	Percentage (%)
Earnings manipulation	38
Expenses manipulation	12
Improper disclosures	12
Liabilities manipulation	8
Assets manipulation	7
Reserves manipulation	7
Bribery and kickbacks	4
Assets misappropriation	3
Accounts receivables manipulation	3
Investments	2
Aiding and abetting	2
Goodwill	2

Table 10.4   Accounting frauds recorded by the SEC in 2008

Recognizing the impact of earnings manipulation to financial statement analysis, Professor Messod Beneish of Indiana University conducted a research in 1999 to explore an effective method to detect earnings manipulation directly from financial statements with an approach similar to Altman's Z-score.

The research suggested that the degree of earnings manipulation could be well explained by eight financial ratios:

$$TATA = \frac{\text{Net income - Cash flow from operations}}{\text{Total assets}}$$

$$DSRI = \frac{Receivables}{Total\ revenue}$$

$$SGI = Total\ revenue$$

$$AQI = \frac{Fixed\ assets - Property,\ plant\ and\ equipment}{Total\ assets}$$

$$LVGI = \frac{Total\ liabilities}{Total\ assets}$$

$$SGAI = \frac{Selling,\ general\ and\ administrative\ expenses}{Income}$$

$$GMI = \frac{Gross\ profit}{Total\ revenue}$$

$$DEPI = \frac{Depreciation}{Depreciation + Property,\ plant\ and\ equipment}$$

The ratios between current and previous year values of these eight explanatory financial ratios are then combined linearly to form an M-score formula:

$$M = 4.84 - 4.679 \times TATA\ current\ year - 0.92 \times \frac{DSRI\ current\ year}{DSRI\ previous\ year}$$

$$- 0.892 \times \frac{SGI\ currrent\ year}{SGI\ previous\ year} - 0.404 \times \frac{AQI\ current\ year}{AQI\ previous\ year}$$

$$+ 0.327 \times \frac{LVGI\ current\ year}{LVGI\ previous\ year} + 0.172 \times \frac{SGAI\ current\ year}{SGAI\ previous\ year}$$

$$- 0.528 \times \frac{GMI\ previous\ year}{GMI\ current\ year} - 0.115 \times \frac{DEPI\ previous\ year}{DEPI\ current\ year}$$

The research further demonstrates that for a corporation, an M-score:

- above 2.22 suggests that the financial statements are subject to a lower degree of earnings manipulation;

- between 1.78 and 2.22 suggests that the financial statements are subject to a moderate degree of earnings manipulation; and

- below 1.78 suggests that the financial statements are subject to a higher degree of earnings manipulation.

Combining the Z-score and M-score, a two-dimensional assessment matrix is constructed. This assessment matrix exhibits to a lender both the credit quality of a borrower and reliability of this estimated credit quality to facilitate the lender's understanding on the risks involved and the decision on whether he should lend to a corporation.

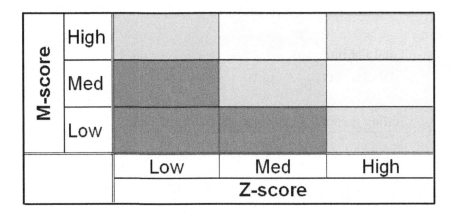

Figure 10.1   Two-dimensional assessment matrix

In emerging markets, the quality of financial statements can never be compatible with that in developed countries. The use of two-dimensional assessment gives more insight to the lenders, thus avoiding the two potential extremities:

- All financial statements are assumed to be unreliable, thus rejecting all lending businesses; or

- All financial statements are assumed to be reliable, thus resulting in potentially large default loss.

PART THREE

CREDIT DERIVATIVES
The New Frontier of Credit Investments

Credit Default Swaps

11

KEY CONCEPTS

- Single name CDS
- Binary CDS
- Basket CDS
- Portfolio CDS

11.1 Default insurance

Default insurance offers protection to a debt investor against the potential loss arising from the default of a credit risky debt. With default insurance, upon the default of a debt, an investor will be compensated an amount that matches largely the default loss of the debt. Thus default insurance serves as an effective and efficient control to mitigate the credit risk.

The most popular default insurance exists in the form of a credit default swap ("CDS"). Many types of CDSs are created by financial institutions to serve the various needs of debt investors. This chapter explains in detail several major types of CDSs, namely: single name CDS, binary CDS, basket CDS and portfolio CDS.

For each type of CDS, the following dimensions are considered from a long position:

- Functional purpose: How to mitigate the credit risk of a debt with this CDS?
- Cash flows: What are the amounts and schedules of cash outflows and inflows?
- Expected protection: Which factors and how these factors impact the expected protection from a CDS?
- Credit risk: How to measure the credit risk of a CDS?

11.2 Single name CDS ★★★

11.2.1 Functional purpose ★★★

A single name CDS is a financial instrument that offers default insurance to an investor on a reference debt. The owner of a single name CDS, referred to as the protection buyer, will receive a default protection equal to the default loss of the principal[28] upon the default of the reference debt, i.e.:

$$\text{Default protection} = \text{Default loss of principal} = \text{Principal} \times \text{LGD}$$

---

[28] A standard CDS offers default protection only to the principal of the reference debt. Please refer to Appendix 11.1 for the default protection covered by some non-standard CDSs.

In order to acquire this insurance benefit, the protection buyer must pay the insurer, referred to as the protection seller, an insurance premium in the form of a series of deterministic cash flows on a regular basis during the protection period until the default event occurs.

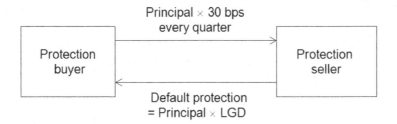

Figure 11.1   Single name CDS

The single name CDS is the simplest form of credit instrument in the financial market. It functions solely in response to the credit quality of a reference debt and serves as a fundamental building block of other credit instruments. Most single name CDSs are traded with lot more liquidity than their corresponding reference debts, thus establishing the contemporary credit market.

With a single name CDS acting as default insurance, a portfolio comprising a reference debt and the corresponding single name CDS is largely equivalent to a risk-free security, except:

- the protection to the default loss of accrued interest is excluded; and
- the schedule of principal payment is accelerated upon default and all the subsequent interest payments are cancelled after default – this works similar to the short position in an early pre-payment option.

Therefore,

> Reference debt + Single name CDS
>
> + Default protection to accrued interest + Pre-payment option
>
> = Risk-free security

For most debts, the total value of default protection to accrued interest and pre-payment option is relatively small, thus resulting in the following approximation:

> Reference debt + Single name CDS ≈ Risk-free security

By arranging terms, the short position in a single name CDS is largely equivalent to a portfolio comprising the long position in a reference debt and the short position in a risk-free security, i.e.:

> - Single name CDS ≈ Reference debt - Risk-free security

Therefore, a debt investor may enter either the long position in a single name CDS to hedge the credit risk of a reference debt or the short position in a single name CDS to invest indirectly in a reference debt, both without upfront cash outflow. Such nice property makes the single name CDS a very convenient tool for either hedging or investing.

11.2.2 Cash flows ★★★

Premium

When a protection buyer acquires a single name CDS on a reference debt, a regular premium is paid, usually in arrears on a quarterly basis,[29] to the protection seller as a cost and service fee for providing the default protection. Upon the default of the reference debt, the protection buyer needs to pay the accrued premium, i.e., the unpaid amount of the regular premium, before the default protection is collected from the protection seller. The accrued premium is calculated as:

$$\text{Accrued premium} = \text{Principal} \times \frac{\text{Premium rate}}{\text{Premium frequency}}$$
$$\times \frac{\text{No. of days since last premium payment day}}{\text{No. of days between last and next premium payment days}}$$

where the number of days follows the day count conventions of corporate bonds. Afterwards, the CDS terminates and the protection buyer stops the scheduled payments of the regular premium.

Physical settlement

If the reference debt survives over the protection period, no default protection will be delivered to the protection buyer. Conversely, if the reference debt defaults during the protection period, for a single name CDS in physical settlement, the protection buyer will deliver the reference debt to the protection seller in exchange for the principal in full. Since the value of the reference debt in default is:

$$(\text{Principal} + \text{Accrued interest}) \times (1 - \text{LGD})$$

The net default protection received by the protection buyer is:

$$\text{Principal} - (\text{Principal} + \text{Accrued interest}) \times (1 - \text{LGD})$$
$$= (\text{Principal} + \text{Accrued interest}) \times \text{LGD} - \text{Accrued interest}$$

---

[29] Since CDSs are traded over-the-counter, the arrangement of premium payments varies in a broad range, subject to the agreement between the protection buyer and protection seller. Some CDSs are entered with a single upfront premium payment while some CDSs are entered with semi-annual premium payments.

Cheapest delivery option

Under the cross default provision, the default of a bond issued by an issuer will trigger the default of all bonds issued by the same issuer. This cross default provision prevents a bond issuer from defaulting selectively certain bonds but maintaining the survival of other bonds, both issued by the same issuer.

To expand the application of a single name CDS, flexibility is incorporated in standard single name CDSs to allow the owner of a single name CDS to deliver any member in a group of similar reference bonds (e.g., same seniority) from the same issuer in order to exchange for the principal in full. In other words, a single name CDS is designed to protect many similar bonds from the same bond issuer.

While the principal is fixed in a single name CDS contract, the accrued interest is determined by the interest rate, interest frequency, last interest payment day, next interest payment day and default day. Obviously, the accrued interest is reduced to zero for a bond that defaults just after an interest payment. This becomes the cheapest candidate to be delivered to the protection seller.

For a bond issuer who has issued many bonds, it is assumed that on any day, at least one of the many bonds issued by the same issuer would have just paid the interest and become zero accrued interest. This essentially encourages the owner of a single name CDS to sell the defaulted reference bond on hand to the distressed debt market to recover a value:

$$(\text{Principal} + \text{Accrued interest}) \times (1 - \text{LGD})$$

and buy from the distressed debt market a reference bond issued by the same bond issuer without accrued interest at a cost:

$$\text{Principal} \times (1 - \text{LGD})$$

in order to pocket a small differential gain:

$$\text{Accrued interest} \times (1 - \text{LGD})$$

The reference bond without accrued interest is then delivered to the protection seller in exchange for the principal in full, resulting in a net default protection:

$$\text{Principal} \times \text{LGD}$$

The total recovered value then becomes:

$$\text{Principal} + \text{Accrued interest} \times (1 - \text{LGD})$$

Because of this cheapest delivery option, the CDS market unifies the default protection of a standard single name CDS to principal only.

Physical settlement is the most popular default settlement approach in the single name CDS market. For many popular reference debts, the outstanding amount of the corresponding single name CDSs are more than the reference debts. This results a very interesting phenomena that when a reference debt defaults, protection buyers will compete in the distressed debt market to acquire the defaulted reference debt and jet up the price of the defaulted reference debt.

Cash settlement

Upon the default of a reference debt, for a single name CDS in cash settlement, the protection buyer will receive from the protection seller an amount equal to:

$$\text{Principal} \times \text{LGD}$$

At the same time, the protection buyer, if owning the reference debt, takes an action to recover from the debt issuer an amount equal to:

$$(\text{Principal} + \text{Accrued interest}) \times (1 - \text{LGD})$$

Combining these two parts, the protection buyer then recovers the entire principal and a certain percentage of the accrued interest:

$$\text{Principal} + \text{Accrued interest} \times (1 - \text{LGD})$$

The cash settlement has an advantage over the physical settlement that it is unnecessary for a protection buyer to own physically the reference debt. This makes the speculation on a reference debt possible. With some creativity, a single name CDS can be originated on a hypothetical reference debt and this arrangement enables a pure speculation on the credit quality of a hypothetical reference debt. Furthermore, the cash settlement also facilitates the extension of default protection to the average accrued interest by acquiring a single name CDS in cash settlement with principal equal to:

$$\text{Debt principal} + \frac{\text{Debt principal} \times \text{Interest rate}}{2 \times \text{Interest frequency}}$$

where $\dfrac{\text{Debt principal} \times \text{Interest rate}}{2 \times \text{Interest frequency}}$ is the average accrued interest.

While cash settlement is not the most common default settlement approach, it is getting popular as a result of its flexibility.

11.2.3 Hedging strategy ★★★

A protection buyer may adopt one of the following three hedging strategies to hedge the credit risk of his debt with a single name CDS:

- Complete static hedge: Complete static hedge is a fully passive risk management strategy which seeks to eliminate totally the EL of the principal of a reference debt using a single name CDS with the principal and protection period identical to the principal and RM of the reference debt. It aims at removing completely in a single transaction the credit risk of the principal of a reference debt.

- Partial static hedge: Partial static hedge is a risk management strategy which seeks to reduce the EL of a reference debt using a single name CDS with; (i) the protection period identical to the RM of the reference debt; and (ii) the principal less than the principal of the reference debt. It aims at removing in a single transaction the credit risk of certain part of the principal of a reference debt.

- Dynamic hedge: Dynamic hedge is an active risk management strategy which seeks to reduce the 1-year EL of a reference debt with the RM longer than one year, using a single name CDS with: (i) the protection period of one year; and (ii) the principal less than the principal of the reference debt. It aims at maintaining the residual 1-year EL after hedging below the protection buyer's tolerance level at a lower immediate hedging cost as a result of the one year only protection period. In general, dynamic hedge is more cost effective than static hedges at a trade off that the protection buyer must review and control the credit risks of his debts at least annually.

When a reference debt is hedged by a single name CDS, this combination will still subject to default loss if the issuer of the reference debt defaults and the protection seller defaults before or together with the reference defaults. Thus a residual credit risk remains exist. Therefore, the combination is subject to a joint PD of the debt issuer and protection buyer.

This joint PD can be estimated using Monte Carlo simulation with over million trials. When the PDs of the debt investor and protection seller are denoted by PD_1 and PD_2 respectively, the lower bound the joint PD is calculated as the arithmetic product of the two PDs, assuming that the debt issuer and protection seller are independent totally. The upper bond of the joint PD is calculated with the formula below by the cumulative bivariate standard normal distribution function, where the CCC is the geometric average of the CCCs of the debt issuer and protection seller:

$$\frac{1}{2\pi\sqrt{1-CCC^2}} \int_{-\infty}^{\Phi^{-1}(PD_1)} \int_{-\infty}^{\Phi^{-1}(PD_2)} \exp\left[-\frac{x^2 + y^2 - 2xy \times CCC}{2\left(1 - CCC^2\right)}\right] dxdy$$

where $CCC = \sqrt{CCC_1 \times CCC_2}$

Table 11.1 shows the upper bound of the joint PDs of the combinations with debt issuers and protection sellers at various credit ratings. Since a higher quality protection seller will result in smaller lower and upper bounds of the joint PD, a single name CDS issued by a higher quality protection seller offers more default protection, is more valuable and is subject to a higher regular premium.

Protection seller →		Rating	AAA	AA	A	BBB
Debt issuer ↓		PD	0.01%	0.0333%	0.0834%	0.3345%
Rating	PD	CCC	0.2394	0.2380	0.2394	0.2215
AAA	0.01%	0.2394	0.00%	0.00%	0.00%	0.00%
AA	0.0333%	0.2380	0.00%	0.00%	0.00%	0.00%
A	0.0834%	0.2394	0.00%	0.00%	0.00%	0.00%
BBB	0.3345%	0.2215	0.00%	0.00%	0.00%	0.01%
BB	2.5652%	0.1533	0.00%	0.00%	0.01%	0.03%
B	7.1682%	0.1233	0.00%	0.01%	0.02%	0.07%
CCC	15.6567%	0.1200	0.00%	0.01%	0.04%	0.12%
CC	29.5270%	0.1200	0.01%	0.02%	0.05%	0.19%
C	63.1597%	0.1200	0.01%	0.03%	0.07%	0.28%

Table 11.1   Joint PDs with investment grade protection sellers

In practice, for hedging purpose, a debt investor will choose a protection seller such that the joint PD approaches 0.01% or below to ascertain that the residual credit risk is neglectable. As such, investment grade financial institutions become the only practitioners in the market of protection sellers. Although a high yield grade debt issuer and a high yield grade protection seller together will also result in a lower joint PD, such combination is not welcome to the credit market.

11.2.4 Expected protection ★★★

The expected protection of a single name CDS is calculated as:

$$\text{Expected protection} = \text{Principal} \times \text{LGD} \times \left[1 - (1 - \text{PD})^{\text{Protection period}} \right]$$

Factor	Impact to expected protection[*]	Variation after origination
Principal	+	No
LGD	+	Moderate
PD	+	Material
Protection period	+	Decreasing gradually

* A "+" means that the expected protection increases when a factor increases.

Table 11.2   Factors impacting the expected protection from a single name CDS

The expected protection increases with increasing principal, LGD, PD and protection period. When a single name CDS is originated, a regular premium scheme is designed to match the expected protection such that the present value of expected premiums is equal to the present value of expected protection. This condition suggests that the regular premium also increases with increasing principal, LGD, PD and initial protection period.

After the origination of a single name CDS, the regular premium remains fixed throughout the life of the single name CDS regardless of the subsequent changes in the LGD, PD and the gradually decreasing protection period.

CDS spread

For a newly originated single name CDS, the annualized regular premium expressed as a percentage of the principal is referred to as the CDS spread.

$$\text{CDS spread} = \frac{\text{Regular premium amount} \times \text{Premium frequency}}{\text{Principal}} \times 100\%$$

For a reference debt with a lower credit quality, there is a higher expectation on default protection which is matched by a series of higher regular premiums, thus resulting in a higher CDS spread. Therefore, the CDS spread of the most recently originated single name CDS serves as an intuitive indicator of the credit quality of a reference debt.

11.2.5 Credit risk ★★★

The protection buyer taking the long position in a single name CDS is entitled to the default protection. Therefore, there is no credit risk.

In contrast, the protection seller taking the short position in a single name CDS must deliver the protection upon the default of a reference debt. Therefore, the short position in a single name CDS is subject to credit risk which is measured by: (i) the EL identical to the expected protection; and/or (ii) the 1-year EL.

$$\text{EL} = \text{Expected protection} = \text{Principal} \times \text{LGD} \times \left[1 - \left(1 - \text{PD} \right)^{\text{Protection period}} \right]$$

$$\text{1-year EL} = \text{Principal} \times \text{LGD} \times \text{Min} \left[\text{PD}, 1 - \left(1 - \text{PD} \right)^{\text{Protection period}} \right]$$

11.3   Binary CDS

11.3.1 Functional purpose

Conceptually, a binary CDS is equivalent to a single name CDS in cash settlement on the principal of a reference debt with LGD 100 percent. A protection buyer acquires a binary CDS by paying a regular premium to a protection seller. Upon the default of the reference institution, the protection seller pays the principal in full to the protection buyer. This simplifies the specification of a single name CDS contingent only on the default of a reference institution instead of a reference debt. Therefore, rather than working as a hedging instrument, a binary CDS is designed primarily for speculating on the default of a reference institution.

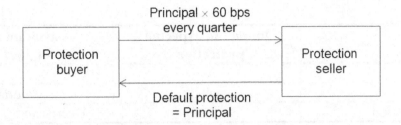

Figure 11.2   Binary CDS

11.3.2 Cash flows

Premium

When a protection buyer acquires a binary CDS on a reference institution, a regular premium is paid, usually in arrears on a quarterly basis, to the protection seller as a cost and service fee for delivering the principal upon the default of the reference institution. When the reference institution defaults, the protection buyer needs to pay the accrued premium, i.e., the unpaid amount of the premium, before the principal is collected from the protection seller. Afterwards, the binary CDS terminates and the protection buyer stops the scheduled payments of the regular premium.

Cash settlement

A binary CDS is settled in cash. Upon the default of a reference institution, the protection buyer receives from the protection seller an amount equal to the principal.

Obviously, for the same principal, reference institution and protection period, a protection seller will demand a higher regular premium on a binary CDS than on a compatible single name CDS since the default protection of the binary CDS is not discounted by the LGD.

11.3.3 Expected protection

The expected protection of a binary CDS is calculated as:

$$\text{Expected protection} = \text{Principal} \times \left[1 - \left(1 - \text{PD} \right)^{\text{Protection period}} \right]$$

The expected protection increases with increasing principal, PD and protection period. Similar to single name CDS, when a binary CDS is originated, a regular premium scheme is designed to match the expected protection. This condition suggests that the regular premium also increases with increasing principal, PD and protection period.

After the origination of a binary CDS, the regular premium is fixed throughout the life of the binary CDS, regardless of the subsequent changes in the PD and the gradually decreasing protection period.

Factor	Impact to expected protection*	Variation after origination
Principal	+	No
PD	+	Material
Protection period	+	Decreasing gradually

* A "+" means that the expected protection increases when the factor increases.

Table 11.3   Factors impacting the expected protection from a binary CDS

11.3.4 Credit risk

The protection buyer taking the long position in a binary CDS is entitled to the default protection. Therefore, there is no credit risk to the long position in a binary CDS.

In contrast, the protection seller taking the short position in a binary CDS must deliver the protection upon the default of a reference institution. Therefore, the short position in a binary CDS is subject to credit risk which is measured by: (i) the EL identical to the expected protection; and/or (ii) the 1-year EL.

$$\text{EL} = \text{Expected protection} = \text{Principal} \times \left[1 - \left(1 - \text{PD} \right)^{\text{Protection period}} \right]$$

$$\text{1-year EL} = \text{Principal} \times \text{Min} \left[\text{PD}, 1 - \left(1 - \text{PD} \right)^{\text{Protection period}} \right]$$

11.4   Basket CDS

11.4.1 Functional purpose

A single name CDS offers a convenient and effective way to mitigate the credit risk of a single debt at a cost, i.e. the regular premium. For an investor owning several debts in a basket, a naive hedging strategy is formed by hedging every debt in the basket with the corresponding single name CDS. This complete protection results in a higher total hedging cost. A debt investor thus seeks an alternative approach to mitigate the credit risk of a basket of reference debts with identical principal at a lower cost. This arrives at the basket CDS which could be in the form of a first-to-default ("1TD") CDS, second-to-default ("2TD") CDS and last-to-default ("LTD") CDS, collectively referred to as an Nth-to-default ("NTD") CDS.

An NTD CDS is a CDS that offers default insurance to a debt investor on the principal of a reference debt to default in the Nth place in a basket of reference debts with the same principal but issued by different issuers. The protection buyer of an NTD CDS will receive a default protection equal to the default loss of the principal upon the Nth default event in a basket of reference debts. In order to acquire this insurance benefit, the protection buyer must pay the protection seller an insurance premium in the form of a series of deterministic cash flow on a regular basis during the protection period until the Nth default event occurs.

A 1TD CDS offers a flexibility to protect the principal of the reference debt to default in the first place without specifying the exact identity of the reference debt in advance. This first default event accounts for the majority of the credit risk in the basket of reference debts.

Similarly, a 2TD CDS offers a flexibility to protect the principal of a reference debt to default in the second place without specifying the exact identity of the reference debt in advance. This second default event accounts for the majority of the residual credit risk in a basket of reference debts not protected by the 1TD CDS.

Finally, an LTD CDS offers a flexibility to protect the principal of the reference debt to default last without specifying the exact identity of the reference debt in advance. The last default event accounts for the worst situation of the basket of reference debts.

11.4.2 Cash flows

Premium

When a protection buyer acquires an NTD CDS on a basket of reference debts, a regular premium is paid, usually in arrears on a quarterly basis, to the protection seller as a cost and service fee for providing the default protection. Upon the Nth default event in the basket of reference debts, the protection buyer needs to pay the accrued premium before the default protection is collected from a protection seller. Afterwards, the NTD CDS terminates and the protection buyer stops the scheduled payments of the regular premium.

Physical settlement

If the basket of reference debts experience only up to N - 1 default events over the protection period, no default protection will be delivered to the protection buyer. If the Nth default event occurs during the protection period, for an NTD CDS in physical settlement, the protection buyer will deliver the defaulted reference debt to the protection seller in exchange for the principal in full.

Cash settlement

When the Nth default event occurs, for an NTD CDS in cash settlement, the protection buyer will receive from the protection seller an amount equal to Principal $\times$ LGD.

11.4.3 Expected protection

Similar to single name CDS and binary CDS, the expected protection from a basket CDS increases with increasing principal, LGD, PD and protection period. In addition, the expected protection is also driven by the protection order, basket size and default dependency among the issuers of reference debts in the basket. Obviously, early default protection is more valuable than late default protection since late default protection will only be triggered by the joint default of several reference debts. Nevertheless, the impacts from basket size and default dependency are less straight forward and determined in accordance with the protection order.

For a basket CDS offering early default protection, a large number of reference debts in the basket will trigger an early default protection at a higher chance. Therefore, the expected protection of a basket CDS with an early protection order increases with increasing basket size. In contrast, for a basket CDS with late protection order, the default protection will be realized only when the joint default of many debts occurs. A large number of reference debts in the basket thus delay the default protection. Therefore, the expected protection of a basket CDS with late protection order decreases with increasing basket size.

Category	Factor	Impact to expected protection*	Variation after origination
Reference debt	Principal	+	No
	LGD	+	Moderate
	PD	+	Material
	Protection period	+	Decreasing gradually
Basket	Protection order	-	No
	Basket size	+ for early protection - for late protection	Mild
	Default dependency	- for early protection + for late protection	Moderate

* A "+" means that the expected protection increases when the factor increases and a "-" means that the expected protection decreases when the factor increases.

Table 11.4   Factors impacting the expected protection from a basket CDS

A higher default dependency suggests that the reference debts tend to default or survive together. Under such situation, a 1TD CDS then works similar to a single name CDS with a fixed principal and results in less flexibility of default protection. Conversely, a lower default dependency suggests that the reference debt tends to default or survive on its own. Then a 1TD CDS works more flexibly to offer default protection to many less dependent potential defaults. An LTD CDS works in the opposite direction. It provides more flexibility of default protection to a basket of reference debts with higher default dependency and less flexibility of default protection to a basket of reference debts with lower default dependency.

Due to the impact from the protection order, basket size and default dependency, the expected protection of a basket CDS cannot be expressed in a closed form. Nevertheless, the qualitative impacts to the expected protection from the risk factors are intuitive and are summarized in Table 11.4.

Similar to other CDSs, the risk factors impact the level of the regular premium in the same way as they impact the expected protection.

11.4.4 Credit risk

The protection buyer taking the long position in a basket CDS is entitled to the default protection. Therefore, there is no credit risk.

In contrast, the protection seller taking the short position in a basket CDS must deliver the protection upon the default of a reference debt matching the protection order. Therefore, the short position in a basket CDS is subject to credit risk.

The credit risk of the short position in a basket CDS is measured by the EL and/or 1-year EL. Due to the effect from the basket size and protection order, the EL and 1-year EL cannot be expressed in closed form formula but has to be derived with Monte Carlo simulation.

11.5   Portfolio CDS ★★★

11.5.1 Functional purpose ★★★

Tranche

A tranche is a continuous sub-portfolio of a debt portfolio determined by a portfolio attachment point ("PAP") and a portfolio detachment point ("PDP"). A PAP is the percentage of portfolio principal from which the tranche starts to suffer from default loss. A PDP is the percentage of portfolio principal up to which the tranche defaults completely. The difference between the PDP and PAP defines the thickness of a tranche. The PAP determines the seniority of a tranche. An equity tranche with a smaller PAP and lower seniority will suffer from default loss early when the debt portfolio starts to deteriorate. A mezzanine tranche with a medium PAP and medium seniority will suffer from default loss when some of the portfolio principal has defaulted. A senior tranche with a larger PAP and higher seniority will suffer from default loss only when the majority of the portfolio principal has defaulted.

When a CDS is designed to offer default protection to the principal of a particular tranche, a portfolio CDS is formed. The protection buyer of a portfolio CDS for a tranche will receive a default protection equal to the loss of the tranche principal upon the default of any debt in that particular tranche. This default insurance ends when the entire tranche has defaulted completely. Similar to other CDSs, in order to acquire this insurance benefit, the protection buyer must pay the protection seller an insurance premium in the form of a series of deterministic cash flow on a regular basis during the protection period, until the entire tranche has defaulted completely.

Therefore, a portfolio CDS for a lower seniority tranche offers a flexibility to protect the portfolio principal to default early without specifying in advance the exact identify of those debts. These early default events account for the majority of the credit risk in a debt portfolio.

Similarly, a portfolio CDS for a higher seniority tranche offers a flexibility to protect the portfolio principal to default late without specifying in advance the exact identity of those debts. These late default events occur only at a severe situation.

Following the same principle, a portfolio CDS for a mezzanine tranche will offer a flexibility to protect the tranche principal to default in between with a moderate chance.

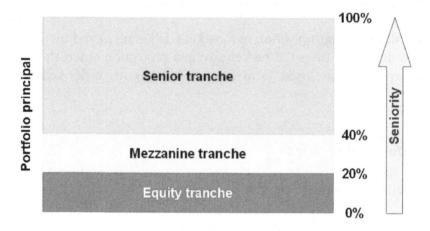

Figure 11.3   Tranching of a debt portfolio

11.5.2 Cash flows ★★★

Premium

When a protection buyer acquires a portfolio CDS, a regular premium is paid, usually in arrears on a quarterly basis, to the protection seller as a cost and service fee for providing the default protection. When the aggregation of a defaulted portfolio principal is above the PAP, the tranche principal starts to default and the regular premium is reduced in proportion to the defaulted tranche principal. This premium reduction continues until the tranche principal defaults completely and the portfolio CDS terminates.

Moreover, upon the default of any debt in the tranche, the protection buyer needs to pay the accrued premium corresponding to the defaulted portfolio principal before the default protection is collected from the protection seller.

Physical settlement

If the full tranche remains in survival, no default protection will be delivered to the protection buyer. Conversely, if part of the tranche defaults, for a portfolio CDS in physical settlement, the protection buyer will deliver the defaulted debts in the tranche to the protection seller in exchange for the corresponding defaulted portfolio principal. This process continues until the tranche defaults completely.

Cash settlement

For a portfolio CDS with cash settlement, the protection buyer will receive from the protection seller an amount equal to:

Defaulted debt principal × LGD

This process continues until the tranche defaults completely.

11.5.3 Expected protection ★★★

Similar to other CDSs, the expected protection of a portfolio CDS increases with increasing portfolio principal, LGD, PD and protection period. In addition, the expected protection is also driven by the PAP, PDP, concentration of debts and default dependency. Obviously, the protection from a portfolio CDS with a smaller PAP is more valuable than that from a portfolio CDS with a larger PAP since a larger PAP will only be reached by the joint default of a larger percentage of the portfolio principal. In addition, a larger PDP essentially suggests that the default protection will continue up to the default of a larger percentage of the portfolio principal. Nevertheless, the impacts from concentration of debts and default dependency are less straight forward and determined in accordance with the PAP.

A higher concentration of debts and default dependency suggests that the portfolio principal tends to survive or default together. Under such situation, a portfolio CDS with a smaller PAP then works similarly to a single name CDS with a fixed principal and results in less flexibility of default protection. Conversely, a lower concentration of debts and default dependency suggests that the portfolio principal tends to default on individual debt basis. Then a portfolio CDS with a smaller PAP works more flexibly to offers default protection to many less dependent potential defaults. A portfolio CDS with a larger PAP works in the opposite direction. It provides more flexibility of default protection to a debt portfolio with a higher concentration of debts and default dependency and less flexibility of default protection to a debt portfolio with a lower concentration of debts and default dependency.

Due to the impacts from the PAP and PDP, the expected protection of a portfolio CDS cannot be expressed in a closed form. Nevertheless, the qualitative impacts to the expected protection from the risk factors are intuitive and are summarized in Table 11.5.

Category	Factor	Impact to expected protection*	Variation after origination
Portfolio	Portfolio principal	+	No
	LGD	+	Moderate
	PD	+	Material
	Protection period	+	Decreasing gradually
	Concentration of debts	- for smaller PAP	Mild
	Default dependency	+ for larger PAP	Moderate
Tranche	PAP	-	No
	PDP	+	No

* A "+" means that the expected protection increases when the factor increases and a "-" means that the expected protection decreases when the factor increases.

Table 11.5   Factors impacting the expected protection of a portfolio CDS

Similar to other CDSs, the risk factors impact the level of the premium in the same way as they impact the expected protection.

11.5.4 Credit risk ★★★

The protection buyer taking the long position in a portfolio CDS is entitled to the default protection. Therefore, there is no credit risk.

In contrast, the protection seller taking the short position in a portfolio CDS must deliver the protection upon the default of the portfolio principal between the PAP and PDP. Therefore, the short position in a portfolio CDS is subject to credit risk.

Neither the EL, the 1-year EL nor the XCL serves as a valid measure to quantify the credit risk of a portfolio CDS since these three credit risk measures do not incorporate the effect from the PAP and PDP.

Appendix 11.1   Non-standard single name CDSs

A standard CDS protects only the principal of a reference debt. Nevertheless, subject to the agreement between a protection buyer and a protection seller, a customized CDS can be tailored to incorporate the additional protection on:

- accrued interest to cover the entire EAD; and/or
- remaining scheduled cash inflows not to be delivered by a defaulted reference debt.

With a single name CDS offering default protection to the entire EAD of a reference debt, a portfolio comprising the reference debt and the single name CDS is largely equivalent to a risk-free security, except that the schedule of the principal payment is accelerated upon default and all the subsequent interest payments are cancelled after default. This works similarly to the short position in an early prepayment option.

Therefore,

Reference debt + Single name CDS + Pre-payment option = Risk-free security

With a single name CDS also offering default protection to the remaining scheduled cash inflows not to be delivered by a defaulted reference debt, a portfolio comprising the reference debt and the single name CDS is equivalent to a risk-free security, i.e.:

Reference debt + Single name CDS = Risk-free security

Appendix 11.2   CDS trading

A CDS contract is a bilateral agreement between a protection buyer and a protection seller. Once entered, a CDS contract must be honoured by both parties until maturity, similar to other contract based financial instruments. Nevertheless, subject to a bilateral netting agreement,[30] a protection buyer may reverse an existing CDS with the original protection seller in order to offset the outstanding potential cash flows of an existing CDS. In order words, the protection buyer now enters the short position of an existing CDS with the original protection seller such that the cash flows arising from the existing CDS is cancelled by the identical cash flows arising from the new short position. This results in the trading of CDSs.

The value of a CDS is the difference between the present value of expected protection and the present value of expected premiums with the premium rate fixed at origination:

$$\text{CDS value} = \text{Present value of expected protection} \\ - \text{Present value of expected premiums}$$

When a CDS is originated, the premium rate is designed such that the two present values are equal. This arrangement eliminates any initial cash outflow from either the protection buyer or the protection seller. Nevertheless, after the origination of a CDS, while the premium rate remains fixed, the expected protection may vary due to the gradually decreasing protection period and changes in the LGD and PD of the reference debts. These continuous changes may increase or decrease the present value of expected protection. A non-zero value, either positive or negative, is thus resulted to the CDS.

When a protection buyer reverses an existing CDS with the protection seller, if the present value of expected protection is higher than the present value of expected premiums, the protection buyer must receive from the protection seller an upfront fee equal to the difference between the two present values. In contrast, if the present value of expected premiums is higher than the present value of expected protection, the protection buyer must pay to the protection seller an upfront fee equal to the difference between the two present values.

---

[30]The ISDA Master Agreement serves as the industry standard in bilateral netting.

Appendix 11.3   EL of a basket CDS

The EL of a basket CDS is derived with Monte Carlo simulation by taking the following steps:

- Derive the hazard rate of the reference debt issuer k as $\lambda_k = -\ln(1 - PD_k)$;

- Generate a common standard normal random number y;

- For the borrower of the reference debt k (k = 1 to NOB),

  - generate a standard normal random number z_k;

  - set $x_k = y\sqrt{CCC_k} + z_k\sqrt{1 - CCC_k}$;

  - calculate the value of the cumulative standard normal distribution function
  $$\Phi(x_k) = \frac{1}{\sqrt{2\pi}} \int_{-\infty}^{x_k} \exp(-\frac{\tau^2}{2})d\tau \; ;$$

  - derive the default time $t_k = -\dfrac{\ln\left[1 - \Phi(x_k)\right]}{\lambda_k}$

  - if $t_k \leq RM$, then reference debt k defaults.

- Count the number of reference debts defaulted;

- If the number of reference debts defaulted is equal to or larger than the protection order, the reference debt matching the protection order is selected and a default loss equal to the arithmetic product of the principal and LGD is registered;

- If the number of reference debts defaulted is less than the protection order, then the default loss is zero; and

- Repeat the above simulation steps for a sufficient large number of times, e.g., hundred thousand times.

The EL of the basket CLN is calculated as the average of the simulated default losses.

CDS Indices

12

KEY CONCEPTS

- CDX index
- iTraxx index

- On-the-run series
- CDS index contract

12.1 CDX and iTraxx indices ★★★

Similar to other financial risks, the credit risk of a debt comprises the systematic risk driven by macro factors common to many debts and specific risk driven by idiosyncratic factors impacting only that particular debt. For internationally active banks, their debt investments are largely diversified due to the huge number of debts issued by many different issuers in the debt portfolio, leaving the systematic risk as the dominating component. Since systematic risk is not observable directly, effort has been made to discover this systematic risk. This drives the development of the CDS indices.

Region	Credit quality/theme	No. of compo-nents	Index
North America	Investment grade	125	CDX.NA.IG
	Investment grade and high volatility	30	CDX.NA.IG.HVOL
	High yield grade	100	CDX.NA.HY
	BB	37	CDX.NA.HY.BB
	B	46	CDX.NA.HY.B
	Crossover	35	CDX.NA.XO
	First lien leveraged loans	100	LCDX
Emerging markets	██████████████	14	CDX.EM
	Diversified	40	CDX.EM Diversified

Table 12.1   CDX indices

A CDS index is the arithmetic average of the updated CDS spreads of a group of liquidly traded and standardized single name CDSs (from three to 125 components) that are originated on specific days in March and September to protect the reference debts issued by a number of different and representative debt issuers with certain common characteristics. After the origination, the CDS spreads of this group of single name CDSs are calculated with respect to the revised premium, subject to the hypothetical assumption that a new zero value single name CDS is originated for the original reference debt, having the same principal, issuer and maturity day but updated LGD, updated PD and reduced protection period. A CDS index serves as a proxy to represent the systematic credit quality of a particular segment in the credit market.

Region	Theme	No. of CDSs	Index
Europe	███████████	125	iTraxx Europe
	High volatility	30	iTraxx Europe HiVol
	Crossover	75	iTraxx Europe Crossover
	First lien loan	40	iTraxx LEVX
	Non-financial	100	iTraxx Non-financials
	Senior subordination financial	25	iTraxx Financials Senior
	Junior subordination financial	25	iTraxx Financials Sub
	Telecommunications, media and technology	20	iTraxx TMT
	Industrial	20	iTraxx Industrials
	Energy industry	20	iTraxx Energy
	Manufacturers of consumer products	30	iTraxx Consumers
	Automobile industry	10	iTraxx Autos
Asia	Ex-Japan investment grade	50	iTraxx Asia
	Ex-Japan high yield	20	iTraxx Asia HY
	Japan	50	iTraxx Japan
	Australia	25	iTraxx Australia
Country	West Europe	15	iTraxx SOVX West Europe
	Central/East Europe, Middle East and Africa	15	iTraxx SOVX CEEMEA
	Asia Pacific	10	iTraxx SOVX Asia Pacific
	Latin America	8	iTraxx SOVX Latin America
	Global liquid investment grade		iTraxx SOVX IG
	G7		iTraxx SOVX G7
	Brazil, Russia, India, China		iTraxx SOVX BRIC

Table 12.2   iTraxx indices

The major CDS indices are operated and published on a daily basis by Mark-it.[31] These CDS indices come in two families:

- The CDX family covers the CDS indices for North America and emerging markets; and
- The iTraxx family covers the CDS indices for Europe, Asia and countries.

In addition to geographical area, CDS indices are also classified by type of debt issuers, credit quality and standard tenor.[32] As such, a number of CDS indices are created to serve the needs of a broad range of investors. The two most popular CDS indices are:

[31] The CDS indices are published by Mark-it on its website with the URL
   http://www.markit.com/markit.jsp?jsppage=indices.jsp
[32] Standard tenors include one, three, five, seven and ten years.

- CDX North America, investment grade and five-year; and
- iTraxx Europe and five-year.

12.1.1 On-the-run series ★★★

Since the protection period of a single name CDS is reduced gradually on a daily basis, the protection period of the component single name CDSs of a CDS index will deviate materially from the original tenor some time after the origination. In addition, some component single name CDSs may terminate due to the default of the corresponding reference debts. Therefore, once every six months in March and September for every CDS index, a revised set of component single name CDSs with a protection period three months longer than the standard tenor are proposed by major CDS traders to form a new on-the-run series of that particular CDS index. Each on-the-run series of a CDX index will last for six months such that the protection period reduces gradually from the standard tenor plus three months to the standard tenor minus three months. For example, the on-the-run period of a CDS index with five-year standard tenor ranges from five years and three months to four years and nine months. The previous series of the CDS index is then labelled as an off-the-run series. The market gives almost no attention to the off-the-run series of a CDX index.

When the new on-the-run series of a CDS index is constructed, the CDS index is quoted as the arithmetic average of the CDS spreads of all component single name CDSs. In case any component single name CDS is terminated during the protection period as a result of the default of any reference debt, the CDS index is revised to the arithmetic average of the CDS spreads of the component single name CDSs remaining active.

12.1.2 Market monitoring

Some practitioners use the on-the-run series of a CDS index as a metric to monitor the systematic credit quality of a particular market segment. Nevertheless, due to the limited life of an on-the-run series, a number of technical issues emerge. In general, CDS indices exhibit the following deficiencies:

- Default effect

  During the life of a CDS index, the CDS spread of a component single name CDS increases sharply when any one of its reference debts is approaching default. The CDS index is then pushed upwards. Upon the default of the reference debt, the CDS index is calculated with the component single name CDSs remaining active. The CDS index thus drops sharply after the default event. Nevertheless, this sudden reduction in the CDS index is driven by the exclusion of the component single name CDS referencing the defaulted debt instead of the improvement in systematic credit quality, thus demonstrating a false signal of improvement in systematic credit quality.

- Discontinuity

  Each on-the-run series of a CDS index lasts for only six months. A revised set of component single name CDSs with a protection period three months longer than the standard tenor are proposed by major CDS traders to form a new on-the-run series of that particular CDS index once every six months. This essentially introduces a discontinuity with an abrupt change of a CDS index on the day when a new on-the-run series becomes effective.

- Selection bias

  An on-the-run series of a CDS index is constructed with component single name CDSs referencing debts that match the credit quality of that particular CDS index. For an investment grade CDS index, a reference debt with the credit quality of its issuer deteriorating below the investment grade during the most recent on-the-run period will trigger all single name CDSs referencing the debts issued by the same issuer to be excluded from the next on-the-run series. Under such situation, the value of a new on-the-run series of the CDS index is likely to be pressed downwards due to the selection of component single name CDSs of higher quality and understate the deterioration in systematic credit quality.

  Conversely, for a high yield grade CDS index, a reference debt with the credit quality of its issuer improving above the high yield grade during the most recent on-the-run period will trigger all single name CDSs referencing the debts issued by the same issuer to be excluded from the next on-the-run series. Under such situation, the value of a new on-the-run series of the CDS index is likely to be pushed upwards due to the selection of component single name CDSs of lower quality and understate the improvement in systematic credit quality.

Therefore, care must be taken when CDS indices are utilized for market monitoring since CDS indices are designed primarily to drive the trading of the CDX index contract instead of for credit risk management.

12.2   CDS index contract

A CDS index contract is a portfolio of standard single name CDSs identical to the construction of a CDS index. For a CDS index contract with N components, each component single name CDS accounts for one-N^{th} of the contractual principal of the CDS index contract and is subject to the same standardized premium rate[33] and protection period. Due to the improvement or deterioration in credit quality of the component reference debts, the component single name CDSs have continuously changing non-zero values. The sum of the values of the component single name CDSs then becomes the value of the CDS index contract. Deterioration in the systematic credit quality will boost the value of a CDS index contract and improvement in the systematic credit quality will suppress the value of a CDS index contract. Since CDS index contracts reflect directly the systematic credit quality of certain major market segments, these contracts are by far the most liquidly traded credit instrument in the financial market.

12.2.1 Functional purpose ★★★

In contrast to its component single name CDSs which are originated for the purpose of credit risk mitigation, a CDS index contract is designed primarily for trading the systematic credit quality of a particular market segment. An investor who expects deterioration in the systematic credit quality of a particular market segment may act as a protection buyer to enter the long position in a CDS index contract when its value is low. Conversely, an investor who expects an improvement in the systematic credit quality of a particular market segment may act as a protection seller to enter the short position in a CDS index contract when its value is high.

12.2.2 Cash flows

Upfront payments

The protection buyer of a CDS index contract acquires an on-the-run CDS index contract[34] from the protection seller by either:

- paying an upfront fee when the present value of expected protection is higher than the present value of expected premiums; or

- receiving an upfront fee when the present value of expected protection is lower than the present value of expected premiums.

---

[33] 100 bps per quarter for an investment grade CDS index contract and 500 bps per quarter for a high yield grade CDS index contract.

[34] An off-the-run CDS index contract has no secondary market. As such, most CDS index contracts are reversed before the expiry of the on-the-run period.

Premium

In addition to the upfront payments, the protection buyer of a CDS index contract needs to pay the protection seller a regular premium on a quarterly basis. The initial regular premium is equal to:

Principal × Standard premium rate

Upon the default of a reference debt in the CDS index, the protection buyer pays the accrued premium:

$$\frac{Principal}{Initial\ number\ of\ reference\ debts} \times Standard\ premium\ rate$$
$$\times \frac{No.\ of\ days\ since\ last\ premium\ payment\ day}{No.\ of\ days\ between\ last\ and\ next\ premium\ payment\ days}$$

and the regular premium is reduced to:

$$Standard\ premium \times \frac{Number\ of\ survival\ debts}{Initial\ number\ of\ reference\ debts}$$

The reduction in regular premium continues until all debts referenced by the component single name CDSs in the CDS index default.

Default protection

A CDS index contract is settled in cash. Upon the default of a reference debt of a component single name CDS in a CDS index, the protection buyer of a CDS index contract will receive from the protection seller a default protection equal to:

$$\frac{Contractal\ principal \times LGD\ of\ defaulted\ debt}{Initial\ number\ of\ reference\ debts}$$

12.2.3 Valuation

The value of a CDS index contract is the difference between the present values of expected protection and expected premiums.

The expected protection is driven by the characteristics of the reference debts. Obviously, a larger contractual principal, larger LGD, larger PD and longer protection period all demand a larger protection. Since all reference debts are protected, the concentration of and default dependency among the reference debts have no impact to the value of a CDS index contract.

In summary, the value of a CDS index contact is determined by the factors listed in Table 12.3.

Category	Factor	Impact to value (long position)*	Variation after origination	Impact to credit risk (short position)*
Reference debt	Contractual principal	+	Mild	+
	LGD	+	Moderate	+
	PD	+	Material	+
	Protection period	+	Decreasing gradually	+
Portfolio	Concentration of debts		Mild	+
	Default dependency		Moderate	+
CDS index	Premium rate	-	No	

* A "+" means that the value or credit risk increases when the factor increases and a "-" means that the value or credit risk decreases when the factor increases.

Table 12.3   Factors impacting the value of a CDS index contract

The principal and premium rate are fixed in a CDS index contract. The protection period is specified initially in the same CDS index contract and reduces on a daily basis. This decreases gradually the value of a CDS index contract. The LGDs and PDs vary during the life of a CDS index contract. They become the two primary factors that drive the uncertainty of the value of a CDS index contract.

12.2.4 Credit risk

Since a single name CDS is largely equivalent to the short position in a debt and the long position in a risk-free security, a CDS index contract, being a portfolio of single name CDSs with equal principal, is largely equivalent to the short position in a debt portfolio and the long position in a risk-free security. The credit risk of the short position in a CDS index contract is largely equivalent to that of the portfolio of debts referenced by the component single name CDSs in the CDS index.

Most factors impacting the value of a CDS index contract also impact the credit risk. In addition, the credit risk also increases with increasing concentration of debts and default dependency. The impacts to credit risk of the short position in a CDS index contract from the risk factors are listed in Table 12.3. The credit risk of a CDS index contract with sufficiently large number of reference entities, e.g., more than thirty, can be measured by the XCL.

12.2.5 Trading

A CDS index contract is a bilateral agreement between a protection buyer and a protection seller. Once entered, a CDS index contract must be honoured by both parties until maturity, similar to other contract based financial instruments. Nevertheless, subject to a bilateral netting agreement, a protection buyer may reverse an existing CDS index contract with the original protection seller in order to offset the outstanding potential cash flows of the existing CDS index contract. In other words, the protection buyer now enters the short position of an existing CDS index contract with the original protection seller such that the cash flows arising from the existing CDS index contract is cancelled by the identical cash flows arising from the new short position. This results in the trading of CDS index contracts.

Credit Linked Notes

13

KEY CONCEPTS

- Single name CLN
- Basket CLN
- Market value CLN

13.1   Financial innovation with CDSs ★★★

The popularity of CDSs realizes financial innovations in the credit market. While the formation of traditional credit products is bounded by the direct demand and supply relationship between debt investors and debt issuers in asset and liability formats, the CDSs serve the financial market as a foundation building block to create new credit products beyond this boundary. By combining various types of CDSs with top quality assets as proxy of risk-free securities, many forms of credit products are created to meet the risk-return preferences of a broad range of investors without a direct matching of supply from debt issuers. These credit products include, among others, credit linked notes ("CLNs") and collateralized debt obligations ("CDOs"). Although CDOs are more complicated than CLNs, they share many commonalities.

For each credit product, the following dimensions are considered:

- Functional purpose: Why does an investor acquire this credit product?
- Cash flows: What are the amounts and schedules of cash outflows and inflows?
- Valuation: Which factors and how do these factors impact the value of this credit product?
- Credit risk: How to measure the credit risk of this credit product?

13.2   Single name CLN

13.2.1 Functional purpose

In its simplest form, a single name CLN is a financial instrument that tracks the cash flows of a reference debt. A single name CLN is issued by a financial institution that seeks to provide an opportunity for an investor to invest in a debt that the investor may not have a convenient channel to acquire due to certain restrictions, e.g., some bonds are traded in: (i) a huge lot size; or (ii) a market in which the investor cannot participate directly.

Since the cash flows of a single name CLN is identical to those of the reference debt, the value and credit risk of a single name CLN are also identical to those of the reference debt. Nevertheless, as a single name CLN is issued by a financial institution, in case the financial institution defaults, the investor of a single name CLN will no longer be paid in accordance with the cash flows of the reference debt. As such, a single name CLN issued by a financial institution is essentially subject to an additional layer of credit risk which is not welcomed to most investors.

13.2.2 Special purpose entity

To eliminate this additional layer of credit risk, a special purpose entity ("SPE"), which is a shell company created by but legally independent of the financial institution, is established with a primary function to issue a single name CLN.

The SPE is first granted a short term loan by the financial institution to acquire the reference debt and issue a single name CLN to match the cash flows of the reference debt. This single name CLN is then divided into many smaller units and sold to many investors. The proceeds from selling the single name CLN are then utilized to settle the short term loan. The cash flows of the single name CLN are identical to those of the reference debt held in the SPE. The SPE is characterized as a bankruptcy remote entity because the SPE is a liability free shell company and independent of the financial institution that establishes the SPE.

13.2.3 Synthetic CLN

Since a reference debt can largely be synthesized by the short position in a single name CDS and the long position in a risk-free security, a single name CLN can also be synthesized with the same approach. Therefore, instead of holding a reference debt, an SPE may synthesize a reference debt by:

- acting as a protection seller to issue a single name CDS to the financial institution; and
- applying a short term loan from the financial institution to purchase some top quality assets.

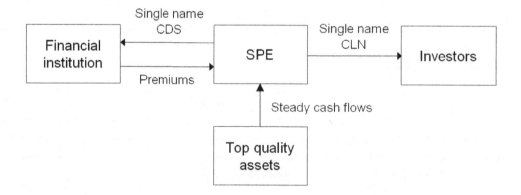

Figure 13.1   Single name CLN issued under an SPE

The SPE then issues a single name CLN to track the cash flows of the reference debt. This single name CLN is divided into many smaller units and sold to many investors. The proceeds from selling the single name CLN are utilized to settle the short term loan. The financial institution acts as a wholesale protection buyer who may enter the short position of the single name CDS with another financial institution in order to transfer the obligation of premium payments.

This convenient alternative allows a single name CLN to be issued in accordance with the preference of an investor in terms of debt issuer, seniority, interest rate and maturity, i.e., the SPE simply issues a single name CDS on a hypothetical reference debt in accordance with the specification from an investor. This arrangement immediately broadens the range of investors in the debt market without the physical existence of a reference debt.

The single name CDS serves as a building block to construct a synthetic CLN. The SPE uses the collected CDS premiums to provide the CLN investors an excess return above the return generated by the top quality assets when the reference debt survives and pays the default protection to the protection buyer by converting some top quality assets into cash upon the default of the reference debt.

13.2.4 Cash flows

Cash outflow

An investor pays an initial amount to acquire a single name CLN.

Cash inflows

When the reference debt survives, the investor will receive the scheduled interests and principal tracking the reference debt. In case the reference debt defaults, the investor will receive the recovered amount of the reference debt through debt collection actions.

13.2.5 Valuation

The value of a single name CLN is determined by the cash inflows identical to those of the reference debt. Therefore, the factors that affect the value of a reference debt will have the same impact to the value of a single name CLN.

The principal and interest rate are fixed in a single name CLN contract. The initial RM is also specified in the same single name CLN contract and reduces on a daily basis. This increases gradually the value of a single name CLN. The LGD and PD thus become the two primary factors that drive the uncertainty of the value of a single name CLN.

Category	Factor	Impact to value[*]	Variation	Impact to credit risk[*]
Reference debt	Principal	+	No	+
	LGD	-	Moderate	+
	PD	-	Material	+
	RM	-	Decreasing gradually	+
CLN	Interest rate	+	No	+

[*] A "+" means that the value or credit risk increases when the factor increases and a "-" means that the value or credit risk decreases when the factor increases.

Table 13.1   Factors impacting the value and credit risk of a single name CLN

13.2.6 Credit risk

The credit risk of a single name CLN is driven by the EAD, LGD, PD and RM of the reference debt. It is measured by the EL and 1-year EL as:

$$EL = EAD \times LGD \times \left[1 - (1 - PD)^{RM} \right]$$

$$\text{1-year EL} = EAD \times LGD \times Min\left[PD, 1 - (1 - PD)^{RM} \right]$$

13.3   Basket CLN   ★★★

13.3.1 Functional purpose   ★★★

A basket CLN facilitates an investor to enhance the nominal yield of his credit investment by investing in several debts simultaneously with a shared principal. It is designed to serve some investors who are willing to take risk simultaneously on several debts of higher quality in order to achieve a more attractive return.

13.3.2 Structuring   ★★★

A basket CLN is designed with its cash flows tracking those of the first to default member in a basket of reference debts from different issuers. The reference debts are equipped with identical principal, interest amount and payment schedule.

This basket CLN can largely be hedged with a 1TD CDS to form a risk-free security, i.e.:

Basket CLN + 1TD CDS ≈ Risk-free security

By arranging terms:

Basket CLN ≈ - 1TD CDS + Risk-free security

This relationship suggests that a basket CLN can be synthesized with the short position in a 1TD CDS and the long position in a risk-free security.

In reality, it is very difficult to form physically a basket of debts from different issuers with identical principal, interest amount and payment schedule. Therefore, the basket of reference debts is synthesized with an SPE by:

- acting as a protection seller to issue a 1TD CDS to the financial institution; and
- applying a short term loan from the financial institution to purchase some top quality assets.

The SPE then issues a basket CLN to track the cash flows of the 1TD member in the basket of reference debts. This basket CLN is divided into many smaller units and sold to many investors. The proceeds from selling the basket CLN are utilized to settle the short term loan. The financial institution acts as a wholesale protection buyer. The 1TD CDS is kept and hedged[35] by the financial institution since the 1TD CDS is highly customized to facilitate the issuance of the basket CLN and unlikely to be acquired directly by other protection buyers.

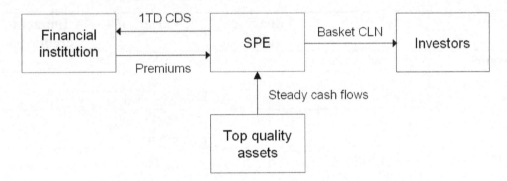

Figure 13.2   Basket CLN issued under an SPE

---

[35] The long position in a 1TD CDS is hedged dynamically with several short positions in single name CDSs in order to transfer indirectly the cost of acquiring the 1TD CDS to other protection buyers.

13.3.3 Cash flows ★★★

Cash outflow

An investor pays an initial amount to acquire a basket CLN.

Cash inflows

When all reference debts in the basket survive, the investor will receive the interests and principal tracking any one of the reference debts. In case any reference debt defaults, the investor will receive the recovered amount of the 1TD reference debt through debt collection actions.

13.3.4 Valuation ★★★

With the approximation

Basket CLN ≈ - 1TD CDS + Risk-free security

there is a reverse relationship between the value of a basket CLN and that of the corresponding 1TD CDS. Therefore, the value of a basket CLN is determined by the factors set out in Table 13.2.

Category	Factor	Impact to value[*]	Variation	Impact to credit risk[*]
Reference debt	Principal	+	No	+
	LGD	-	Moderate	+
	PD	-	Material	+
	RM	-	Decreasing gradually	+
Basket	Basket size	-	No	+
	Default dependency	+	Moderate	-
CLN	Interest rate	+	No	+

* A "+" means that the value or credit risk increases when the factor increases and a "-" means that the value or credit risk decreases when the factor increases.

Table 13.2   Factors impacting the value of a basket CLN

The principal, interest rate and basket size are fixed in a basket CLN contract. The initial RM is also specified in the same basket CLN contract and reduces on a daily basis. This gradually increases the value of a basket CLN. The LGD, PD and default dependency thus become the three primary factors that drive the uncertainty to the value of a basket CLN.

13.3.5 Probability of first default ★★★

The probability of first default ("P1D") of a basket CLN is the chance that any one of the reference debts in the basket defaults in the following year. The actual P1D can be derived using Monte Carlo simulation with over million trials. The lower bound of the P1D is estimated subject to the condition that there is a perfect default dependency among the reference debts in the basket, i.e., all reference debts will either default or survive together. Under this condition, the lower bound of the P1D is simply equal to the maximum of the PDs of the reference debts in the basket. The upper bound of the P1D is estimated subject to the condition that there is totally no default dependency among the reference debts in the basket, i.e. the reference debts in the basket will default or survive on their own. When there are N default independent reference debts in the basket, the survival of the basket CLN in one year is driven by the survival of all reference debts in one year and the probability of survival is:

$$\left(1 - PD_1\right) \times \left(1 - PD_2\right) \times \left(1 - PD_3\right) \times ... \times \left(1 - PD_N\right)$$

Under this condition, the upper bound of the P1D is simply equal to the sum of the PDs of the reference debts in the basket.

$$1 - \left(1 - PD_1\right) \times \left(1 - PD_2\right) \times \left(1 - PD_3\right) \times ... \times \left(1 - PD_N\right)$$
$$< PD_1 + PD_2 + PD_3 + ... + PD_N$$

13.3.6 Credit risk ★★★

Since

Basket CLN ≈ - 1TD CDS + Risk-free security

the credit risk of a basket CLN is largely equivalent to that of the short position in a 1TD CDS. The factors impacting the value of a basket CLN also impact the credit risk in the opposite direction. The impacts to credit risk from the risk factors are set out in Table 13.2.

The credit risk of a basket CLN is measured by the EL and/or 1-year EL. Due to the effect from the basket size, the EL and 1-year EL cannot be expressed in closed form formula but has to be derived with Monte Carlo simulation.

When the reference debts are also equipped with the same LGD in addition to the same EAD and same RM, the P1D of the CLN, which has incorporated the impacts from the PD of the reference debts, basket size and default dependency, can be derived with Monte Carlos simulation and the EL and 1-year EL can be expressed in closed form formulas as:

$$EL = EAD \times LGD \times \left[1 - \left(1 - P1D \right)^{RM} \right]$$

$$\text{1-year } EL = EAD \times LGD \times Min \left[P1D, 1 - \left(1 - P1D \right)^{RM} \right]$$

13.4   Market value CLN

In order to create a synthetic CLN, the SPE holds a portfolio of top quality assets that are initially acquired with an intention to generate the cash flows to be distributed to the CLN investors.

In the situation where the market has a higher demand on top quality assets, the SPE may sell part of the top quality assets above their acquisition cost in order to realize a profit. Afterwards, when the market has a lower demand on top quality assets, the SPE may acquire some similar top quality assets below the previous selling price. This selling high and buying low process is repeated continuously with an aim to push up the overall value of the assets in the SPE until the maturity of the CLN. Upon the default of any reference debt, the profit arising from the active trading offsets part of the default loss arising from the reference debt and forms part of the recovered amount to be distributed to the CLN investor. A synthetic CLN with its top quality assets operating under this active trading scheme is referred to as a market value CLN. If all reference debts survive until the maturity of the CLN, the profit arising from the active trading will also be distributed to the CLN investors.

The creation of a market value CLN essentially demands a more sophisticated SPE manager who is capable of delivering a profit through the trading of top quality assets. In case the SPE creates a loss as a result of the trading activities, the trading loss will also be transferred to the CLN investors. Therefore, a market value CLN is subject to an additional layer of trading risk and thus deserves a higher return. In summary, a market value CLN is a hybrid instrument with its return driven by both the credit risk of the reference debts and the trading risk of the top quality assets.

Appendix 13.1   EL of a basket CLN

The EL of a basket CLN is derived with Monte Carlo simulation by taking the following steps:

- Derive the hazard rate of the reference debt issuer k as $\lambda_k = - \ln(1 - PD_k)$;

- Generate a common standard normal random number y;

- For each reference debt issuer k (k = 1 to N),

    - generate a standard normal random number z_k;

    - set $x_k = y\sqrt{CCC_k} + z_k\sqrt{1 - CCC_k}$;

    - calculate the value of the cumulative standard normal distribution function
    $$\Phi\left(x_k\right) = \frac{1}{\sqrt{2\pi}} \int_{-\infty}^{x_k} \exp(-\frac{\tau^2}{2})d\tau ;$$

    - derive the default time $t_k = - \dfrac{\ln\left[1 - \Phi\left(x_k\right)\right]}{\lambda_k}$

    - if $t_k \leq RM$, then reference debt k defaults.

- If any reference debt defaults within the RM, a default loss equal to the arithmetic product of the EAD and LGD of the reference default defaulted first is registered;

- If no reference debt defaults within the RM, then the default loss is zero; and

- Repeat the above simulation steps for a sufficient large number of times, e.g., hundred thousand times.

The EL of the basket CLN is calculated as the average of the simulated default losses.

Collateralized Debt Obligations

KEY CONCEPTS

- Cash flow CDO
- Synthetic CDO

- Market value CDO
- CDO rating

14.1 Credit securitization

In general, credit risky debts have an illiquid secondary market primarily due to the following two reasons:

- There is a persistent mis-match between demand and supply of debts in terms of risk-return characteristics. In general, there is a strong demand on high quality debts but only a very limited supply on high quality debts; and

- The information asymmetry on a debt creates a large spread between the bid and ask prices. An owner who has invested in a debt for some time has more understanding on the specific risk of a debt and demands a higher ask price. An investor who intends to acquire a debt from the secondary market has limited understanding on the specific risk of a debt and offers a lower bid price.

Through the process of credit securitization over a debt portfolio, structured credit instruments in the form of collateralized debt obligations ("CDOs") are created and tailored to match the demands from investors. The specific risks of individual debts are diversified away, leaving only the systematic risk on which most investors have a common understanding.

14.2 Structuring

14.2.1 Cash flow CDO ★★★

At its origination, a CDO family, supported by a debt portfolio well approximated by an infinite homogeneous portfolio,[36] comprises several CDO tranches, each with its own tranche principal, tranche interest rate and seniority. The sum of all tranche principals, referred to as the total tranche principal, is equal to the portfolio principal and the total interest amount to be distributed to the CDO tranches is equal to the sum of interests generated by the portfolio principal.

---

[36] The theories for modelling CDOs created by a heterogeneous portfolio are not well developed. The high model error makes such kind of CDOs less welcome to the CDO market, in particular after the financial tsunami 2008.

A CDO tranche is specified by a portfolio attachment point ("PAP") and a portfolio detachment point ("PDP") of the portfolio principal. A PAP is the percentage of portfolio principal from which the CDO tranche starts to suffer from default loss in the tranche principal. A PDP is the percentage of portfolio principal up to which the CDO tranche will suffer from total default loss. The most junior tranche has a PAP 0 percent while the most senior tranche has a PAP 100 percent but no detachment point.

Alternatively, a CDO tranche can be specified by a tranche attachment point ("TAP") and a tranche detachment point ("TDP") of the portfolio principal. A TAP is the percentage of total tranche principal from which the CDO tranche starts to suffer from default loss in the tranche principal. A TDP is the percentage of total tranche principal up to which the CDO tranche will suffer from total default loss. The most junior tranche has a TAP 0 percent while the most senior tranche has a TDP 100 percent.

Obviously, the TAP and PAP are connected with the relationship:

$$TAP = PAP \times LGD$$

and, except for the ultra senior tranche, the TDP and PDP are connected with the relationship:

$$TDP = PDP \times LGD$$

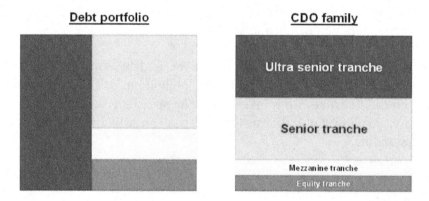

Figure 14.1   Cash flow re-distribution through credit securitization

On an interest payment day, the most senior tranche has the priority to collect the interests generated from the debt portfolio until either the entitled tranche interest amount is collected in full or the interests from the debt portfolio are exhausted, i.e.:

$$Min\left(\begin{array}{c} \text{Tranche principal} \times \dfrac{\text{Tranch interest rate}}{\text{Interest frequency}}, \\ \text{Portfolio principal} \times \dfrac{\text{Portfolio interest rate}}{\text{Interest frequency}} \end{array} \right)$$

After the interest payment of the most senior tranche has been satisfied, the second most senior tranche has the priority to receive the interests from the debt portfolio until either the tranche interest amount is collected in full or the interests from the debt portfolio are exhausted, i.e.:

$$\text{Min} \left(\begin{array}{l} \text{Tranche principal} \times \dfrac{\text{Tranch interest rate}}{\text{Interest frequency}}, \\[2ex] \text{Portfolio principal} \times \dfrac{\text{Portfolio interest rate}}{\text{Interest frequency}} \\[2ex] \text{- Interests paid to the most senior tranche} \end{array} \right)$$

After the interest payments on the most and second most senior tranches have been met, the third most senior tranche has the priority to receive the interests from the debt portfolio until either the tranche interest amount is collected in full or the interests from the debt portfolio are exhausted, i.e.:

$$\text{Min} \left(\begin{array}{l} \text{Tranche principal} \times \dfrac{\text{Tranch interest rate}}{\text{Interest fequency}}, \\[2ex] \text{Portfolio principal} \times \dfrac{\text{Portfolio interest rate}}{\text{Interest fequency}} \\[2ex] \text{- Interests paid to more senior tranches} \end{array} \right)$$

This cash waterfall scheme continues onto other CDO tranches consecutively until either all tranche interest amounts are received in full or the interests from the debt portfolio are exhausted.

This tranche based interest distribution process repeats on every interest payment day. Nevertheless, the tranche and portfolio principals may decrease in between two interest payment days as a result of defaults in the debt portfolio. When there is any default of the portfolio principal:

- the portfolio principal is reduced;
- the interest will only be generated from the survival portfolio principal; and
- the amount recovered from the defaulted portfolio principal will be returned to the ultra senior tranche and result a deduction of the principal of the ultra senior tranche.

Therefore, for each CDO tranche, the tranche interest amount is revised to:

$$\text{Min} \begin{pmatrix} \text{Survival tranche principal} \times \dfrac{\text{Tranch interest rate}}{\text{Interest frequency}}, \\[2ex] \text{Survival portfolio principal} \times \dfrac{\text{Portfolio interest rate}}{\text{Interest frequency}} \\[2ex] \text{- Interests paid to more senior tranches} \end{pmatrix}$$

At maturity, each CDO tranche is distributed with the principal according to a similar cash waterfall scheme, i.e.:

$$\text{Min} \begin{pmatrix} \text{CDO tranche principal,} \\ \text{Survival portfolio principal} \\ \text{- Principal paid to more senior tranches} \end{pmatrix}$$

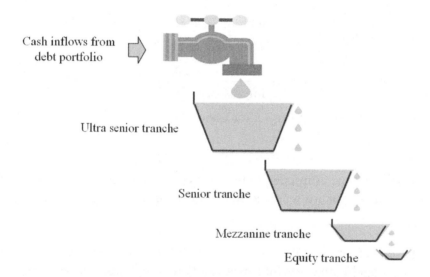

Cash inflows from debt portfolio

Ultra senior tranche

Senior tranche

Mezzanine tranche

Equity tranche

Figure 14.2   Cash waterfall of a CDO family

The total interest generated by the survival portfolio principal reduces continuously over the life of the debt portfolio as a result of the defaults in the debt portfolio. Therefore, a higher seniority tranche is subject to a higher stability of cash inflows and deserves a lower return while a lower seniority tranche is subject to a higher uncertainty of cash inflows and deserves a higher return. This essentially creates a number of new credit instruments with a broad range of risk-return characteristics from a debt portfolio with a uniform risk-return characteristic.

The CDO tranche with the highest priority is the ultra senior tranche with its principal supported by the recovered amount of the initial portfolio principal. Under the most extreme situation where the entire portfolio principal defaults, the principal of an ultra senior tranche will be paid in full. This indeed creates an almost risk-free security from a portfolio of credit risky debts.[37]

The CDO tranche with the second highest priority is the senior tranche which has stable cash inflows with high certainty. The equity tranche is the CDO tranche with the lowest priority which will be distributed with interests and principal only after the interest and principal requirements of all other CDO tranches have been met. In other words, the equity tranche has the lowest claim priority to the cash flows generated from the debt portfolio, similar to the shareholders' equity in the asset structure of a corporation. Therefore, in general, the equity tranche is acquired by the financial institution originating the CDO family at a lower price due to its extremely high risk. The CDO tranches in between the senior and equity tranches are referred to as mezzanine tranches.

The tranche principal of the ultra senior tranche is:

$$\text{Tranche principal} = \text{Portfolio principal} \times (1 - \text{LGD})$$

and the tranche principal of other tranches is:

$$\text{Tranche principal} = \text{Portfolio principal} \times (\text{PDP} - \text{PAP}) \times \text{LGD}$$
$$= \text{Portfolio principal} \times (\text{TDP} - \text{TAP})$$

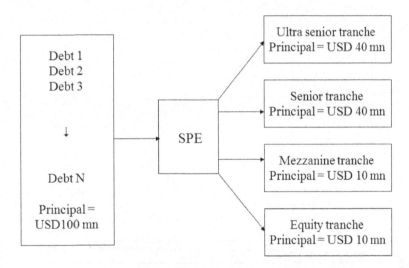

Figure 14.3   Cash flow CDO

Similarly to a CLN, to eliminate the additional layer of credit risk of a CDO issuer, the CDO tranches are issued by an SPE which is granted a short term loan by a financial institution to acquire the debt portfolio and issues CDO tranches backed up by the cash

---

[37] In practice, an ultra senior tranche seldom exists in its generic format in the financial market. It is often combined with the senior tranche to form a large "senior tranche" in order to ascertain that this combined "senior tranche" is the most senior member in the CDO family.

flows from the debt portfolio. Each CDO tranche is divided into a number of smaller units and sold to many investors. The proceeds from selling the CDO tranches are then utilized to settle the short term loan. The cash flows of the CDO tranches are matched by those of the debt portfolio in the SPE.

Through the mechanisms of debt portfolio and cash waterfall, the default loss of credit investments is re-distributed. For the same principal invested in:

- a single debt, the default occurs at a moderate confidence level with loss rate LGD;

- a debt portfolio, a stable default loss occurs in most situations and the default loss rate is bounded below the LGD;

- an equity tranche, a large default loss occurs even at a very low confidence level and increases rapidly towards 100 percent;

- a mezzanine tranche, the default loss emerges after the PAP and increases stably towards 100 percent at the PDP;

- a senior tranche, the default loss occurs only at a very high confidence level; and

- an ultra senior tranche, default loss of the principal never occurs.

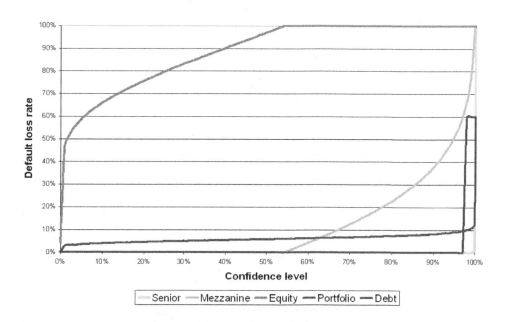

Figure 14.4   Default loss re-distribution

14.2.2 Synthetic CDO ★★★

A CDO tranche can be hedged by a portfolio CDS to form a largely risk-free security, i.e.:

CDO tranche + Portfolio CDS ≈ Risk-free security

By arranging terms,

CDO tranche ≈ - Portfolio CDS + Risk-free security

This relationship suggests that a CDO tranche can be synthesized with the short position in a portfolio CDS and the long position in a risk-free security. In addition, the synthesis of a CDO tranche is separated totally from its family members. This allows the production of a CDO tranche to match completely the preference of an investor without creating any side products.

Thus a CDO tranche can be synthesized with an SPE by:

- acting as a protection seller to issue a portfolio CDS to a financial institution; and
- applying a short term loan from the financial institution to purchase some top quality assets.

The SPE then issues a CDO tranche to match the cash flows of the portfolio CDS and top quality assets. This CDO tranche is divided into many smaller units and sold to many investors. The proceeds from selling the CDO tranche are utilized to settle the short term loan. The financial institution acts as a wholesale protection buyer. The portfolio CDS is kept and hedged [38] by the financial institution since the portfolio CDS is highly customized to facilitate the issuance of the CDO tranche and unlikely to be acquired directly by other protection buyers.

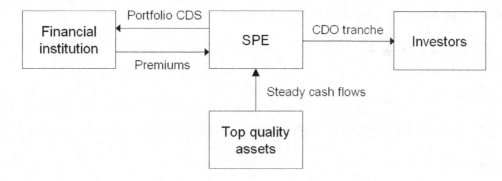

Figure 14.5 Synthetic CDO

---

[38] The long position in a portfolio CDS is hedged dynamically with CDS index contracts in order to transfer indirectly the premium of acquiring the portfolio CDS to other protection buyers.

A synthetic CDO tranche performs similar to a cash flow CDO tranche with an advantage that a synthetic CDO tranche can be tailored to meet the specific requirements of an investor in a much shorter period of time without the acquisition of a debt portfolio physically.

14.2.3 Market value CDO

To create a cash flow CDO, the SPE holds a portfolio of credit risky debts. To create a synthetic CDO, the SPE holds a portfolio of top quality assets. These portfolios are referred to as collaterals of the CDO family. The collaterals are initially acquired with an intention to generate cash flows that will be distributed to the CDO tranches.

In the situation where the market has a higher demand on collaterals, the SPE may sell part of the collaterals above their acquisition cost in order to realize a profit. Afterwards, when the market has a lower demand on collaterals, the SPE may acquire some similar collaterals below the previous selling price. This selling high and buying low process is repeated continuously with an aim to push up the overall value of assets in the SPE until the maturity of the CDO tranches. At maturity, the profit arising from the active trading offsets part of the default loss and forms part of the portfolio principal to be distributed to the CDO tranches. A CDO family with its collaterals operating under this active trading scheme is referred to as a market value CDO.

The creation of a market value CDO essentially demands a more sophisticated SPE manager who must be capable to ensure that the collaterals, after being partially converted into cash, remain sufficient to meet the interest payments of various CDO tranches. In case the SPE creates loss as a result of the trading activities, the trading loss will also be transferred to the CDO tranches. Therefore, a market value CDO is subject to an additional layer of trading risk and thus deserves a higher return. In summary, a market value CDO is a hybrid instrument with its return driven by both the credit risk of the debt portfolio and the trading risk of the collaterals.

14.3   Cash flows   ★★★

Cash outflow

An investor pays an initial amount to acquire a CDO tranche.

Cash inflows

When the tranche principal survives in full, the investor will receive the interests and principal in accordance with the schedule set out in a CDO contract. In case the tranche principal defaults partially, the scheduled interests will be reduced in proportion to the defaulted tranche principal. At maturity, the investor will receive the survived tranche principal.

14.4 Valuation ★★★

With the approximation

CDO tranche ≈ - Portfolio CDS + Risk-free security

there is a reverse relationship between the value of a CDO tranche and that of the corresponding portfolio CDS. Therefore, the value of a CDO is determined by the factors set out in Table 14.1. The ultra senior tranche is a special case in which the value of the CDO tranche depends primarily on the portfolio principal, LGD and interest rate.

The tranche principal, interest rate and PAP are fixed in a CDO contract. The initial RM is specified in the same CDO contract and reduces on a daily basis. This increases gradually the value of a CDO tranche. The LGD, PD and CCC vary during the life of a CDO tranche and become the three primary factors that drive the uncertainty of the value of a CDO tranche.

Category	Factor	Impact to value[*]	Variation	Impact to credit risk[*]
Debt portfolio	LGD	-	Moderate	+
	PD	-	Material	+
	RM	-	Decreasing gradually	+
	CCC	+ for smaller PAP - for larger PAP	Moderate	- for smaller PAP + for larger PAP
Tranche	Principal	+	Decreasing	+
	Interest rate	+	No	+
	PAP	+	No	-

* A "+" means that the value or credit risk increases when the factor increases and a "-" means that the value or credit risk decreases when the factor increases.

Table 14.1   Factors impacting the value and credit risk of a CDO tranche

14.5 Credit risk ★★★

Since

CDO tranche ≈ - Portfolio CDS + Risk-free security

the credit risk of a CDO tranche is largely equivalent to that of the short position in a portfolio CDS.

Most factors impacting the value of the CDO tranche also impact the credit risk. The impacts to credit risk from the risk factors are set out in Table 14.1. Neither the EL, the

1-year EL nor the XCL serves as a valid measure for the credit risk of a CDO tranche due to the effects from the PAP and the PDP implied by the tranche principal and LGD.

14.6   Functional purpose

14.6.1 Broadening of credit market ★★★

CDO tranches are created and tailored to meet the demand from investors without the requirements matched directly by the supply from debt issuers. The credit quality is customized in accordance with seniority. As such, a large amount of senior tranches are created for insurance companies and pension funds which demand credit investments with very stable cash inflows. The ultra senior tranches, virtually having the same credit quality as treasuries, can be acquired at a cost lower than treasuries due to the lack of liquid secondary market and privilege to act as collaterals for borrowing from central banks. They may serve as an alternative proxy of risk-free security.

14.6.2 Credit risk mitigation ★★★

Through credit securitization, a financial institution can convert part of its debt portfolio into cash within a shorter period of time by setting up an SPE to acquire a largely homogeneous part of the financial institution's debt portfolio and package this sub-portfolio into CDO tranches which are then sold to CDO investors. This essentially reduces the credit risk of the original debt portfolio owned by the financial institution when the financial institution considers that the original portfolio credit risk is beyond its tolerance level. The same disposal of the sub-portfolio is difficult to be accomplished in an ordinary illiquid secondary debt market. A CDO family that is created with a primary purpose to reduce portfolio credit risk is referred to as a balance sheet CDO.

14.6.3 Diversification arbitrage ★★★

A trading strategy can be constructed by:

- acquiring many similar debts, each at a lower cost with its credit risk comprising both the systematic and specific risks;

- combining the debts into a portfolio with most of the specific risk diversified away; and

- packaging the debt portfolio into a CDO family and selling to many debt investors of different risk-return preferences. This CDO family is subject to a higher total selling price due to the reduction in total risk as a result of the elimination of specific risks.

The differential between the higher selling price of the CDO family and the lower acquisition cost of the debt portfolio then contributes an arbitrage profit to the SPE. This arbitrage profit will eventually be pocketed as management fee by the financial institution which creates the SPE. A CDO family that is created with a primary purpose to generate a profit from price-cost differential is referred to as an arbitrage CDO. A large proportion of the CDO tranches in the market are arbitrage CDOs due to this profit making opportunity under which a financial institution can generate steady profits through the recipe of forming an SPE, buying low, diversifying, tranching and selling high.

14.7 CDO rating ★★★

Since the risk of a CDO tranche is driven by the certainty of the cash inflows arising from the cash waterfall, it becomes very technical to assess the quality of a CDO tranche. To facilitate the common interest of investing in the CDO tranches, some credit rating agencies use their own proprietary methodology to conduct an assessment on the cash inflows stability of a CDO tranche and assign a CDO rating to the CDO tranche. A CDO rating characterizes the ability of the debt portfolio and tranche structure to meet the commitment of the scheduled interest and principal payments.

The CDO ratings are incompatible with the corporate credit ratings. A CDO rating[39] characterizes the chance of violation to scheduled interests and principal while a credit rating represents only the default likelihood of a corporation. Nevertheless, the symbolic similarity between these two rating scales creates a common mis-understanding from many investors that the CDO rating and corporate credit rating carry the same economic meaning.

In contrast to corporate credit ratings, the Basel III framework does not set out any guideline on CDO ratings. This results in different treatments from different credit rating agencies and different interpretations from different investors on CDO ratings. The CDO ratings are defined qualitatively in Table 14.2.

---

[39] For the CDO ratings between AA and B, modifiers "+" and "-" are supplemented to further differentiate the credit quality at a higher granularity, with "+" being the best in the same group and "-" being the worst in the same group.

Rating	Description
AAA	A CDO tranche rated AAA has the highest quality. The capacity of the debt portfolio and tranche structure to meet the interests and principal to the CDO tranche is extremely strong.
AA	A CDO tranche rated AA differs from the highest rated CDO tranches only to a small degree. The capacity of the debt portfolio and tranche structure to meet the interests and principal to the CDO tranche is very strong.
A	A CDO tranche rated A is somewhat more susceptible to the adverse effects of changes in circumstances and economic conditions than the CDO tranches in higher rated categories. However, the capacity of the debt portfolio and tranche structure to meet the interests and principal to the CDO tranche is still strong.
BBB	A CDO tranche rated BBB is subject to adequate protection to the payment schedule. However, adverse economic conditions or changing circumstances are more likely to lead to a weakened capacity of the debt portfolio and tranche structure to meet the interests and principal to the CDO tranche.
BB	A CDO tranche rated BB is less vulnerable to violation of payment schedule than other speculative issues. However, it faces major on-going uncertainties or exposure to adverse business, financial or economic conditions that could lead to inadequate capacity of the debt portfolio and tranche structure to meet the interests and principal to the CDO tranche.
B	A CDO tranche rated B is more vulnerable to violation of payment schedule than the CDO tranches rated BB but the debt portfolio currently has the capacity to meet the interests and principal to the CDO tranche. Adverse business, financial or economic conditions will likely impair the capacity of the debt portfolio and tranche structure to meet the interests and principal to the CDO tranche.
CCC	A CDO tranche rated CCC is currently vulnerable to violation of payment schedule and is dependent upon favourable business, financial and economic conditions for the debt portfolio to meet the interests and principal to the CDO tranche. In the event of adverse business, financial and/or economic conditions, the debt portfolio and tranche structure is unlikely to have the capacity to meet the interests and principal to the CDO tranche.
CC	A CDO tranche rated CC is currently highly vulnerable to violation of payment schedule.
C	A C rating is assigned to a CDO tranche that is currently highly vulnerable to violation of payment schedule or has payment arrearages allowed by the terms of the documents.

Table 14.2   Definition of CDO ratings

14.8   CDO assessment

The mechanisms of the CDO ratings from the credit rating agencies are not transparent. It is unclear how credit rating agencies consolidate all the factors which drive the risk of a CDO tranche. To better assess the risk of a CDO tranche, there is a need to develop a theoretically sounded CDO assessment framework to quantify the risk of a CDO tranche.

Similar to credit assessment, the process of CDO assessment aims at characterizing in simple language the quality of a CDO tranche, i.e., the certainty of cash inflows generated from a CDO tranche, since a CDO tranche is a relatively complex financial instrument with a sophisticated cash waterfall scheme that drives the value and risk of the CDO tranche.

So far, there is no universal standard to assess the quality of a CDO tranche. The following sections propose four simple approaches to facilitate the characterization of the quality of a CDO tranche, riding on the theories of credit assessments for debts.

14.8.1 Probabilities of loss

When the concern is focused on the loss of tranche principal, the quality of a CDO tranche can be assessed by two probabilities of loss:

- The probability of total loss ("PTL") is the chance that the tranche principal will lose totally in the following ONE year. The PTL is calculated as:

$$PTL = 1 - \Phi\left[\frac{\Phi^{-1}(PDP)\sqrt{1 - CCC} - \Phi^{-1}(PD)}{\sqrt{CCC}} \right]$$

- The probability of first loss ("P1L") is the chance that the tranche principal will start to suffer from loss in the following ONE year. The P1L is calculated as:

$$P1L = 1 - \Phi\left[\frac{\Phi^{-1}(PAP)\sqrt{1 - CCC} - \Phi^{-1}(PD)}{\sqrt{CCC}} \right]$$

Obviously, the P1L must be larger than the PTL since the first loss must occur earlier than the total loss.

14.8.2 CDO quality

The relationship between the CDO quality and the probabilities of loss is similar to the relationship between the credit quality of a borrower and the PD. Obviously, a good quality CDO tranche must equip with lower PTL and P1L. In contrast, a bad quality CDO tranche must equip with higher PTL and P1L. Nevertheless, when a CDO tranche is thick such that the PTL and P1L fall into different ranges, there is a need to describe the CDO quality with two parameters, i.e., good to moderate, good to bad or moderate to bad.

Combining three ranges of the PTL and three ranges of the P1L, and subject to the condition that the quality indicated by the P1L must be lower than that indicted by the PTL, there are a total of six feasible combinations which are listed in Table 14.2.

Probabilities of loss (%)		PTL		
		Below 1	Between 1 and 10	Above 10
		Good	Moderate	Bad
P1L	Below 1 — Good	Good		
	Between 1 and 10 — Moderate	Good to moderate	Moderate	
	Above 10 — Bad	Good to bad	Moderate to bad	Bad

Table 14.2   CDO quality

14.8.3 Dual rating

Under the ECAI Plus rating scale, each credit rating is associated with a PD. This PD can be interpreted as the central tenancy of a group of PDs of the borrowers with similar credit quality. Therefore, the relationship between a credit rating and a PD can be extended to the relationship between credit rating and a PD range. For example, the credit rating A covers the PD range from 0.0532 percent to 0.1707 percent while 0.0834 percent represents the central tendency. Conversely, when a PD of a borrower is calculated and falls within the PD range of a credit rating, the borrower can be classified under that credit rating. For example, if the PD borrower of a borrower is 0.1%, then the credit rating of the borrower is A.

Credit rating	PD (%)	Probit	Probit range		PD range (%)	
			From	To	From	To
AAA	0.0100	-3.7190	-∞	-3.5609	0	0.0185
AA	0.0333	-3.4028	-3.5609	-3.2733	0.0185	0.0532
A	0.0834	-3.1437	-3.2733	-2.9278	0.0532	0.1707
BBB	0.3345	-2.7119	-2.9278	-2.3304	0.1707	0.9892
BB	2.5652	-1.9489	-2.3304	-1.7061	0.9892	4.3990
B	7.1682	-1.4634	-1.7061	-1.2360	4.3990	10.8225
CCC	15.6567	-1.0087	-1.2360	-0.7734	10.8225	21.9655
CC	29.5270	-0.5381	-0.7734	-0.1010	21.9655	45.9782
C	63.1597	0.3361	-0.1010	∞	45.9782	100

Table 14.3   Credit ratings vs PD ranges

Since the PD is highly skewed, it is less appropriate to adopt the mid-point between the PDs of two adjacent credit ratings as the boundary. Therefore, the PDs are first converted into Probits and the mid-point between the Probits of two adjacent credit ratings is set as the boundary. This arrives at the PDs range in Table 14.3.

With this established relationship between the credit ratings and PD ranges, the concept of CDO quality can be extended to dual rating with which the quality of a CDO tranche is characterized by two ratings, the first corresponding to the PTL and the second corresponding to the P1L. When both the PTL and P1L fall into the same range, the dual rating can be simplified into one CDO rating covering both the PTL and P1L. The financial industry prefers a CDO tranche with single CDO rating to avoid the complication of interpreting two ratings. In fact, dual rating is not used in practice. CDO issuers design CDO tranches which can be labelled with a single CDO rating.

The relationships among the PTL, P1L and dual ratings of selected CDO tranches are set out in Table 14.4.

Probabilities of loss (%)				**PTL**			
			From	**0**	**0.0185**	**0.0532**	**0.1707**
			To	**0.0185**	**0.0532**	**0.1707**	**0.9892**
	From	**To**	**Rating**	**AAA**	**AA**	**A**	**BBB**
	0	**0.0185**	**AAA**	AAA			
	0.0185	**0.0532**	**AA**	AAA to AA	AA		
	0.0532	**0.1707**	**A**	AAA to A	AA to A	A	
	0.1707	**0.9892**	**BBB**	AAA to BBB	AA to BBB	A to BBB	BBB
P1L	**0.9892**	**4.399**	**BB**	AAA to BB	AA to BB	A to BB	BBB to BB
	4.399	**10.8225**	**B**	AAA to B	AA to B	A to B	BBB to B
	10.8225	**21.9655**	**CCC**	AAA to CCC	AA to CCC	A to CCC	BBB to CCC
	21.9655	**45.9782**	**CC**	AAA to CC	AA to CC	A to CC	BBB to CC
	45.9782	**100**	**C**	AAA to C	AA to C	A to C	BBB to C

Table 14.4 Dual ratings of selected CDO tranches

14.8.4 Preventive rating

The dual rating scheme set out in the previous section suffers from a major issue that the ratings are not stable. In other words, the assignment of a dual rating needs to be reviewed on an on-going basis. This phenomenon arises from the continuous defaults of the debts in the underlying portfolio, thus increasing the probabilities of loss on an on-going basis. When either the PTL or P1L increases and shifts to a lower PD range, the dual rating has to be changed.

Naturally, the financial industry prefers a more stable rating methodology which allows the rating assignment to be stable within an effective period, e.g., one year or longer. This requirement arrives at the preventive rating which presents that the quality of a CDO tranche is expected to be at least as good as demonstrated by the dual rating even at the end of the effective period. In other words, the preventive rating seeks to derive a dual rating which demonstrates the quality of a CDO tranche at the end of the effective period, having taken into account the expected default of the debts in the underlying portfolio during the effective period.

If the preventive rating is expected to be effective for a period of T years, the expected default rating ("EDR") within the effective period is simply:

$$EDR = 1 - (1 - PD)^T$$

This EDR is then used to scale up the PDP and PAP, referred to as the preventive PAP and preventive PDP, of a CDO tranche to:

$$Preventive\ PDP = EDR + PDP \times (1 - EDR)$$
$$Preventive\ PAP = EDR + PAP \times (1 - EDR)$$

Then the PTL and P1L are calculated from the preventive PDP and preventive PAP respectively.

$$PTL = 1 - \Phi\left[\frac{\Phi^{-1}(Preventive\ PDP)\sqrt{1 - CCC} - \Phi^{-1}(PD)}{\sqrt{CCC}}\right]$$

$$P1L = 1 - \Phi\left[\frac{\Phi^{-1}(Preventive\ PAP)\sqrt{1 - CCC} - \Phi^{-1}(PD)}{\sqrt{CCC}}\right]$$

Therefore, for an effective period of one year, the probabilities of loss in Table 14.4 are scaled down in Table 14.5.

Probabilities of loss (%)			PTL			
		From	0	0.0060	0.0167	0.0519
		To	0.0060	0.0167	0.0519	0.2843
From	To	Rating	AAA	AA	A	BBB
0	0.0060	AAA	AAA			
0.0060	0.0167	AA	AAA to AA	AA		
0.0167	0.0519	A	AAA to A	AA to A	A	
0.0519	0.2843	BBB	AAA to BBB	AA to BBB	A to BBB	BBB
0.2843	1.1990	BB	AAA to BB	AA to BB	A to BB	BBB to BB
1.1990	2.8606	B	AAA to B	AA to B	A to B	BBB to B
2.8606	5.7064	CCC	AAA to CCC	AA to CCC	A to CCC	BBB to CCC
5.7064	12.0352	CC	AAA to CC	AA to CC	A to CC	BBB to CC
12.0352	39.5346	C	AAA to C	AA to C	A to C	BBB to C

(Left column vertical label: P1L)

Table 14.5   Preventive ratings of selected CDO tranches

14.9   CDO design

14.9.1 Tranching

The preventive rating scheme suggests a very good mechanism for a CDO issuer to design a family of CDO tranches with the preventive PAPs and preventive PDPs with a single stable CDO rating within an effective period.

When a CDO tranche is characterized by a single CDO rating which is expected to be stable for a period of T years, with the PTL and P1L chosen as the lower and upper bounds of a rating, the corresponding preventive PDP and preventive PAP are calculated as:

$$PDP = \Phi \left[\frac{\Phi^{-1}(PD) + \Phi^{-1}(1 - PTL)\sqrt{CCC}}{\sqrt{1 - CCC}} \right]$$

$$PAP = \Phi \left[\frac{\Phi^{-1}(PD) + \Phi^{-1}(1 - P1L)\sqrt{CCC}}{\sqrt{1 - CCC}} \right]$$

$$EDR = 1 - \left(1 - PD\right)^{T}$$

$$\text{Preventive PDP} = EDR + PDP \times \left(1 - EDR\right) = 1 - \left(1 - PD\right)^{T} + PDP \times \left(1 - PD\right)^{T}$$

$$\text{Preventive PAP} = EDR + PAP \times \left(1 - EDR\right) = 1 - \left(1 - PD\right)^{T} + PAP \times \left(1 - PD\right)^{T}$$

Therefore, when a CDO family is created from a corporate debt portfolio well approximated by an infinite homogeneous portfolio, the rating, preventive PDP and preventive PAP are determined in accordance with the following scheme:

- An AAAA (four As) rating is assigned to an ultra senior tranche with a preventive PAP 100 percent which also serves as the preventive PDP of the AAA rated CDO tranche. The ultra senior tranche is virtually risk-free, thus deserving an AAAA CDO rating higher than all corporate bonds.

- The AAA rated CDO tranche is equipped with a preventive PDP 100% and a preventive PAP:

$$1 - \left(1 - PD\right)^{T} + \Phi\left[\frac{\Phi^{-1}\left(PD\right) + \Phi^{-1}\left(1 - 0.0185\%\right)\sqrt{CCC}}{\sqrt{1 - CCC}}\right] \times \left(1 - PD\right)^{T}$$

This preventive PAP also serves as the preventive PDP of the AA rated CDO tranche.

- The AA rated CDO tranche is equipped with a preventive PAP:

$$1 - \left(1 - PD\right)^{T} + \Phi\left[\frac{\Phi^{-1}\left(PD\right) + \Phi^{-1}\left(1 - 0.0531\%\right)\sqrt{CCC}}{\sqrt{1 - CCC}}\right] \times \left(1 - PD\right)^{T}$$

This preventive PAP also serves as the preventive PDP of the A rated CDO tranche.

- The A rated CDO tranche is equipped with a preventive PAP:

$$1 - \left(1 - PD\right)^{T} + \Phi\left[\frac{\Phi^{-1}\left(PD\right) + \Phi^{-1}\left(1 - 0.1707\%\right)\sqrt{CCC}}{\sqrt{1 - CCC}}\right] \times \left(1 - PD\right)^{T}$$

This preventive PAP also serves as the preventive PDP of the BBB rated CDO tranche.

This process is repeated until the preventive PAPs and preventive PDPs for all CDO tranches are calculated.

14.9.2 Re-balancing

Similar to credit assignment, CDO assignment needs to be conducted on a regular basis or when there is a material deterioration of the debts in the underlying portfolio in order to monitor effectively the quality of CDO tranches. When the assessment results suggest that a CDO tranche has deteriorated below the quality demonstrated by its current preventive rating, the issuer has to downgrade the rating' of the CDO tranche. Alternatively, the issuer may choose to improve the quality of the CDO tranche by re-balancing the structure of the CDO family.

The idea of re-balancing is very simple. In order to improve the quality of a CDO tranche, the percentage of the more senior tranches should be reduced to enhance the stability of the cash inflows generated by the underlying debt portfolio while the percentage of the less senior tranches should be increased to absorb the default loss arising from the underlying debt portfolio. This allocation of tranches can be achieved by acquiring from the market certain amount of senior tranches which are then put into the equity tranche with the lowest priority among the cash waterfall.

Within a CDO family, the tranche with the lowest rating always has the most urgent need of re-balancing. Also, the reduction of the senior tranche will always improve the quality of all CDO tranches. In practice, since the changes to the PDPs and PAPs are not uniform across all CDO tranches, a CDO issuer may choose to acquire several amounts from different CDO tranches, as long as the qualities of the CDO tranches are improved to match their expected preventive ratings.

Appendix 14.1   Universal credit risk measure

In order to measure the credit risk of a financial instrument in the form of neither a single debt nor a debt portfolio, a more sophisticated universal credit risk measure is developed with a two-dimensional presentation:

[Expected loss, loss standard deviation]

abbreviated as:

[EL, LSD]

While the EL measures the central tendency of default loss, the LSD measures the dispersion of default loss around the EL.

For a single debt, the [EL, LSD] are calculated as

$$EL = EAD \times LGD \times \left[1 - \left(1 - PD \right)^{RM} \right]$$

$$LSD = EAD \times LGD \times \sqrt{\left(1 - PD \right)^{RM} \times \left[1 - \left(1 - PD \right)^{RM} \right]}$$

For a homogeneous debt portfolio with the RMs unified to one year, the [EL, LSD] are calculated as:

$$EL = \text{Portfolio EAD} \times LGD \times PD$$

$$LSD = \text{Portfolio EAD} \times LGD$$

$$\times \sqrt{\frac{1}{2\pi\sqrt{1 - CCC^2}} \int_{-\infty}^{\Phi^{-1}(PD)} \int_{-\infty}^{\Phi^{-1}(PD)} \exp\left[-\frac{x^2 + y^2 - 2xy \times CCC}{2\left(1 - CCC^2 \right)} \right] dxdy - PD^2}$$

For other financial instruments, the [EL, LSD] are estimated conveniently by Monte Carlo simulation.

The [EL, LSD] are applicable to quantify the credit risk of almost all financial instruments, including a debt basket with only a few members and most credit derivatives. The credit risk increases with increasing EL and LSD. Nevertheless, due to its two-dimensional presentation, the [EL, LSD] is less convenient to be applied in practice.

Table 14.6 summaries the types of credit instruments described in this book and their corresponding effective credit risk measures.

	Credit instrument	Credit risk measure	
		Long position	Short position
	(A) Debt		
1.	Single debt	EL, 1-year EL	
2.	Debt portfolio	XCL	
	(B) Credit default swap		
3.	Single name CDS		EL, 1-year EL
4.	Binary CDS		
5.	Basket CDS		
6	Portfolio CDS		[EL, LSD]
7.	CDS index contract		XCL# or [EL, LSD]
	(C) Credit structuring		
8.	Single name CLN	EL, 1-year EL	
9.	Basket CLN		
10.	Market value CLN		
11.	Cash flow CDO	[EL, LSD]	
12.	Market value CDO		

The XCL is only applicable to a CDS index contract with a sufficient large number of component single name CDSs.

Table 14.6   Credit risk measures

Financial Tsunami 2008

15

KEY CONCEPTS

- Subprime mortgage
- Deregulation

- Lehman Brothers and AIG
- Regulatory reform

15.1   How did we get here?

The financial tsunami in 2008 was not an act of god but the bursting of bubbles with mishaps and misconducts accumulated over the last few decades. While the financial tsunami shares the same ingredients with other financial crises in the pass, first by greed and then by fear, the following causes were recognized by many as forces pushing the global financial markets and economies to a near collapse by the end of 2008.

15.1.1 Excessive borrowing in the United States

The crisis was originated in the United States when "bamboo curtain" countries, like China, opened their markets and companies like General Motors and US Steel, which had all long been the core of American industries, moved their manufacturing base together with their jobs to those countries. Jobs which remained in the United States were mostly in the technology and service sectors that required an advanced set of technical skills. Retraining to acquire those skills was hampered by the high tuition fees charged by universities. American families responded to these changes in two ways: by working longer hours and by going into debt. They borrowed to finance on almost everything: their cars, their health cares, their children's education, and above all, their homes.

15.1.2 Subprime mortgages

Home ownership has been and still is an American dream and that of many people across Europe. "Buy to live," "buy to let" and "buy to sell" were believed to be recipes for quick wealth. Fuelled by low interest rates and the boom in securitization of mortgages and other loan products, banks first lent to borrowers with high credit quality, then to those with moderate credit quality and ultimately to anyone with total disregard of their credit quality. This resulted in the subprime mortgages, the primary cause of the financial tsunami 2008.

Banks were no longer concerned about the credit risk of their loans because through the securitization of mortgages, the credit risks associated with these mortgages were transferred to the CDO investors. Banks started to offer mortgages to borrowers with low credit quality. Indeed, banks preferred subprime mortgages consciously because the borrowers are charged higher interest rates. Borrowers were needlessly placed in expensive subprime mortgages and many mortgages were granted to people who could not repay them. From 2000 to 2003, bank loans quadrupled in the United States, a substantial number of which were subprime mortgages. Immediately before the collapse of the property market, Countrywide Finance alone had entered with their customers over USD 90 bn in subprime mortgages.

Figure 15.1   Property market in the United States peaked in 2006

15.1.3 Credit maniac

Commercial banks sold mortgages, credit cards and other credit assets to investment banks and used the sales proceeds collected from the investment banks to extend more loans to other borrowers. Investment banks then securitized these credit assets in the form of CDOs and sold to investors around the world.

To facilitate the sale of the CDOs to investors, investment banks paid credit rating agencies to assess the credit qualities. Problems arose when the CDOs would invariably be awarded with the highest investment grades while the underlying mortgages were in fact of lower credit qualities. When these subprime mortgages were revealed, no one knew exactly how to estimate the fair value of the derived CDOs. Once the darlings of the investors, the CDOs were then seen as toxic and junk assets.

Worse still, many CDO issuers (investment banks) misled investors to buy CDOs by presenting to them the merchantable quality of these assets. Behind the investors, they made bets against the loss of the CDOs by entering the CDSs with protection sellers. If the underlying mortgages defaulted, investors of the CDOs would see reduction in their value and hence suffer a loss. These CDO issuers would then collect payoffs from the protection sellers for making the right bet against the loss of the CDOs. The total compensation was so large that it resulted in the collapse of American International Group ("AIG") which acted as a gigantic protection seller during the financial tsunami 2008.

15.1.4 Deregulation

The United States and many European countries, the United Kingdom in particular, witnessed some thirty years of boom and prosperity in financial markets. Investment banks went public, giving them huge amounts of shareholders' equity. People working on Wall Street started to get rich. By the late nineties, the US financial sector had consolidated itself into a few gigantic firms, each of them being so large that failure of any one could threaten the whole financial system.

Governments, either by themselves or succumbing to lobbyists, were convinced to let the financial markets run their own cause. Instead of regulation, the regulators advocated deregulation on the belief that participants in the financial markets could govern themselves through self-regulation. However, as it now turns out, many players, including some in the biggest financial firms, had been caught laundering money, defrauding customers, cooking their books, etc., again and again without the notice of the regulators. Whilst the culprits settled the regulatory claims against them by paying hefty fines, they did not have to admit any wrong doings.

15.1.5 Financial executives' greed

The structure of remuneration to financial executives encouraged them to take risks. The remuneration, which comprises awarded bonuses and other incentives, was prorated to the immediate profit that the financial executives made for the financial institutions. Risks of longer term losses to their customers were not of their primary concern.

Well before the financial tsunami 2008, numerous warnings on the risk prone pay structure were given by critics, including that from the International Monetary Fund ("IMF"). Regrettably, the warnings were taken heed of by neither the financial markets nor the regulators. Financial executives, who destroyed their institutions and plunged the world into crisis, walked away from the wreckage with their pay package intact. The top five executives of Lehman Brothers made over USD 1 bn between 2000 and 2007. When the institution went bankrupt, they kept all of their money. In 2008, AIG Financial Products Corp. lost USD 11 bn. Under the institution's special incentive plan, senior executives of the company could retain their rights to all payments due to them.

15.1.6 Unethical practices

The unethical practices of some credit rating agencies and economists contributed to the crisis. For credit rating agencies, it is their clients, many of them being investment banks, who pay for the credit rating services. The credit ratings therefore reflect more on the dominance of their clients than on the credit quality of the rated institution. Lehman Brothers and the AIG were still classified as investment grade companies by the major global credit rating agencies at the time of their collapses in 2008.

For academic economists, many of them quietly made fortunes by helping shape public debates and economic policies. They were blamed for their blatant conflicts of interest and corrupt views as they were discovered to have given biased views on economic policies and financial matters – biased towards their clients who remunerate them in the form of hefty consultation fees, advisory fees, speaker's fees and directorship fees.

15.2   The bubble

The above irregularities were built up not just in the United States but also in other western economies, particularly in Europe. When the bubbles burst, the contagion effect meant that they burst together across the globe.

15.2.1 Property bubble

In the United States, predatory lending practices means that prior to the bursting of the property bubble, practically any one could get a mortgage to buy a house prior. The Federal Reserve took no action to control subprime lending.   The Securities and Exchange Commission conducted no major investigations on the investment banks during the bubble. Housing prices skyrocketed. The United States saw property prices double and reach their peak in 2006. Then the bubble burst in 2008.

European countries had built up bubbles similar to those in the United States over the years prior to 2008. The low interest rates, predatory lending practices and home dreams all added up to be a booster of the property prices, Spain and the United Kingdom in particular.

15.2.2 High leverage ratio

During the bubble, investment banks borrowed heavily to acquire more loans and create more CDOs. Some banks had seen their leverage ratio (liabilities as a multiple of shareholders' equity) increased above thirty, meaning that a tiny decrease in the asset base would lead them into insolvency.

Lehman Brothers was a typical example. The bank borrowed significant amounts to fund its investments in the years leading to bankruptcy in 2008. The leverage ratio increased approximately to 31 in 2007 from 24 in 2003. While generating tremendous profits during the boom, this vulnerable position meant that just a 3.3 percent decline in the value of the bank's assets would eliminate entirely the shareholders' equity.

15.2.3 Financial derivatives

The AIG sold huge quantities of CDSs not only to investors for insuring against loss in their debts but also to speculators who did not own the reference debts. The AIG acted as a protection seller of the CDSs against investment banks who bet against the loss of CDOs sold to their customers. Since the CDSs were unregulated, the AIG did not have to put aside capital to cover these CDSs. The AIG's financial services in London issued some USD 5 bn worth of CDSs during the bubble while many of them were entered for

CDOs backed by subprime mortgages. The AIG's management chose to ignore the risk of the CDSs and paid the executives huge bonuses as soon as the contracts were entered.

15.2.4 Iceland

Seen as an experimental deregulation of financial markets in the turn of the twentieth century, Iceland privatized the country's three largest banks, namely: Landsbanki, Kaupthing and Glitnir. In five years after their privatization, these three banks, which had never operated outside Iceland, borrowed some USD 120 bn, ten times the size of the country's economy. Banks showered monies on themselves and one another. The banks' auditors found nothing wrong with them. In 2007, the banks received AAA ratings from the credit rating agencies. Equity prices went up. Property prices rose more than double.

When the banks collapsed at the end of 2008, the unemployment rate tripled in six months. Depositors lost their savings. Everybody in Iceland was impacted by the crisis. The Financial Supervisory Authority, the country's financial regulator, was seen as doing nothing to prevent the crisis from happening.

15.2.5 European government debts

Another time bomb built in Europe was government debts – overspending by European governments. Many European countries simply could not afford the social security and retirement programmes so that in an economic downturn, the tax income was not enough to meet their expenses. As it now transpires, Europe suffered a hard hit by the financial crisis. Exports fell and the unemployment rate rose. One country after another, Greece, Spain, Portugal, Italy, Ireland, sought bailout funds from European Central Bank and the IMF.

15.3   The crisis

The collapse of Lehman Brothers triggered the financial tsunami in September 2008 when the bank filed for bankruptcy after the Federal Reserve declined to participate in creating a financial support facility for the bank, citing that a huge volume of toxic assets at Lehman Brothers made the rescue impossible. The damage to financial markets by Lehman Brothers' collapse was colossal, huge losses to investors worldwide who had invested in financial products from or linked to the bank. The loss itself and the fear of further loss brought chaos to the financial markets.

Also in September 2008, the AIG collapsed. The company, with significant participation in the CDS markets, announced a liquidity crisis following the downgrade of its credit rating. The Federal Reserve offered credit facilities to the AIG and became the major shareholder of the company.

Beginning with the failures of large financial institutions in the United States, the local financial crisis rapidly evolved into a global crisis. For banks, many failed and required bailout by their governments. They faced a credit crunch which further accelerated the liquidity crisis. Banks' failure to lend led to many company collapses and a global recession, resulting in significant reductions in the market value of equity and commodities worldwide, loss of trillions of dollars in terms of investment failures, loss of income by employees and more importantly, loss of some twelve million jobs worldwide. In the United States, loss of income of Americans led to a collapse in the housing market, resulting in material house price reductions, evictions and foreclosures. In Europe, the financial tsunami 2008 created another crisis – the government debt crisis.

Faced with lashes of their economies by the financial tsunami 2008, financial regulators, individually and together, implemented prompt measures to contain the damage, including:

- conservatorship of government sponsored mortgage enterprises, e.g., in the United States, the Federal Housing Finance Agency placed Federal National Mortgage Association and Federal Home Loan Mortgage Corporation into conservatorship;

- purchase of illiquid mortgage backed securities from financial institutions with the intent to increase the liquidity of the secondary mortgage markets and reduce potential losses encountered by financial institutions owning the securities;

- nationalization of banks, e.g., the Landsbanki and Glitnir were seized by the Iceland government and the government of the Netherlands took over the Dutch operations of Fortis Bank;

- suspension of trading in the equity and commodity markets, resulting from the sharp drop in the share and commodities prices led to suspension by the governments of trading in the equity markets in Brazil, Russia, etc.;

- guarantee of bank deposits by the governments of the United Kingdom, Ireland, Greece, Denmark, Austria, Germany, etc.;

- capitalizing the banks, e.g., the Britain government announced that it would arrange an injection of GBP 25 bn as tier one capital to Abbey, Barclays, HBOS, HSBC Bank plc, Lloyds TSB, Nationwide Building Society, Royal Bank of Scotland, Standard Chartered Bank, etc.;

- cutting interest rates to boost lending and spending by Federal Reserve, European Central Bank, Bank of England, Bank of Canada, Swedish Riksbank, Swiss National Bank and The People's Bank of China; and

- suspension of the short selling of equities by financial authorities, e.g., the Financial Services Authority in the United Kingdom and the Securities and Exchange Commission in the United States.

15.4   Accountability and oversight

15.4.1 Banks

Banks suffered huge losses in the financial tsunami 2008, in terms of: loss to customers and shareholders, compensations and settlements in law suits, and penalties for criminal acts like money laundering.

- About forty-three thousand Hong Kong investors bought an estimated USD 1.8 bn of Lehman Brothers' minibonds. In the few years after the bank collapsed, investors protested almost daily outside bank branches in Hong Kong that sold the minibonds to them, banging cymbals and blaring pre-recorded statements from bullhorns.

Figure 15.2   Protest outside major banks in Hong Kong between 2010 and 2012

- Citigroup paid USD 730 mn to settle a class action suit by bond investors brought over the financial tsunami 2008. The bank was alleged to have misled bond buyers to acquire excessive exposure to subprime mortgages and other higher risk securities between 2006 and 2008;

- In December 2012, the HSBC announced that it had agreed to record a USD 1.92 bn settlement with the US government authorities. The bank was faced with accusations that it transferred billions of dollars for nations like Iran and enabled Mexican drug cartels to move money illegally through its American subsidiaries;

- On 18 March 2013, Goldman Sachs suffered a defeat as the US Supreme Court let stand a decision forcing it to defend against claims in which it misled investors about losses in mortgage backed securities during the financial tsunami 2008. This US Supreme Court decision allows the NECA-IBEW Health & Welfare Fund, which owned mortgage backed securities underwritten by Goldman Sachs, to sue on behalf of investors in securities that Goldman Sachs did not own but were backed by mortgages from the same lenders. This case will now proceed towards a possible trial.

United States

On 7 May 2009, in a speech titled "Lessons of the Financial Crisis for Banking Supervision," Mr. Bernard Bernanke, Chairman of Federal Reserve, said:

> "The events of the past two years have revealed weaknesses in both private sector's risk management and the public sector's oversight of the financial system. It is imperative that we apply the lessons of this experience to strengthen our regulatory system, both at the level of its overall architecture and in its daily execution. Indeed, although reform of the current system is necessary, much can be done within the current framework. The Federal Reserve has engaged in extensive introspection and review of the lessons of the crisis and is working diligently to implement what has been learned. As the past two years have brought home to everyone, the development of a more stable and sound financial system should be of the highest priority."

Mr. Bernanke highlighted the following banking practices as top priorities for oversight by Federal Reserve to:

- strengthen banks' capital adequacy, liquidity sufficiency and risk management;

- consolidate supervision of banks to assure that all systemically important financial institutions should be subject to a robust regulatory framework; and

- enhance the stability of the financial system as a whole.

Mr. Bernanke said:

> "I believe a more macro prudential approach to supervision, one that supplements the supervision of individual institutions to address risks to the financial system as a whole, could help to enhance overall financial stability. Our regulatory system must include the capacity to monitor, assess and, if necessary, address potential systemic risks within the financial system. Elements of a macro prudential agenda include:
>
> - monitoring large or rapidly increasing exposures such as subprime mortgages across institutions and markets rather than only at the level of individual institutions or sectors;
>
> - assessing the potential systemic risks implied by evolving risk management practices, broad based increases in financial leverage or changes in financial markets or products;

- analyzing possible spillovers between financial institutions or between institutions and markets, such as the mutual exposures of highly inter-connected institutions;

- ensuring that each systemically important financial institution receives oversight commensurate with the risks that its failure would pose to the financial system;

- providing a resolution mechanism to safely wind down failing systemically important financial institutions;

- ensuring that the critical financial infrastructure, including the institutions that support trading, payments, clearing and settlement, is robust;

- working to mitigate pro-cyclical features of capital regulation and other rules and standards; and

- identifying possible regulatory gaps, including gaps in the protection of consumers and investors which pose risks for the system as a whole."

In respect of foreign banks, the Federal Reserve proposed to tighten the leash on them to protect taxpayers from having to bail them out. The plan would force foreign banks to group all their subsidiaries under a holding company subject to the same capital standards as a US holding company. These largest banks would also need to hold liquidity buffers.

Executives' remuneration

The Basel Committee on Banking Supervision ("BCBS") issued a report on aligning bankers' pay with risk and performance. The report was intended to enhance banks' and supervisors' understanding of risk adjusted remuneration. By providing clarification on the design of risk adjusted remuneration schemes, the BCBS aimed at promoting greater adoption of sound compensation practices in the banking sector. The endeavours were echoed in Europe where legislation was in place to establish European Central Bank as a bank supervisor to monitor remuneration practices and policies.

Liquidity sufficiency

On liquidity of banks, the BCBS finalized in December 2010 a regulatory guideline titled "Basel III: International Framework for Liquidity Risk Measurement, Standards and Monitoring," proposing among others, two complementary liquidity risk measures for promoting stronger liquidity buffers at financial institutions. This regulatory guideline is a giantic step towards implementing the BCBS's previous guideline "Principles for Sound Liquidity Risk Management and Supervision" promulgated in September 2008. The regulatory guideline makes a bold attempt in procuring consistency and granularity in liquidity risk management by banks at an international scale against the backdrop of efforts by financial regimes worldwide to prevent another financial turmoil from destabilizing the financial systems, including the banking system.

Capital adequacy

The Basel III framework is the latest endeavour by the BCBS to strengthening bank capital requirements by increasing bank liquidity and limiting bank leverage. The framework was developed in response to the deficiencies in financial regulations revealed by the financial tsunami 2008. It was intended to set a global and voluntary regulatory standard on bank capital adequacy, stress testing and liquidity risk. The approaches to measure credit risk under the Basel framework are discussed in Part IV of this book.

15.4.2 Credit rating agencies

Credit rating agencies, being blamed for their reckless ratings of companies and governments before the crisis, are subject to stringent oversight. For example:

- In Canada, the Canadian Securities Administrators, while recognizing the significant role credit rating agencies play in today's global credit markets, has adopted a new regulatory framework that requires credit rating agencies to apply for the status of "designated rating organization" in Canada;

- In the European Union, rules are now in place requiring credit rating agencies to adhere to a code of conduct so as to reduce conflicts of interest between them and rated entities; and

- In Hong Kong, credit rating is a regulated activity obliging credit rating agencies to obtain a licence from the Securities and Futures Commission before they can conduct credit rating activities in the city.

15.4.3 Regulators

The fact that regulators were behind the curve in the financial tsunami 2008 is the evidence of a systemic failure that warrants fundamental reforms. The biggest reform is in the United Kingdom where the Financial Services Authority was abolished and replaced by two successor organizations:

- The Prudential Regulation Authority, which is responsible for ensuring the stability of financial services firms and to be part of the Bank of England; and

- The Financial Conduct Authority, which now becomes the country's behavioural watchdog.

The Bank of England has also gained direct supervision of the entire banking system through its powerful Financial Policy Committee which can instruct the two new regulators.

15.4.4 Financial derivatives

Financial derivatives had become "weapons of mass destruction" in the financial tsunami 2008. They were used for speculation instead of hedging. They spread rather than mitigate financial risks. The destructive power of the financial derivatives has convinced regulators that financial derivatives should be regulated in a way similar to, if not stricter than, the underlying assets. For example,

- In the United States, as part of the overhaul under the Dodd-Frank Act, most financial institutions have to register their derivatives business with the Commodity Futures Trading Commission. The rule captured the biggest banks in the world, requiring them to register as swap dealers by the end of 2012. The designation requires that banks, among others, adopt internal risk management controls, bolster disclosures to trading partners and meet certain record keeping requirements. They must also turn over in real time the data from their trading book. The disclosures posted on the website of the Depository Trust and Clearing Corporation include the volume, time and price of each derivatives trade.

- In Singapore, the Monetary Authority of Singapore has issued the revised Code on Collective Investment Schemes, among others, to strengthen safeguards on the use of financial derivatives and counterparty requirements.

15.5   Where are we now?

15.5.1 Global rescue

The financial tsunami 2008 hit the global economy severely. Never in history have we seen global leaders making such large scale and concerted efforts to contain the damage and bring economic order to the financial markets. While the Group of 20 nations founded the Financial Stability Board to strengthen the financial system at an international level, countries, individually and at regional levels, saw fit to introduce measures to improve their economies.

15.5.2 United States

On 29 September 2008, the US President Barack Obama said:

> "The error of greed and irresponsibility of Wall Street and Washington has led us to a financial crisis as serious as any we faced since the great depression ... Our lack of oversight ... is what exactly got us into this mess ... We need to change the Wall Street's culture ...."

In 2010, the US government promulgated the Volker Rule to limit engagement of banks in proprietary trading. Between 2009 and 2010, legislations were passed to address consumer protection, executive pay, bank's capital requirements, shadow banking and derivatives and enhanced authority for the Federal Reserve to safely wind down systemically important financial institutions. The major acts include the Wall Street Reform and Consumer Protection Act of 2009, the Restoring American Financial Stability Act of 2010, the Dodd-Frank Wall Street Reform and Consumer Protection Act of 2010.

The Dodd-Frank Wall Street Reform and Consumer Protection Act brought the most significant changes to financial regulation in the United States since the regulatory reform following the great depression. It made changes in the American financial regulatory environment that affected all federal financial regulatory agencies and almost every part of the country's financial services industry, including:

- the consolidation of regulatory agencies, elimination of the national thrift charter and new oversight council to evaluate systemic risk;

- regulation of financial markets, including increased transparency of derivatives;

- consumer protection reforms, including a new consumer protection agency and uniform standards for plain vanilla derivatives as well as strengthened investor protection;

- tools for financial crises, including a "resolution regime" complementing the existing Federal Deposit Insurance Corporation to allow for orderly winding down of bankrupt firms and to allow the Federal Reserve to grant extensions of credit in unusual or exigent circumstances; and

- measures aimed at increasing international standards and co-operation, including proposals related to improved accounting and tightened regulation of credit rating agencies.

To stimulate sustainable economic growth, the Federal Reserve chose to suppress interest rates. They took the view that low interest rates were also helping other countries instead of damaging them. If the currency of an advanced nation weakened against competitive exporters, its goods became relatively cheaper, giving it a price advantage. Mr. Bernanke said: "Because stronger growth in each advanced economy confers beneficial spillovers to trading policies, these policies are not 'beggar thy neighbour' but rather 'enrich thy neighbour' actions.'"

The US interest rates have been maintained in the range between 0 percent and 0.25 percent since December 2008. The Federal Reserve has pledged to keep the rates at the record low level until the US unemployment rate falls below 6.5 percent. However, critics say that low interest rates are cutting the value of currencies of advanced nations and put the developing world at a disadvantage.

15.5.3 Europe

While suppressing interest rates seems to be a consensual cure, either voluntarily or as directed by the European Commission, some members of the European Union adopted austerity measures to cut public spending to put public finances in order and carry out overdue reforms. Critics say that austerity has led to reductions in demand which lead to reductions in output. Reductions in output will lead to further downwards revisions – not just in current output but in projections regarding the economy's future. So far, the measures have not been encouraging. Indeed, Europe remains broadly in recession. The Euro zone shrank by 0.2 percent in the first quarter in 2013 and is expected to register negative growth for 2013 as a whole.

15.5.4 Asia

Economic slowdown in the United States and Europe impacts export countries in Asia, especially China and Japan. The export loss resulted in massive layoff of factory workers. Facing the challenge, to maintain employment and economic growth, China introduced unprecedented infrastructure projects in the country to boost domestic demand. The huge fiscal stimulus package, amounting to some USD 600 bn (about 20 percent of China's GDP), was launched in November 2008 in conjunction with calls for the nation's banks to boost their lending rates. The quite restrictive monetary stance of the People's Bank of China since then stood in sharp contrast to the continued easy money policies of the United States which initiated yet more quantitative easing between 2010 and 2011 to address the lacklustre growth in employment in the country.

Figure 15.3   The People's Bank of China

Japan had been in recovery in the middle of the decade of the 2000s but slipped back into recession and deflation in the financial tsunami 2008. The recession intensified in the fourth quarter of 2008 with a GDP growth of -12.7 percent and deepened further in the first quarter of 2009 to a GDP growth of -15.2 percent.

In January 2013, Japan announced a USD 117 bn stimulus package, including among others, expansion of the purchase of government debts by the Bank of Japan. The arrangement aimed to jumpstart the failing Japanese economy for the past two decades with beefing up inflation to 2 percent and devaluating JPY to boost exports as their targets.

15.5.5 "Spending approach" or "austerity approach"?

The aftermath of the financial tsunami 2008 is far from over. Many countries are still facing severe and prolonged stagnant economic growth. Weakness in the real economy means less tax income, hence higher budget deficits and government debts. Each country has its own economic problems and there is no "one size fits all" solution. It remains to be seen which approach: the "spending approach," the "austerity approach" or others approaches, proves to be effective in resolving those problems. Meanwhile, financial leaders and regulators must continue to show humility for failing to predict the financial crisis, admitting that they underestimated how the interaction of a multitude of distortions could affect the global financial system.

Appendix 15.1   Subprime mortgages and CDOs

A subprime mortgage is a property loan offered from a bank to a retail borrower with his FICO score falling into the range of subprime or deep subprime category. Subprime mortgage was a very popular credit product in the US retail lending market in early 2000 when the property prices kept going up due to the low interest rate policy mandated by the Federal Reserve.

A subprime mortgage is designed to facilitate a borrower to purchase a property with minimum monthly payments from the borrower during the first few years after the purchase of the property. The characteristics of a subprime mortgage are very different from those of a conventional mortgage.

Cash flows

At the origination of a subprime mortgage, an amount of at least 95 percent of the property price is lent to the borrower.

During the first two to three years after the drawdown of the subprime mortgage, the borrower needs only to pay the interest at a lower interest rate on a monthly basis without any principal amortization incorporated. After the interest only period, the borrower starts to follow the conventional principal amortization scheme to pay a small part of the principal plus the interest at a much higher interest rate on a monthly basis.

Prepayment

The cash flow arrangement of a subprime mortgage essentially encourages a borrower to acquire a property as long as he can afford to pay the monthly interest payment at a lower interest rate during the first few years after the purchase of the property. As a result, after the interest only period:

* If the financial condition of the borrower is improved, the borrower is likely to redeem the subprime mortgage at a material prepayment penalty and enter a conventional mortgage to avoid the interest payments at a much higher interest rate;

* If the financial condition of the borrower is not improved and the borrower cannot afford the monthly payments at a much higher interest rate but the property price is substantially higher than the acquisition cost, the borrower is likely to sell the property and redeem the entire subprime mortgage. Alternatively, the borrower may enter a new subprime mortgage with another bank and make use of the new drawdown amount to pay off the existing subprime mortgage in order to continue to enjoy the lower interest rate of a flash subprime mortgage. The new drawdown amount, supported by the appreciated property price, is sufficient to pay off both the old subprime mortgage amount and the material prepayment penalty; and

- If the financial condition of the borrower is not improved, the borrower cannot afford the monthly payment at a much higher interest rate and the property price is below the acquisition cost, the borrower is likely to be in default.

Therefore, although the contractual initial RM of a subprime mortgage is long, the practical life of a subprime mortgage only lasts for three to five years.

Credit risk

In line with other major credit products, the credit risk factors of a subprime mortgage comprise the EAD, LGD, PD and RM. Nevertheless, they behave differently from those of a conventional mortgage.

Obviously, the EAD of a subprime mortgage is large in order to match the property price. Additionally, the conventional principal amortization scheme does not take place in a subprime mortgage within the interest only period.

The LGD of a subprime mortgage is totally driven by the expectation to property market. All subprime mortgages are originated with an optimistic expectation that the property market will continue to go up, and the property price will increase above the mortgage amount and result in a zero LGD. Nevertheless, the financial tsunami 2008 demonstrated that this subjective expectation was not realized.

By definition, a subprime mortgage is offered to a borrower with a lower FICO score. Therefore, the PD of a subprime mortgage is large.

The contractual initial RM of a subprime mortgage is long but the practical initial RM of a subprime mortgage will only be in the range of three to five years.

Due to the zero expected LGD, a zero EL is resulted for all subprime mortgages at origination regardless of the large EAD and PD of the subprime mortgage.

The credit quality of a subprime mortgage is dependent strongly on the property market. Since subprime mortgages are supported by properties as collaterals, the downturn of the property market will drive the increases in the LGD. This phenomenon applies to all subprime mortgages.

For many subprime mortgages, the EL has a strong primary dependency on the property price. When the property price is above the mortgage amount, the zero LGD drives a zero EL. When the property price is below the mortgage amount, the LGD rises above zero and the PD approaches one rapidly. Together with the large EAD, the credit risk factors result in a material EL.

Subprime mortgage portfolio

A subprime mortgage portfolio is a collection of subprime mortgages among which there is a high default dependency due to their strong relationship with the property market. During the downturn of the property market driven by an economic recession, the default dependency increases together with the PDs. As such, the constant CCC 0.15 and the CCC formula for other retail exposures set out by the BCBS are not applicable to subprime mortgage portfolios.

Subprime CDO

When credit securitization is applied to a subprime mortgage portfolio, a family of subprime CDOs is constructed. Due to the strong relationship between the default of subprime mortgages and the property market, the theory of homogeneous portfolio is not applicable to characterize subprime CDOs, in particular during the downturn of the property market.

When the property market goes up, the LGDs of the subprime mortgages in the portfolio are virtually zero. Both the senior and subordinated tranches will suffer from very limited default loss. Therefore, the difference between the economic values of a senior tranche and a subordinated tranche is less obvious than the situation in a conventional CDO family.

When the property market goes down as a result of economic recession, the LGDs rise above zero and the PDs approach one rapidly. Both the senior and subordinated tranches will suffer from large default loss. Therefore, the difference between the economic values of a senior tranche and a subordinated tranche is also less obvious than the situation in a conventional CDO family.

PART FOUR

CREDIT REGULATIONS
The International Credit Standards

The IFRS 9

16

KEY CONCEPTS

- Model value
- Book value

- Credit provision
- Interest income

16.1   International financial reporting standard

The International Financial Reporting Standard version 9 ("IFRS 9") is an accounting framework promulgated by the International Accounting Standards Board, with an aim to address the major accounting issues of financial instruments through a set of unified practices in order to ensure the level playing field among financial institutions.

The IFRS 9 began as a joint project with the Financial Accounting Standards Board which promotes accounting standards in the United States.   These two accounting organizations published jointly a discussion paper in March 2008, proposing an eventual goal of reporting all financial instruments at fair value, with all changes in fair value reported in profit and loss.   As a result of the financial tsunami 2008, these two organizations decided to revise their accounting standards for financial instruments to address the perceived deficiencies which were believed to have contributed to the magnitude of the financial tsunami 2008.

The IFRS 9 is designed for major financial instruments, including credit risky debts which are not traded actively in the market.   Certain parts of the IFRS 9 are developed to address this unique characteristic of credit risky debts.   This chapter highlights the treatments to the accounting issues of credit risky debts, covering the valuation, credit provision and interest income.

16.2   Valuation

Valuation is the process of determining the amount of cash to be received in case a financial instrument is disposed immediately in the market. This assumption is far from reality because many financial instruments do not have liquid markets in which the financial instruments are traded.   Therefore, several methods have been proposed to proxy the value of a financial instrument, including market value, model value and book value.

16.2.1 Market value

The market value of a financial instrument is simply equal to the market price of the financial instrument when it is traded actively in the market. This is the general practice of valuating an equity which is traded on a stock exchange, assuming that the current holding of equity can be disposed in the very near future at the same price.

16.2.2 Model value

The model value of a financial instrument is calculated by a quantitative model using some independent variables which can be observed directly or indirectly from the market. The model value serves as an alternative to the market value when a financial instrument is not traded actively in the market.

The model value is used frequently to valuate government bonds. For example, while on-the-run US treasuries are traded liquidly in the market, off-the-run US treasuries are traded illiquidly in the market. Thus the market price of an on-the-run US treasury is used to derive the internal rate of return ("IRR") through the discounted cash flow model.

$$\text{Market price} = \sum_{k=1}^{N} \frac{CF_N}{(1 + IRR)^k}$$

This IRR, observed indirectly from the market, is then used as the discount rate to calculate the model value of an off-the-run US treasury with similar interest payments, payment schedule and maturity.

Set   Discount rate = IRR

$$\text{Model value} = \sum_{k=1}^{N} \frac{CF_N}{(1 + \text{Discount rate})^k}$$

16.2.3 Book value ★★★

The illiquid market of credit risky debts imposes a challenge to the valuation of credit risky debts. Since loans are not traded individually in the market and corporate bonds are not traded actively in the secondary market, there is no representative market price of a credit risky debt and there is no representative price of a similar debt which can be used to derive the IRR in order to valuate a credit risky debt through the discounted cash flow model. As such, the book value mandated by the IFRS 9 is used to proxy the value of a credit risky debt which is intended to be held until maturity.

For a loan originated by a lender or corporate bond acquired at principal by an investor, the book value is simply equal to the outstanding principal throughout the life of the debt. The book IRR, i.e. the IRR which is used throughout the life of the debt, is simply equal to the periodic interest rate.

$$\text{Book IRR} = \frac{\text{Interest rate}}{\text{Interest frequency}}$$

For a corporate bond acquired at premium or discount by an investor, the book IRR is derived first using the acquisition cost as the market price of the corporate bond, with the discounted cash flow model.

$$\text{Acquisition cost} = \sum_{k=1}^{N} \frac{CF_N}{\left(1 + \text{Book IRR}\right)^k}$$

This book IRR can be calculated easily in Microsoft Excel with the function IRR(...).

$$\text{Book IRR} = \text{IRR}\left(-\text{Acquisition cost}, CF_1, CF_2, CF_3, ... CF_N\right)$$

The initial book value is equal to the acquisition cost of the credit risky debt.

$$\text{Book value}_0 = \text{Acquisition cost}$$

On the first interest payment day after the first interest payment is received by the investor, the book value is updated to:

$$\text{Book value}_1 = \text{Book value}_0 \times \left(1 + \text{Book IRR}\right) - \text{Interest amount}$$

where

$$\text{Interest amount} = \text{Principal} \times \frac{\text{Interest rate}}{\text{Interest frequency}}$$

On the second interest payment day after the second interest payment is received by the investor, the book value is updated to:

$$\text{Book value}_2 = \text{Book value}_1 \times \left(1 + \text{Book IRR}\right) - \text{Interest amount}$$

The update to the book value continues on every interest payment day such that on the kth interest payment day after the kth interest payment is received by the investor, the book value is updated to:

$$\text{Book value}_k = \text{Book value}_{k-1} \times \left(1 + \text{Book IRR}\right) - \text{Interest amount}$$

If the corporate bond is acquired at a premium, i.e., the acquisition cost is above the principal, the book IRR is smaller than the periodic interest rate and the book value will converge downwards to the principal throughout the life of the corporate bond. In contrast, if the corporate bond is acquired at a discount, i.e., the acquisition cost is below the principal, the book IRR is larger than the periodic interest rate and the book value will converge upwards to the principal throughout the life of the corporate bond.

The book value addresses the issue of lacking an IRR by using one book IRR throughout the life of a corporate bond, at a shortcoming that this constant book IRR fails to incorporate the continuous change of credit risk throughout the life of the corporate bond.

16.3   Credit provision ★★★

Credit provision is the present value of expected loss ("PVEL") of a debt arising from the default of the debt, using the book IRR as the discount rate.

For a debt paying interest periodically, define period k as the time between the k-1th and kth interest payments. If the default is only observable on the interest payment days, then the default loss in any period is calculated as:

$$\text{Default loss} = \text{EAD} \times \text{LGD} = \text{Principal} \times \left(1 + \frac{\text{Interest rate}}{\text{Interest frequency}} \right) \times \text{LGD}$$

The discount factor of the default loss observed on the kth interest payment day is:

$$\text{Discount factor}_k = \frac{1}{\left(1 + \text{Book IRR} \right)^k}$$

The default chance in period k is:

$$\text{Default chance}_k = \left(1 - \text{PD} \right)^{T_{k-1}} - \left(1 - \text{PD} \right)^{T_k}$$

Then the PVEL in period k is:

$$\text{PVEL}_k = \text{Default loss} \times \text{Discount factor}_k \times \text{Default chance}_k$$

The total PVEL is the sum of the PVELs in all periods:

$$\text{Total PVEL} = \sum_{k=1}^{N} \text{PVEL}_k$$

The IFRS 9 mandates the credit provision to be assigned according to the credit risk level of a debt:

- When the debt is acquired at a lower credit risk, the credit provision is calculated as the 1-year PVEL. This arrangement reflects the situation where the cost of the debt has incorporated the prevailing credit risk. The credit provision calculated in this scenario is classified as a general provision;

- After the acquisition of the debt, if the credit risk of the debt has increased to a moderate level, the credit provision is calculated as the RM-year PVEL. This arrangement reflects the situation where the cost of the debt has not yet incorporated the additional credit risk arising from the deterioration. The credit provision calculated in this scenario is classified as a general provision; and

- Subsequently, if the credit risk of the debt has increased to a higher level, the credit provision is calculated as the RM-year PVEL. This arrangement reflects the situation where the cost of the debt has not yet incorporated the additional credit risk arising from the further deterioration. The credit provision calculated in this scenario is classified as a specific provision.

The IFRS does define what contributes to lower, moderate and higher credit risk. If the EAD, LGD and RM are well controlled by the lender, inline with the ECAI credit rating scale, a credit risky debt with the borrower's PD:

- below 1 percent is classified as lower risk;
- between 1 percent and 10 percent is classified as moderate risk; and
- above 10 percent is classified as higher risk.

16.4   Interest income

Interest income is received as a result of the interest payment from a debt on the interest payment day. The cash flow of the interest income is calculated as the arithmetic product of the principal and interest rate per period. Nevertheless, the IFRS 9 mandates the interest income to be recognized according to the credit risk level of the debt, using the book value and book IRR as major independent variables:

- When the debt is acquired at a lower credit risk, the interest income is calculated is as the arithmetic product of the book value and book IRR;

- After the acquisition of the debt, if the credit risk of the debt has increased to a moderate level, the interest income is calculated as the arithmetic product of the book value and book IRR; and

- Subsequently, if the credit risk of the debt has increased to a higher level, the interest income is calculated the arithmetic of (i) the book value less the RM-year PVEL; and (ii) the book IRR.

16.5   Extensions to the CDOs and government bonds

The rules of book value, credit provision and interest income in the IFRS 9 are also applicable to the CDOs and government bonds which are acquired by investors with an intention to hold these financial instruments until maturity. These financial instruments have the cash flow patterns similar to those of credit risky debts.

The Basel III Framework

KEY CONCEPTS

- Credit contagion
- Capital charge
- Basel Committee

- Basel III framework
- Standardized approach
- Regulatory capital

17.1   Credit contagion ★★★

Although banks seek to lend to corporations of higher credit quality with lower financial leverage, banks themselves are a group of highly leveraged corporations. While a small part of a bank's assets are funded by shareholders in the form of equity, the majority of its assets are funded by depositors who put monies into the bank and investors who acquire bonds issued by the bank. The bank then uses monies from both shareholders and debt investors (including depositors and bond investors) to conduct investments, including loans and bonds. In case the bank's investments are profitable, the debt investors will receive the fixed nominal yields, and the shareholders will pocket the proceeds in the forms of dividend and equity appreciation after satisfying all payments to debt investors. On the other hand, if the bank's investments suffer from a loss, under a severe situation, the bank will lose all monies from shareholders and certain monies from debt investors. In such case, the debt investors cannot collect in full the interim interests and/or principals at maturity and the bank defaults. This asymmetric payoff with bounded downside loss but unlimited upside profit potential to a bank's shareholders essentially encourages the bank to make investments of the highest return with least funding from shareholders.   This arrangement is virtually equivalent to making investments of the highest risk with most funding from debt investors.

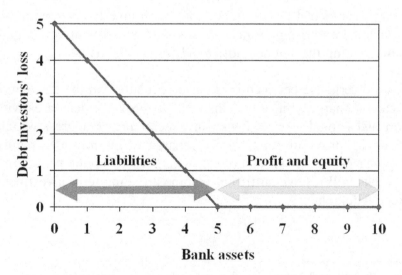

Figure 17.1   Debt investors' loss vs bank assets

In addition, banks have strong credit relationships with one another. The largest lender of a bank is usually another bank whilst the largest borrower of a bank is often another bank. This relationship results in a credit contagion effect that the default of a bank will trigger the default of another bank, either for financial reasons or depositors' behavioural reasons arising from a lack of confidence. The propagation of defaults among a number of banks together will cause the collapse of the entire banking system.

Therefore, in order to prevent such banking system crisis, every bank must confine its investment loss to shareholders and ensure that its debt investors can be paid in full on schedule. In other words, a bank must reserve sufficient shareholders' monies to absorb the potential investment loss even under an extreme scenario. The larger the investment losses to be registered in an extreme scenario, the more the shareholders' monies are reserved.

17.2   Credit provision and capital charge

Credit provision is a proxy of the 1-year EL arising from debt investments. It is treated as a cost and deducted from the income when a bank calculates its profit. The credit provision and income are primarily estimated in accordance with the IFRS 9 and other related accounting rules, with supplementary guidelines from regulators.

Capital charge is a prudent estimate of the unexpected loss ("UL") of a debt, defined as the difference between the XCL and 1-year EL arising from a debt investment.

UL = XCL - 1-year EL

Capital charge is matched by the long term investment funding to a bank. The capital charge and long term investment funding are estimated in accordance with the rules set out in the Basel III framework.[40]

Such arrangement ensures that the profit and long term investment funding are sufficient to absorb the default loss arising from a bank's debt investments even under a severe situation, thus minimizing the potential loss to a bank's debt investors.

There is always a divergence between banks and regulators on the calculations of credit provision and capital charge. Since the financial performance decreases with increasing credit provision and capital charge, banks in general prefer aggressive approaches to minimize the credit provision and capital charge. In contrast, regulators prefer conservative approaches to arrive at prudent estimates of credit provision and capital charge so that banks will reserve sufficient income and long term investment funding to absorb the potential default loss.

---

[40] If a bank uses the IRB approach to calculate the capital charge for credit risk, the bank must also follow the IRB approach to calculate the benchmark of credit provision for the relevant debts.

17.3 Basel Committee and Basel Accord

While the credit provision of a bank's debt investments has been addressed by the IFRS 9, the treatment to the capital charge remains outstanding. This triggers regulators to set out guidelines to ensure that a bank maintains sufficient long term investment funding, most of which is shareholders' equity, to match the capital charge.

Before 1988, determination on sufficiency of shareholders' equity varied among different countries. Many regulators required banks under their purview to maintain the shareholders' equity not less than 5 percent of the total assets. Nevertheless, the calculation of shareholders' equity and total assets varied from country to country due to differences in domestic accounting standards. Moreover, some countries enforced their regulations less diligently than others in order to make their banking industry more attractive to international banking groups.

However, the explosion of over-the-counter derivatives trading in the eighties made the total asset value a less effective basis for determining the minimum shareholders' equity since most derivatives are registered as off balance sheet items and outside the coverage of assets. Moreover, the large amount of debts invested in less developed countries of lower credit quality, such as Mexico, Brazil and Argentina, by internationally active banks necessitated another review on the sufficiency of shareholders' equity.

The Basel Committee on Banking Supervision ("BCBS") was founded in 1974 by the bank regulators from the G10 countries. The members meet regularly in the city Basel, Switzerland under the patronage of the Bank for International Settlements. The BCBS published in 1988 the "International Convergence of Capital Measurement and Capital Standards," simply referred to as the Basel Accord, which aims at setting a global standard to assess a bank's ability to absorb the UL arising from its debt investments without incurring loss to the bank's debt investors. The first standard, referred to as Basel I, was adopted by over one hundred bank regulators in the world.

The Basel I framework was revised in 1996 to incorporate market risk management and further expanded to the Basel II framework in 2006 to cover operational risk management and the contemporary issues in credit risk management. After the financial tsunami in 2008, the Basel II framework was once again enhanced to the Basel III framework to include the developments of liquidity risk management.

According to the Basel Accord, the ability of a bank to match the total UL arising from its debt investments is measured by comparing:

- the total capital charge, which is a prudent estimate of the total UL of a bank's investments; and

- the regulatory capital, which is the amount of long term investment funding (the majority of which being shareholders' equity) to a bank, both calculated in accordance with a set of unified regulatory rules. A bank is required to maintain sufficient regulatory capital to match the total capital charge.

The major calculations of capital charge for credit risk and regulatory capital in the Basel Accord are described in the following chapters. Since the full details of the calculations are very tedious with many exceptions and with many contents outside credit risk management, a full coverage of the Basel Accord is beyond the scope of this book. Instead, this book uses a scale down and reader friendly version of the Basel III framework to illustrate the critical calculations of capital charge for credit risk and regulatory capital. This mini Basel III framework focuses on those important aspects in relation to common credit products and facilitates a comparison between the standardized and internal ratings based approaches. This arrangement aims at providing a clear understanding on the Basel III framework with a minimum effort. Readers should refer to the full set of updated Basel III guidelines issued by the BCBS when working on an industrial implementation of the Basel III framework.

17.4   Basel I framework

Under the Basel I framework, a bank's debt investments are classified into four categories which are then assigned different capital charge ratios:

- A capital charge ratio of 0 percent is assigned to residential mortgages of higher quality and debts issued by the member countries of Organization for Economic Co-operation and Development ("OECD");

- A capital charge ratio of 1.6 percent is assigned to debts issued by banks and public sector entities in the member countries of the OECD. These include debts issued by government agencies like Fannie Mae, Freddie Mac and municipalities;

- A capital charge ratio of 4 percent is assigned to residential mortgages of lower quality; and

- A capital charge ratio of 8 percent is assigned to other debts.

The capital charge of a debt is then calculated as the arithmetic product of the principal and capital charge ratio.

Capital charge = Principal × Capital charge ratio

The sum of all capital charges then becomes a prudent estimate of the total UL arising from a bank's debt investments.

The Basel I framework allows the capital charge to be calculated in a very simple setting. However, the Basel I framework is over simplified to the extent that it results in little differentiation in the real credit risk among debts of different credit quality. For example, while a loan to Microsoft, an AAA-rated global software giant, is assigned a capital charge ratio 8 percent, the same loan to Tencent, a BBB-rated Chinese technology firm, is also assigned a capital charge ratio 8 percent. Moreover, a government bond issued by Greece, a CCC-rated country as a member of the OECD, is assigned a 0 percent capital charge ratio. Thus, the Basel I framework essentially encourages banks to seek capital arbitrage opportunities by investing in debts with lower capital charge ratio but higher credit risk in order to capture a higher return at a lower capital charge ratio.

Furthermore, the Basel I framework does not recognize the effort of credit risk controls. A debt hedged perfectly by a CDS will be subject to the standard capital charge ratio and a debt supported fully by collaterals will be treated in the same way as a debt without any collateral. This further creates an incentive for banks not to control their credit risk.

Finally, the Basel I framework does not cover the impacts from market, operational and liquidity risks which were later the major exposures of critical financial crisis, e.g., the collapse of global equity markets in 1987, the 911 terrorist attack in 2001 and the financial tsunami in 2008.

All these deficiencies in the Basel I framework suggest that there is a need to improve this simple framework into a more comprehensive version. Several major evolutions occurred during the last two decades and resulted in the latest Basel III framework, being started to implement in 2013.

17.5   Basel III framework

The Basel III framework comprises four major building blocks to address the different aspects of a bank's risk management functions. These building blocks are referred to as the four pillars of the Basel III framework:

- Pillar 1: Minimum capital requirements;
- Pillar 2: Supervisory review process;
- Pillar 3: Public disclosure; and
- Pillar 4: Liquidity sufficiency.

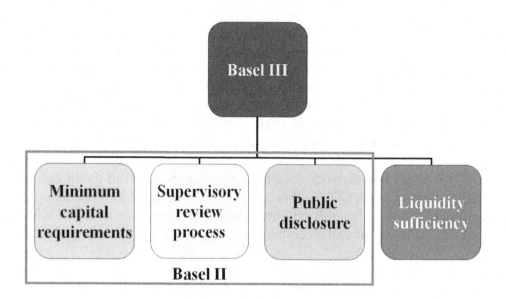

Figure 17.2   Basel III framework

17.5.1 Minimum capital requirements ★★★

The Basel III framework proposes a number of quantitative approaches to:

- calculate the capital charges that aim at quantifying the credit, market and operational risks arising from a bank's investments and operations;

- calculate the regulatory capital which is the long term investment funding to a bank; and

- match the total capital charge with regulatory capital.

Having considered the business models of individual banks, the Basel III framework offers for each risk two or three approaches for a bank to select, taking into account the bank's resources and expertise. A bank that seeks to adopt a more sophisticated approach must obtain the approval from its regulator.

Risk	Simple approach	Sophisticated approach*
Credit	Standardized approach	Internal ratings based approach
Market	Standardized approach	Internal models approach
Operational	Basic indicator approach	Standardized approach Advanced measurement approach

* A bank using any sophisticated approach to calculate the capital charges must seek the approval from its regulator.

Table 17.1   Capital charge calculation approaches

17.5.2 Supervisory review process

The Basel III framework proposes four major principles for a regulator to review a bank's risk management practices:

- A bank should have a process in place to assess its overall capital adequacy in relation to its risk profile and a strategy to maintain its level of capital;

- A regulator should review and evaluate a bank's internal capital adequacy assessments and strategies as well as the bank's ability to monitor and ensure compliance with capital sufficiency. A regulator should take appropriate supervisory action if it is not satisfied with the result of a bank's process;

- A regulator should expect a bank to operate above the minimum regulatory capital sufficiency and should be able to request a bank to hold additional regulatory capital; and

- A regulator should seek to intervene at an early stage to prevent a bank's regulatory capital from falling below the minimum level and mandate a bank to take rapid remedial action if the regulatory capital is not maintained or restored.

The implementation of the supervisory review process varies among different regulators. Some regulators issue guidelines as an implementation while some regulators use score cards to assess a bank's level of compliance.

17.5.3 Public disclosure

The Basel III framework proposes the major risk management topics that a bank should disclose to the general public. These include, among others:

- the organization structure of a banking group, the entities covered by the Basel III framework and the entities excluded from the Basel III framework;

- the terms and conditions of the major features of the financial instruments that are qualified as regulatory capital;

- the financial instruments qualified as common equity and additional tier one capital;

- the total amount of tier two capital;

- the capital charges arising from the credit, market and operational risks;

- the general information of other risks to which a bank is exposed and the relevant methods that the bank has applied in managing these risks; and

- the structure and operations of a bank's risk management function.

17.5.4 Liquidity sufficiency

The liquidity sufficiency requirements became a major part of the Basel Accord after the financial tsunami in 2008 from which the BCBS recognized that the liquidity sufficiency had the same importance as capital adequacy in banking stability. The liquidity sufficiency aims at strengthening and standardizing a bank's liquidity measurement framework by setting out the following quantitative requirements:

- A bank must hold sufficient high quality liquid assets to meet the net cash outflow over a period of thirty calendar days under an acute liquidity stress scenario; and

- A bank must match its required amount of out-going stable funding with sufficient available incoming funding from stable funding sources.

In addition, the Basel III framework also proposes a set of common monitoring tools for a regulator to monitor a bank's funding liquidity. These include:

- contractual maturity profile, which provides an initial and simple baseline of contractual commitments;

- concentration of funding, which assesses the extent of liquidity risk caused by excessive reliance on a single or several funding sources;

- available unencumbered assets, which help a bank be better aware of its potential capacity to raise additional secured funds; and

- financial market monitoring tools, which cover the market data such as currency rates, interest rates, equity prices, commodity prices, credit spreads, liquidity spreads and others that can be accessed easily by a bank to monitor its liquidity situations.

17.6   Standardized approach for credit risk

Under the standardized approach, the capital charge arising from the UL is calculated on an individual debt basis. For each debt, a bank is required to estimate an EAD with a set of simplified rules and assign a capital charge ratio that captures the effect of the LGD or PD. The impact from the RM is not incorporated in the standardized approach.

17.6.1 Exposure at default ★★★

For a debt registered on the balance sheet, the EAD is estimated as the principal less specific provision. This avoids the double counting of the unrealized default loss that has been captured by specific provision.

EAD = Principal - Specific provision

For a commitment on which a bank makes a promise to lend up to a certain amount, the EAD is calculated as the sum of: (i) the drawdown amount less specific provision; and (ii) the arithmetic product of the difference between the credit limit and the drawdown amount, and a credit conversion factor. Table 17.2 sets out the credit conversion factors for various types of commitment.

EAD = Drawdown amount - Specific provision
+ (Credit limit - Drawdown amount) × Credit conversion factor

	Type of commitment	CCF (%)
1.	Direct credit substitutes	100
2.	Transaction related contingencies	50
3.	Trade related contingencies	20
4.	Asset sales with recourse	100
5.	Forward asset purchases	100
6.	Partly paid-up securities	100
7.	Forward forward deposits placed	100
8.	Note issuance and revolving underwriting facilities	75
9.	Commitments that are unconditionally cancellable without prior notice	0
10.	Other commitments	20/50

Table 17.2   Commitments and credit conversion factors

On balance sheet netting and financial collaterals can be applied as credit risk controls to reduce the EAD.

17.6.2 Capital charge ratio

For a loan offered to a retail borrower, the capital charge ratio is assigned in accordance with the exposure type. For a debt issued by an institution, the capital charge ratio is assigned in accordance with the credit rating and issuer type.

17.6.2.1 Retail exposure ★★★

A retail exposure is a loan offered to an individual person or a small business with annual revenue less the EUR 5 mn and the total loan amount from the lending bank less than EUR 1 mn. For each retail exposure, a capital charge ratio is assigned according to the exposure type, as illustrated in Table 17.3.

The capital charge ratios are independent of the PD and RM. This results in a side effect which encourages banks to lend to retail borrowers with lower credit quality and/or longer maturity.

Exposure	Capital charge ratio (%)
Residential mortgage	2.8
Qualifying revolving retail exposure	6
Other retail exposure	6

Table 17.3   Capital charge ratios for retail exposures

17.6.2.2 Institution exposure ★★★

An institution exposure is a debt issued by a corporation, bank or country. For each institution exposure, a capital charge ratio is assigned according to credit rating and issuer type, as illustrated in Table 17.4. A set of smaller capital charge ratios are applied to a debt issued by a bank, with short contractual maturity at origination.

Rating	Corporation (%)	Bank (%)		Country (%)
		≤ 3 months*	> 3 months*	
AAA	1.6	1.6	1.6	0
AA	1.6	1.6	1.6	0
A	4	1.6	4	1.6
BBB	8	1.6	4	4
BB	8	4	8	8
B	12	4	8	8
CCC to C	12			
Unrated	8	1.6	4	8

* Contractual maturity at origination.

Table 17.4   Capital charge ratios for institution exposures

The capital charge ratio is independent of the RM. This results in a side effect which encourages banks to invest in debts with longer maturity. It is also interesting to observe that a debt issuer without credit rating has a capital charge ratio lower than that of a debt issuer with poor credit rating. Capital arbitrage may thus be resulted by investing in a debt issued by an institution of lower credit quality but without credit rating.

The credit ratings must be issued by an external credit assessment institution recognized by the bank's regulator. In general, these include the three major global credit rating agencies and the major domestic credit rating agencies in the bank's own country. If a debt issuer is assigned different credit ratings by several credit rating agencies and results in:

- two different capital charge ratios, the larger capital charge ratio is adopted; or
- more than two capital charge ratios, the second smallest capital charge ratio is adopted.

For a CLN with multiple reference debts, the capital charge ratios of issuers of the reference debts are first looked up and then the capital charge ratio of the CLN is assigned with the largest capital charge ratio among the issuers of the reference debts.

Default insurance can be applied as a credit risk control to reduce the capital charge ratio.

17.6.3 Capital charge ★★★

The capital charge is the arithmetic product of the EAD and capital charge ratio. Hence, the capital charge increases with increasing EAD and capital charge ratio.

$$\text{Capital charge} = \text{EAD} \times \text{Capital charge ratio}$$

17.6.4 Credit risk mitigation

The standardized approach recognizes the credit risk mitigation through three credit risk controls: on balance sheet netting, financial collaterals and default insurance.

17.6.4.1 On balance sheet netting ★★★

Subject to a valid bilateral netting agreement, a bank acting as both a lender and a borrower of a counterparty is allowed to offset the lending EAD with the borrowing principal and subject to a currency haircut if the currencies of lending EAD and borrowing principal are different. In many cases, the currency haircut is set to 8 percent.

$$\text{Net EAD} = \text{Max}\left[\text{Lending EAD - Borrowing principal} \times (1 - \text{Currency haircut}), 0\right]$$

17.6.4.2 Financial collaterals ★★★

The standardized approach recognizes certain financial instruments as collaterals to reduce the credit risk. With financial collateral, the effective EAD of a debt is reduced to:

$$\text{Effective EAD} = \text{Max}\left[\begin{array}{l} \text{EAD without collateral} \\ \text{- Collateral value} \times \left(\begin{array}{l} 1 \text{ - Collateral haircut} \\ \text{- Currency haircut} \end{array}\right), \\ 0 \end{array}\right]$$

The collateral haircuts are listed in Table 17.5.

Collateral and credit rating		Residual maturity or constituent	Corporation and bank (%)	Country (%)
Debt	AAA to AA	Up to 1 year	1	0.5
		From 1 to 5 years	4	2
		Longer than 5 years	8	4
	A to BBB	Up to 1 year	2	1
		From 1 to 5 years	6	3
		Longer than 5 years	12	6
	BB			15
Equity of a listed company		Constituent of a major equity index	15	
		Not a constituent of major equity indices	25	
Others		100		
Mutual fund		The largest haircut among the investment components		

Table 17.5   Collateral haircuts

17.6.4.3 Default insurance ★★★

A bank may apply default insurance in the form of credit guarantee or CDS to improve the credit quality of a debt issued by an institution. To be recognized, the credit guarantor/protection seller must be independent of the debt issuer.

With default insurance, the lower capital charge ratio between the debt issuer and the credit guarantor/protection seller is adopted as the capital charge ratio of the debt.

$$\text{Capital charge ratio} = \text{Min}\begin{bmatrix} \text{Capital charge ratio of debt issuer,} \\ \text{Capital charge ratio of credit guarantor/protection seller} \end{bmatrix}$$

In case the default insurance covers only part of the EAD, the entire debt is divided into the protected and unprotected parts, and the capital charges on these two parts are calculated separately. Only the protected part is subject to default insurance.

17.6.4.4 Currency and maturity mis-matches

In case the currency of a credit risk control is different from that of the debt, the protection to the debt is discounted by a currency haircut, in most cases, 8 percent.

In case the protection period of the credit risk control is shorter than the RM of the debt,

- for a debt with the RM longer than 0.25, the protected part of the debt is reduced to:

EAD of the protected part without maturity mis-match

$$\times \frac{\text{Min}\left[\text{Protection period of credit risk control, 5}\right] - 0.25}{\text{Min}\left[\text{RM of debt, 5}\right] - 0.25}$$

- for a debt with the RM shorter than or equal to 0.25, the effect from the credit risk control is ignored simply.

17.7 Regulatory capital ★★★

Regulatory capital is the long term funding from a bank's investors who have the lowest claim priority during the liquidation of a bank. A bank must maintain sufficient regulatory capital to match the UL of the potential loss arising from its debt investments under a severe condition.

The regulatory capital includes retained earnings and the funds raised from financial instruments issued by a bank in the form of common shares, preferred shares and subordinated debts. Their contributions to regulatory capital are calculated in accordance to the rules set out in the Basel III framework in order to maintain consistency among different countries. The qualities of the regulatory capitals are classified in accordance with the seniority of the financial instruments.

Common equity tier one capital

Common equity tier one capital includes retained earnings and common shares. They are the monies belonging to a bank's shareholders.

Additional tier one capital

Additional tier one capital includes non-cumulative perpetual preferred shares to which dividends must be paid prior to common shares.

Tier two capital

Tier two capital includes:

- cumulative perpetual preferred shares; and
- subordinated debts with contractual maturity longer than five years.

A bank is considered to have been equipped with sufficient regulatory capital if the following layers of regulatory capital requirements are satisfied:

$$\text{Tier one capital} = \text{Common equity tier one capital}$$
$$+ \text{ Additional tier one capital}$$
$$\text{Total capital} = \text{Tier one capital} + \text{Tier two capital}$$
$$\text{Regulatory capital} = \text{Min}\left[\text{Total capital, Tier one capital} \times 2\right]$$

$$\text{Regulatory capital} \geq \text{Total capital charge}$$
$$\text{Tier one capial} \geq \text{Total capital charge} \times 75\%$$
$$\text{Common equity tier one capital} \geq \text{Total capital charge} \times 56.25\%$$

Appendix 17.1   Risk weight, risk weighed amount and capital adequacy ratio[41] ★★★

A risk weight is defined as the capital charge ratio multiplied by 12.5. A risk weighted amount is defined as the capital charge multiplied by 12.5.

$$\text{Risk weight} = \text{Capital charge ratio} \times 12.5$$
$$\text{Risk weighted amount} = \text{Capital charge} \times 12.5$$
$$= \text{EAD} \times \text{Capital charge ratio} \times 12.5$$

The ratio between the regulatory capital and total risk weighted amount is referred to as the capital adequacy ratio. To ensure that there is sufficient regulatory capital to match the total capital charge, the capital adequacy ratio must be greater than or equal to 8 percent, i.e.:

$$
\begin{aligned}
\text{Capital adequacy ratio} &= \frac{\text{Regulatory capital}}{\text{Total risk weighted amount}} \\
&= \frac{\text{Regulatory capital}}{\text{Total capital charge} \times 12.5} \\
&= \frac{\text{Regulatory capital}}{\text{Total capital charge}} \times \frac{1}{12.5} \\
&\geq 1 \times 8\% \\
&\geq 8\%
\end{aligned}
$$

Although less intuitive, the terms risk weight, risk weighted amount and capital adequacy ratio appear frequently in many literatures about the Basel III framework. They are inherited from the Basel I framework in which the risk weighted amount is the primary metric to quantify the UL.

Using the risk weighted amount instead of capital charge, a bank is considered to have been equipped with sufficient regulatory capital if the following layers of regulatory capital requirements are satisfied:

$$\text{Regulatory capital} \geq \text{Total risk weighed amount} \times 8\%$$
$$\text{Tier one capital} \geq \text{Total risk weighed amount} \times 6\%$$
$$\text{Common equity tier one capital} \geq \text{Total risk weighed amount} \times 4.5\%$$

---

[41]Appendix 17.1 is applicable to both the standardized and IRB approaches.

Internal Ratings Based Approach 18

KEY CONCEPTS

- Retail IRB approach
- Advanced IRB approach
- Foundation IRB approach

- Credit risk mitigation
- Industry implementation

18.1 Theory of the IRB approach ★★★

Under the Basel III framework, subject to the approval from its regulator, a bank with sufficient quantitative expertise may adopt a more sophisticated methodology, referred to as the internal ratings based ("IRB") approach, to calculate the credit provision and capital charge for credit risk of its debt investments.

The IRB approach assumes that a bank holds a well diversified debt portfolio comprising a large number of debts with smaller EADs from many debt issuers. In general, this assumption is representative for describing the debt investments of an internationally active bank. Under this assumption, the bank's debt investments can be well approximated by an infinite homogeneous debt portfolio.

When the RMs of the debt investments are unified to one year,

$$\text{Portfolio XCL} = \text{Portfolio EAD} \times \text{LGD} \times \text{XCDR}$$
$$\text{Portfolio 1-year EL} = \text{Portfolio EAD} \times \text{LGD} \times \text{PD}$$
$$\text{Portfolio UL} = \text{Portfolio XCL} - \text{Portfolio 1-year EL}$$

For each debt k, define:

$$\text{XCL}_k = \text{EAD}_k \times \text{LGD}_k \times \text{XCDR}_k$$
$$\text{1-year EL}_k = \text{EAD}_k \times \text{LGD}_k \times \text{PD}_k$$
$$\text{UL}_k = \text{XCL}_k - \text{1-year EL}_k$$

Under these definitions, the XCDR_k, XCL_k and UL_k follow a pure mathematical treatment without any economic meaning.

If there are NOB individual debts, then:

$$\sum_{k=1}^{\text{NOB}} \text{EAD}_k = \text{Portfolio EAD}$$

$$LGD_k \approx LGD$$
$$XCDR_k \approx XCDR$$
$$PD_k \approx PD$$

The portfolio UL can be well approximated as:

$$\text{Portfolio UL} = \text{Portfolio XCL} - \text{Portfolio 1-year EL}$$

$$= \text{Portfolio EAD} \times LGD \times XCDR - \text{Portfolio EAD} \times LGD \times PD$$

$$= \left(\sum_{k=1}^{NOB} EAD_k \right) \times LGD \times XCDR - \left(\sum_{k=1}^{NOB} EAD_k \right) \times LGD \times PD$$

$$= \sum_{k=1}^{NOB} \left(EAD_k \times LGD \times XCDR \right) - \sum_{k=1}^{NOB} \left(EAD_k \times LGD \times PD \right)$$

$$\approx \sum_{k=1}^{NOB} \left(EAD_k \times LGD_k \times XCDR_k \right) - \sum_{k=1}^{NOB} \left(EAD_k \times LGD_k \times PD_k \right)$$

$$= \sum_{k=1}^{NOB} \left(XCL_k - \text{1-year EL}_k \right)$$

$$= \sum_{k=1}^{NOB} UL_k$$

This relationship suggests that the portfolio UL is approximately equal to the sum of the ULs of individual debts. When each debt is treated as a hypothetical infinite homogeneous portfolio, an XCL is calculated and divided into the 1-year EL and UL. In most situations, the 1-year EL is assigned as the credit provision of the debt. The sum of all credit provisions for individual debts then becomes the total credit provision of the bank's debt investments and is treated as the bank's unrealized loss. The UL, after taking into account the characteristics of various debts, including loan type, issuer type, firm size and the RM, is further scaled up by a safety factor to arrive at a capital charge. The sum of all capital charges for individual debts then becomes the total capital charge of the bank's debt investments and is matched by the bank's regulatory capital.

In summary,

Single debt $\Leftrightarrow$ Hypothetical infinite homogeneous portfolio

$$XCL = EAD \times LGD \times XCDR$$
$$\text{1-year EL} = EAD \times LGD \times PD$$
$$UL = XCL - \text{1-year EL}$$

$$\text{Credit provision} = \text{1-year EL}$$
$$\text{Capital charge} = UL \times \text{Safety factor}$$

18.2   Regulatory treatments to credit risk factors

In general, the IRB approach follows the credit risk measurement framework of an infinite homogeneous portfolio to calculate the hypothetical XCL of a single debt. This hypothetical XCL is then utilized to derive the credit provision and capital charge. The major input parameters to the IRB approach are the fundamental credit risk factors EAD, LGD, PD and RM. Nevertheless, under the IRB approach, some specific regulatory treatments are applied to the credit risk factors when the credit provision and capital charge are calculated.

18.2.1 Exposure at default

For a debt registered on the balance sheet, the EAD is estimated simply as the sum of principal and accrued interest.

For a commitment with which a bank makes a contractual promise to lend up to a certain amount, the EAD is calculated as the sum of: (i) the drawdown amount; and (ii) the arithmetic product of the difference between the credit limit and drawdown amount, and a credit conversion factor.

EAD = Drawdown amount
+ (Credit limit - Drawdown amount) × Credit conversion factor

The credit conversion factor is estimated by a bank's internal quantitative model.

On balance sheet netting can be applied as a credit risk control to reduce the EAD.

18.2.2 Loss given default

The LGD is estimated by a bank's internal quantitative model. As a result of the conservative lending practices in most banks, the number of defaults is relatively small. This makes the development of an LGD prediction model difficult.

Collaterals are used as the most common credit risk control to reduce the LGD. In general, debts without collaterals exhibit a higher LGD while debts with collaterals exhibit a lower LGD as a result of the excessive amount of collaterals above the EAD demanded by a bank.

18.2.3 Probability of default

Each debt issuer is assigned a PD which is derived in accordance with a bank's internal ratings system. The PD must be above or equal to 0.03 percent for a debt issuer other than a country that has sole discretion on its currency policy. All debts issued by the same debt issuer are subject to a single PD. Default insurance can be applied as a credit risk control to reduce the PD.

For a CLN with multiple reference debts, the PD is assigned as the largest PD among the issuers of reference debts.

18.2.4 Residual maturity

The RM is defined as the expected cash flow weighted tenor of the debt.

$$RM = \frac{\sum_{k=1}^{N}\left(CF_k \times Tenor_k\right)}{\sum_{k=1}^{N}CF_k}$$

In case the expected cash flows and/or tenors of a debt cannot be determined, the contractual RM can be adopted as a prudent substitution. In addition, if the RM is below one year, it is adjusted upwards to one year. If the RM is above five years, it is adjusted downwards to five years.

18.3   The IRB formulas

Under the IRB approach, there are six sets of formulas, each for one loan type or issuer type, to calculate the credit provision and capital charge. These formulas are summarized in Figure 18.1.

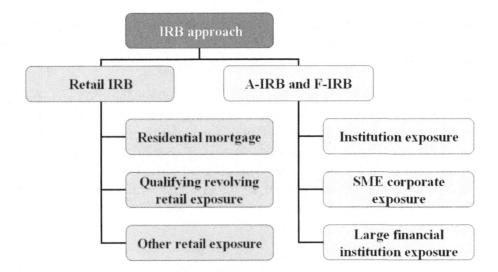

Figure 18.1   The IRB formulas

These IRB formulas adopt a number of abbreviations in Table 18.1 to simplify the presentation.

	Abbreviation	Description
1.	EAD	Exposure at default
2.	LGD	Loss given default
3.	PD	Probability of default
4.	RM	Residual maturity
5.	CCC	Copula correlation coefficient
6.	XCDR	Extreme case default rate
7.	XCL	Extreme case loss
8.	1-year EL	One-year expected loss
9.	UL	Unexpected loss
10.	CP	Credit provision
11.	CC	Capital charge
12.	CCR	Capital charge ratio
13.	b	Maturity adjustment
14.	MAF	Maturity adjustment factor
15.	DDF	Double default factor

Table 18.1   Abbreviations used in the IRB formulas

18.4   Retail IRB approach

The retail IRB approach is applicable to retail loans lent to individual persons and/or small businesses. A small business is a company with total annual revenue less than EUR 5 mn and a total loan amount from the lending bank less than EUR 1 mn.

These retail loans are managed on a pool basis. Although there is no regulatory definition on a pool, in order to arrive at a meaningful XCL from a retail IRB formula, a pool is considered to be a finite homogeneous portfolio with at least three hundred borrowers. Each pool is estimated with its own EAD, LGD and PD, and the credit provision and capital charge are then calculated on a pool basis.

Loans to retail borrowers are classified into residential mortgage, qualifying revolving retail exposure and other retail exposure. The credit provision and capital charge for each type of retail exposure are calculated by a specific set of IRB formulas. Under the retail IRB approach, the RM has no impact to the calculation of credit provision and capital charge.

18.4.1 Residential mortgages ★★★

The credit provision and capital charge of a pool of residential mortgages are calculated with the following set of IRB formulas:

$$CCC = 0.15$$

$$XCDR = \Phi\left[\frac{\Phi^{-1}(PD) + \Phi^{-1}(99.9\%)\sqrt{CCC}}{\sqrt{1 - CCC}}\right]$$

$$XCL = EAD \times LGD \times XCDR$$
$$\text{1-year EL} = EAD \times LGD \times PD$$
$$UL = XCL - \text{1-year EL}$$

$$CP = \text{1-year EL}$$
$$CC = 1.06UL$$

$$CCR = \frac{CC}{EAD}$$

For residential mortgages, the LGD floor is set to 10 percent. A safety factor of 1.06 is multiplied to the UL in order to arrive at the capital charge. Residential mortgages have a higher CCC 0.15 among most retail exposures as property values are generally driven by macroeconomic factors common to all residential mortgages.

18.4.2 Qualifying revolving retail exposures ★★★

The credit provision and capital charge of a pool of qualifying revolving retail exposures are calculated with the following set of IRB formulas:

$$CCC = 0.04$$

$$XCDR = \Phi\left[\frac{\Phi^{-1}(PD) + \Phi^{-1}(99.9\%)\sqrt{CCC}}{\sqrt{1 - CCC}}\right]$$

$$XCL = EAD \times LGD \times XCDR$$
$$\text{1-year EL} = EAD \times LGD \times PD$$
$$UL = XCL - \text{1-year EL}$$

$$CP = 1\text{-year EL}$$
$$CC = 1.06UL$$

$$CCR = \frac{CC}{EAD}$$

These IRB formulas are applicable to credit cards, credit lines and other revolving loans. A lower CCC 0.04 illustrates the relatively lower default dependency among qualifying revolving retail exposures.

18.4.3 Other retail exposures ★★★

Any retail exposure other than residential mortgage and qualifying revolving retail exposure is classified as other retail exposure. The credit provision and capital charge of a pool of other retail exposures are calculated with the following set of IRB formulas:

$$CCC = 0.16 - 0.13\left[\frac{1 - \exp(-35PD)}{1 - \exp(-35)}\right] \approx 0.03 + 0.13\exp(-35PD)$$

$$XCDR = \Phi\left[\frac{\Phi^{-1}(PD) + \Phi^{-1}(99.9\%)\sqrt{CCC}}{\sqrt{1 - CCC}}\right]$$

$$XCL = EAD \times LGD \times XCDR$$
$$1\text{-year EL} = EAD \times LGD \times PD$$
$$UL = XCL - 1\text{-year EL}$$

$$CP = 1\text{-year EL}$$
$$CC = 1.06UL$$

$$CCR = \frac{CC}{EAD}$$

The CCC varies between 0.03 and 0.16, and decreases with increasing PD.

18.5   Advanced IRB approach

The advanced IRB approach is applicable to debts issued by institutions. A maturity adjustment factor is applied to incorporate the impact to the capital charge from the RM. In general, the CCC in the advanced IRB approach falls into a range higher than that in the retail IRB approach. Moreover, a larger institution is subject to a CCC formula that will result in a larger CCC.

18.5.1 Institution exposures ★★★

The credit provision and capital charge of an institution exposure are calculated with the following set of IRB formulas:

$$CCC = 0.24 - 0.12\left[\frac{1 - \exp(-50PD)}{1 - \exp(-50)}\right] \approx 0.12\left[1 + \exp(-50PD)\right]$$

$$XCDR = \Phi\left[\frac{\Phi^{-1}(PD) + \Phi^{-1}(99.9\%)\sqrt{CCC}}{\sqrt{1 - CCC}}\right]$$

$$XCL = EAD \times LGD \times XCDR$$
$$\text{1-year EL} = EAD \times LGD \times PD$$
$$UL = XCL - \text{1-year EL}$$

$$b = \left[0.11852 - 0.05478\ln(PD)\right]^2$$
$$MAF = \frac{1 + (RM - 2.5)b}{1 - 1.5b}$$

$$CP = \text{1-year EL}$$
$$CC = 1.06UL \times MAF$$

$$CCR = \frac{CC}{EAD}$$

The CCC is calculated in accordance with a formula similar to but different from that for other retail exposures. The CCC varies between 0.12 and 0.24, and decreases with increasing PD.

18.5.2 SME corporate exposures ★★★

A corporation is classified as a small and medium enterprise ("SME") corporate if its annual revenue is between EUR 5 mn and EUR 50 mn. An SME corporate has less dependency on the systematic credit risk due to its smaller firm size. Therefore, the annual revenue (S) in EUR mn is incorporated in the CCC formula to result in a smaller CCC. The credit provision and capital charge of an SME corporate exposure are calculated with the following set of IRB formulas:

$$CCC = 0.24 - 0.12\left[\frac{1 - \exp(-50PD)}{1 - \exp(-50)}\right] + \frac{S - 50}{1125}$$

$$\approx 0.12\left[1 + \exp(-50PD)\right] + \frac{S - 50}{1125}$$

$$XCDR = \Phi\left[\frac{\Phi^{-1}(PD) + \Phi^{-1}(99.9\%)\sqrt{CCC}}{\sqrt{1 - CCC}}\right]$$

$$XCL = EAD \times LGD \times XCDR$$
$$\text{1-year EL} = EAD \times LGD \times PD$$
$$UL = XCL - \text{1-year EL}$$

$$b = \left[0.11852 - 0.05478\ln(PD)\right]^2$$
$$MAF = \frac{1 + (RM - 2.5)b}{1 - 1.5b}$$

$$CP = \text{1-year EL}$$
$$CC = 1.06UL \times MAF$$

$$CCR = \frac{CC}{EAD}$$

The CCC varies between 0.0756 and 0.24, and decreases with increasing PD and decreasing annual revenue.

18.5.3 Large financial institution exposures ★★★

A financial institution is classified as a large financial institution if its total asset value is above USD 100 bn. A large financial institution acts as a substantial component of an economy and has a material impact to the systematic credit risk due to its large firm size. Therefore, a multiplier 1.25 is applied to the CCC formula for institution exposure to result in a larger CCC. The credit provision and capital charge of a large financial institution exposure are calculated with the following set of IRB formulas:

$$CCC = 1.25\left\{0.24 - 0.12\left[\frac{1 - \exp(-50PD)}{1 - \exp(-50)}\right]\right\} \approx 0.15\left[1 + \exp(-50PD)\right]$$

$$XCDR = \Phi\left[\frac{\Phi^{-1}(PD) + \Phi^{-1}(99.9\%)\sqrt{CCC}}{\sqrt{1 - CCC}}\right]$$

$$XCL = EAD \times LGD \times XCDR$$
$$\text{1-year EL} = EAD \times LGD \times PD$$
$$UL = XCL - \text{1-year EL}$$

$$b = \left[0.11852 - 0.05478\ln(PD)\right]^2$$
$$MAF = \frac{1 + (RM - 2.5)b}{1 - 1.5b}$$

$$CP = \text{1-year EL}$$
$$CC = 1.06UL \times MAF$$

$$CCR = \frac{CC}{EAD}$$

The CCC varies between 0.15 and 0.3, and decreases with increasing PD.

18.6   Credit risk mitigation

The retail and advanced IRB approaches recognize the credit risk mitigation through three credit risk controls: on balance sheet netting, collaterals and default insurance.

18.6.1 On balance sheet netting ★★★

Subject to a valid bilateral netting agreement, a bank that acts both as a lender and a borrower of a counterparty is allowed to offset the lending EAD with the borrowing EAD of the debts registered on the balance sheet, subject to a currency haircut if the currencies of lending EAD and borrowing EAD are different. In many cases, the currency haircut is set to 8 percent.

$$\text{Net EAD} = \text{Max}\left[\text{Lending EAD} - \text{Borrowing EAD} \times (1 - \text{Currency haircut}), 0\right]$$

18.6.2 Collaterals ★★★

A bank can apply collaterals to arrive at a final LGD of a debt after taking into account the reduction on default loss from selling collaterals.

18.6.3 Default insurance ★★★

A bank can apply default insurance in the form of credit guarantee or CDS to reduce the PD of a debt issuer. To be recognized as a credit risk control, the credit guarantor/protection seller must be independent of the debt issuer.

In case the default insurance covers only part of the EAD, the entire debt is divided into the protected part and unprotected part, and the credit provisions and capital charges on these two parts are calculated separately. Only the protected part is subject to default insurance.

When using default insurance as a credit risk control, a bank may choose to apply either the substitution framework or double default framework to calculate the credit provision and capital charge.

18.6.3.1 Substitution framework ★★★

The substitution framework is applicable to both the retail and advanced IRB approaches. Under the substitution framework, the PD of the debt issuer is replaced with the smaller PD of a credit guarantor/protection seller. The PD of the credit guarantor/protection seller then becomes the effective PD of the debt.

The substitution framework simply assumes that the default of a debt is driven by the default of the credit guarantor/protection seller. Nevertheless, this assumption is conceptually inconsistent with the fact that a bank will suffer from loss only when both the debt issuer and credit guarantor/protection seller default together.

18.6.3.2 Double default framework ★★★

The double default framework is applicable only to the advanced IRB approach. The double default framework seeks to recognize the fact, with a revised set of IRB formulas, that the bank will suffer from loss only when both the debt issuer and credit guarantor/protection seller default together. With the PD_o denoting the PD of the debt issuer and the PD_g denoting the PD of the credit guarantor/protection seller, the credit provision and capital charge are calculated with the following set of double default IRB formulas:

$$\text{CCC} \approx 0.12\left[1 + \exp\left(-50\text{PD}_o\right)\right] \qquad \text{or}$$

$$\text{CCC} \approx 0.12\left[1 + \exp\left(-50\text{PD}_o\right)\right] + \frac{S - 50}{1125} \quad \text{or}$$

$$\text{CCC} \approx 0.15\left[1 + \exp\left(-50\text{PD}_o\right)\right]$$

$$\text{XCDR} = \Phi\left[\frac{\Phi^{-1}\left(\text{PD}_o\right) + \Phi^{-1}\left(99.9\%\right)\sqrt{\text{CCC}}}{\sqrt{1 - \text{CCC}}}\right]$$

$$\text{XCL} = \text{EAD} \times \text{LGD} \times \text{XCDR}$$
$$\text{1-year EL} = \text{EAD} \times \text{LGD} \times \text{PD}_o$$
$$\text{UL} = \text{XCL} - \text{1-year EL}$$

$$b = \left\{0.11852 - 0.05478\ln\left[\text{Min}\left(\text{PD}_o, \text{PD}_g\right)\right]\right\}^2$$

$$\text{MAF} = \frac{1 + \left(\text{RM} - 2.5\right)b}{1 - 1.5b}$$
$$\text{DDF} = 0.15 + 160\text{PD}_g$$

$$\text{CP} = 0$$
$$\text{CC} = 1.06\text{UL} \times \text{MAF} \times \text{DDF}$$

$$\text{CCR} = \frac{\text{CC}}{\text{EAD}}$$

The credit provision is set artificially to zero, subject to the argument that the joint PD is extremely small in the situation where the double default framework is applied.

The double default framework will result in a capital charge lower than that calculated with the substitution framework only when both the debt issuer and credit guarantor/protection seller are subject to higher credit quality. To maximize the benefit of default insurance to the calculation of capital charge, a bank may calculate two capital charges by both the substitution and double default frameworks and select the smaller one as the final capital charge.

18.6.4 Currency and maturity mis-matches

In case the currency of a credit risk control is different from that of a debt, the protection to the debt is discounted by a currency haircut, in most cases, 8 percent.

In case the protection period of the credit risk control is shorter than the RM of the debt,

- for a debt with the RM longer than 0.25, the protected part of the debt is reduced to:

$$\text{EAD of the protected part without maturity mis-match} \times \frac{\text{Min}\left[\text{Protection period of credit risk control, 5}\right] - 0.25}{\text{Min}\left[\text{RM of debt, 5}\right] - 0.25}$$

- for a debt with the RM shorter than or equal to 0.25, the effect from the credit risk control is ignored simply.

18.7 Foundation IRB approach

The Basel III framework allows a bank to adopt a simplified version of the advanced IRB approach, referred to as the foundation IRB approach, under which the bank must estimate the PDs with its internal ratings system but the EAD, LGD and RM with a set of explicit regulatory rules set out in the Basel III framework. The foundation IRB approach facilitates as a transition stage for a bank to migrate to advanced IRB approach from standardized approach by focusing firstly on the development of the PD rating systems.

The major simplifications to the foundation IRB are described in the follow sections.

18.7.1 Exposure at default

Under the foundation IRB approach, the credit conversion factors for various types of commitments are set out in Table 18.2.

18.7.2 Loss given default

The LGD is set artificially to 45 percent and 75 percent for senior and subordinated debts respectively. In case a senior debt is supported with recognized collaterals, the LGD is revised according to a set of regulatory rules. Nevertheless, the LGD of a subordinated debt is always 75 percent, regardless whether it is supported by recognized collaterals.

	Type of commitment	CCF (%)
1.	Direct credit substitutes	100
2.	Transaction-related contingencies	50
3.	Trade-related contingencies	20
4.	Asset sales with recourse	100
5.	Forward asset purchases	100
6.	Partly paid-up securities	100
7.	Forward forward deposits placed	100
8.	Note issuance and revolving underwriting facilities	75
9.	Commitments that are unconditionally cancellable without prior notice	0
10.	Other commitments	75*

* Different from the standardized approach.

Table 18.2 Commitments and credit conversion factors

18.7.2.1 Financial collaterals

The financial collaterals recognized under the standardized approach are also recognized under the foundation IRB approach in accordance with the same set of collateral haircuts. With recognized financial collaterals, the LGD of a senior debt is reduced to:

$$45\% \times \frac{\text{Max}\left[\begin{array}{l}\text{EAD - Collateral value}\\ \times\ (1 - \text{Collateral haircut - Currency haircut}), 0\end{array}\right]}{\text{EAD}}$$

18.7.2.2 IRB collaterals

In addition to financial collaterals, subject to certain conditions, the foundation IRB approach also allows the following types of assets to be recognized as the IRB collaterals:

- financial receivables;
- real estate; and
- physical assets.

The LGD subject to recognized IRB collaterals is calculated by following simplified set of rules:

- A ratio C between the collateral value and the EAD is calculated;

- A lower bound C*, upper bound C** and collateral LGD are looked up from a table of recognized IRB collaterals;

- If C is less than C*, then the collateral value is small and the LGD without collateral 45% is used;

- If C is larger than C**, then the collateral value is large and the collateral LGD 35% or 40% is used; and

- If C is between C* and C**, then the collateral value is moderate and the effective LGD is interpolated as:

$$45\% \times \left(1 - \frac{C}{C^{**}}\right) + \text{Collateral LGD} \times \frac{C}{C^{**}}$$

	Lower bound C* (%)	Upper bound C** (%)	Collateral LGD (%)
Financial receivables	0	125	35
Real estate	30	140	35
Physical assets	30	140	40

Table 18.3   The IRB collaterals

18.7.3 Residual maturity

The RM is fixed to 2.5 years. Subject to the approval from its regulator, a bank may adopt a foundation IRB approach with the RMs estimated by the bank internally. This flexibility facilitates a bank with an overall shorter horizon of debt investments to reduce its total capital charge.

18.8   Credit provision

So far, two different credit provisions are calculated from two separate frameworks: the IFRS 9 and IRB approach. These two credit provisions are different due to the differences between the two underlying framework. While banking laws mandate that IFRS 9 take precedence, a bank must also treat its total credit provision calculated by the IRB approach as unrealized loss and the difference is handled with tier two capital. In case the capital charge calculated by the IRB approach is lower than that calculated by the IFRS 9, the bank must reduce the tier two capital by an amount equal to the difference. Conversely, if the capital charge calculated by the IRB approach is higher than that calculated by the IFRS 9, the bank should increase its tier two capital by the difference. The total surplus over total credit provision is capped at 7.5 percent of the total tier two capital.

18.9   Implementation of the IRB approach ★★★

Subject to the approval from its regulator, a bank may choose one of the four implementations to calculate its capital charges, taking into account the bank's own quantitative expertise versus the level of sophistication of each capital charge calculation approach.

Sophistication	Approach		Internal model	Regulatory rule
High	Retail IRB*	Advanced IRB	EAD, LGD, PD, RM	███████
Medium		Foundation IRB	PD, RM	EAD, LGD
			PD	EAD, LGD, RM
Low	Standardized			EAD, capital charge ratio

* The RM is not applicable to the retail IRB approach.

Table 18.4   Capital charge calculations

18.9.1 Benefits of the IRB approach ★★★

A comparison is made in Table 18.5 between the capital charge ratios calculated by the IRB and standardized approaches among different exposures, LGDs and credit qualities:

Exposure	LGD (%)	RM (yr)	Approach	AA (%)	A (%)	BBB (%)	BB (%)	B (%)
Retail	90	████	IRB	0.82	1.66	4.32	10.38	11.79
			Std.	6	6	6	6	6
Institution	45	1	IRB	0.70	1.39	3.52	8.84	12.95
			Std.	1.6	4	4	8	8
	75	1	IRB	1.16	2.32	5.86	14.73	21.58
			Std.	1.6	4	4	8	8

Table 18.5   Capital charge ratios calculated
by the IRB and standardized approaches

In general, for a bank investing in debts of higher credit quality, the IRB approach will result in less capital charge than the standardized approach, in particular, for retail exposures.

Moreover, a bank adopting the IRB approach also demonstrates to its stakeholders that the bank is equipped with the most advanced credit risk management expertise.

18.9.2 Internal ratings system

Although the PD of each debt issuer can be estimated directly by a quantitative model, in many practical situations, the PD is compared with the debt issuer's external credit rating (if available) and further reviewed by a specialist in order to capture the impacts from those qualitative factors that have not been incorporated in a quantitative model. After the specialist review, the debt issuer is assigned an internal credit rating associated with an average PD which is then applied to the IRB formulas. An internal credit rating scale should consist of at least seven grades for survival debt issuers. Benchmarking on the rating scale from major credit rating agencies, many banks design their internal credit rating scales in accordance with the definitions of the rating grades AAA to C (CCC, CC and C are combined into one rating) to form a seven-level internal credit rating scale or including modifiers + and - for the ratings between AA to B to form a nineteen-level internal credit rating scale.

A similar treatment is applied to the LGD. An LGD, after calculated by a quantitative model, is further reviewed by a specialist in order to capture the impacts from those qualitative factors that have not been incorporated in a quantitative model. This expert opinion, together with the LGD, facilitates a bank to assign a debt with an internal LGD rating that is equipped with an average LGD. This average LGD is then applied to the IRB formulas. In contrast to the internal credit rating scale, there is no minimum number of levels on internal LGD rating. In general, an internal LGD rating scale comprises two to six levels.

18.9.3 Capital charge engine

The complete Basel III framework for the calculations of credit provision and capital charge for credit risk is far more complicated than the descriptions in this book. In addition, the large number of debts in a bank makes the manual calculations of credit provision and capital charge extremely time consuming. Practically, a bank acquires an IRB capital charge engine which is a piece of application software specializing in the calculations of credit provision and capital charge. The capital charge engine is fed with, for each debt, the EAD, LGD, PD, RM and credit risk controls. The credit provisions and capital charges are then derived. Moreover, the final figures, together with the intermediate calculations, are formatted into some standard templates mandated by the bank's regulator.

Moody's Fermet, IBM Algorithmics' Algo Capital, SunGard's Basel III Capital Manager, SAS's Risk Management for Banking and Oracle's Basel III Reporting are the major capital charge engines serving many internationally active banks. They can be customized flexibly to match the localized requirements from national regulators in addition to the international standards set out in the Basel III Framework.

Regulatory IRB Validation

KEY CONCEPTS

- Model validation

- Regulatory validation

19.1 Model validation

Model validation is the process of assessing the accuracy of the estimates derived from a quantitative model, using historical data. For example, to assess the accuracy of a quantitative model which predicates the closing price of an equity on the next trading day, the model closing prices derived from the quantitative model are compared with the corresponding empirical closing prices observed from the equity market. If on most trading days, the model closing prices are close to the empirical closing prices, the quantitative model is considered to be accurate.

This assessment is formalized through statistical hypothesis testing:

Null hypothesis: Empirical closing price - Model closing price $= 0$
Alternative hypothesis: Empirical closing price - Model closing price $\neq 0$

With a sufficiently large size of samples and at a significantly high confidence level, if the alternative hypothesis is rejected, then the quantitative model may be adopted for production.

Banks using quantitative models to derive estimates of credit risk factors, in particular, the PD. Therefore, these quantitative models should be subject to similar statistical hypothesis testing in order to ensure that a bank can measure its credit risk with sufficient accuracy. Nevertheless, it is difficult to conduct statistical hypothesis testing of quantitative models which derive estimates of credit risk factors, primarily because:

- There is a lack of historical default records due to banks' conservative lending practices;

- Empirical default is a binary process (0 or 1) which cannot be used directly to validate a PD having any value between 0 and 1; and

- The empirical CCC is unobservable.

These limitations prevent the development of a rigorous and universal standard on model validation for credit risk factors. Regulators therefore adopt an alternative methodology, which comprises both qualitative and quantitative requirements, to assess whether a bank is technically competent to use the IRB approach to calculate the capital charge for credit risk. This mixed assessment process is referred to as the regulatory IRB validation.

19.2   Principles of regulatory IRB validation

In 2005, the Validation Subgroup of the BCBS's Accord Implementation Group published a paper which elaborated the concept of regulatory IRB validation in six principles:

- A bank has the primary responsibility for the regulatory IRB validation;

- Regulatory IRB validation is fundamentally about assessing the predictive ability of a bank's credit risk estimates and the use of ratings in credit processes;

- There is no single method of regulatory IRB validation;

- The regulatory IRB validation is an iterative process;

- The regulatory IRB validation should encompass both qualitative and quantitative elements; and

- The regulatory IRB validation processes and outcomes should be subject to independent review.

Nevertheless, many specific areas concerning the regulatory IRB validation remain unclear, and the public documents issued by most regulators in the major financial markets have taken the form of research studies, working papers and/or studies of practices adopted by the financial industry. Explicit guidance from regulators on the regulatory IRB validation remains outstanding. To address this issue, this chapter takes a more prescriptive approach to describe the regulatory IRB validation, with an aim to reduce the grey areas in the regulatory IRB validation process.

19.3   Components of the validation process

Broadly speaking, the regulatory IRB validation process seeks to demonstrate that a bank's IRB systems can deliver estimates of credit risk factors with sufficient accuracy. The BCBS believes that by satisfying certain qualitative and quantitative requirements around the IRB systems, these IRB systems are considered to be qualified.

19.3.1 Board and senior management oversight

A bank should place substantial emphasis on the systems and controls environment in which its IRB systems are developed, implemented and operated. In particular, an effective oversight by the bank's Board of Directors ("Board") and senior management is the key to sound IRB systems. Also the Board and senior management of the bank should be involved actively in the implementation of the IRB approaches, both before and after inception.

The Board should have a general understanding of the regulatory requirements for using the IRB approach and know how their bank proposes to meet such requirements according to a defined timeframe. In addition, the Board should be responsible for the approval of the key elements of the IRB systems, based on the information provided by the senior management who should have reviewed the technical aspects with support from internal experts and/or external specialists. The Board should also establish an effective Basel III project management framework and ensure that sufficient resources are provided to support this project management framework.

Similarly, a bank's senior management also have their specific roles and responsibilities in the implementation of the IRB systems. They are responsible for the day-to-day operations and therefore should have a good understanding of the design and operation of the IRB systems to ensure that these systems will work consistently and continually as intended. Some key responsibilities of the senior management include allocating and maintaining sufficient resources for the IRB implementation, delineating and assigning responsibilities and accountabilities to different functions of the bank, and ensuring sufficient training to the relevant staff. The senior management should also be responsible for making necessary changes to existing policies and procedures, including systems and controls, to ensure that the IRB systems can be integrated into the bank's credit risk management process and culture. The senior management need to ensure that the IRB systems will be used properly in the bank's decision making and monitoring of credit risk.

The senior management should also approve and track material deviations of actual practice from the established policies and review regularly the performance of the IRB systems through management information reports. They should meet regularly with relevant staff to discuss issues, such as the performance and operation of the IRB systems, and advise the Board on these issues as appropriate.

Because the regional and/or head offices of some international banks may lead the implementation of the IRB systems, certain oversight responsibilities may be taken up by the regional and/or head offices. However, in some areas, such as monitoring the progress of local implementation and ensuring that sufficient resources are allocated to the subsidiaries, local efforts must be made to meet the requirements.

19.3.2 Transparency

Transparency refers to the extent to which third parties, such as rating system reviewers, internal auditors, external auditors and regulators, are able to understand the design, operations and accuracy of a bank's IRB systems and evaluate whether the IRB systems are performing as intended. Transparency should be a continuing requirement and achieved through documentation. A bank should update its documentation in a timely manner when modifications are made to the IRB systems.

When a bank allows human judgements to override results derived from an algorithm, the overall IRB systems may become less transparent due to the personal experience and subjective assessments used in the overriding process. In these cases, the bank should offset the shortcomings of human judgement by certain compensating measures, including greater independency in the rating approval process and/or a strengthened system review.

19.3.3 Accountability

A bank should have policies in place to identify functions responsible for rating accuracy and rating system performance. The responsibilities, authority and reporting lines of the functions must be specific and defined clearly. Staff involved in particular aspects of the IRB systems, for example rating assignment, validation and annual review, must be held accountable for complying with the bank's relevant policies, ensuring that those aspects of the IRB systems under their control are unbiased and accurate.

A bank should also establish measurable performance standards for staff, with incentive compensation tied to these standards. For example, performance measures of personnel responsible for rating assignment may include the number and frequency of rating errors, significancy of errors and consistent application of rating criteria.

A bank using quantitative models to derive estimates of credit risk factors should maintain an up-to-date inventory of quantitative models and an accountability chart showing the roles of the functions within the bank responsible for the major aspects of the quantitative models, such as design, development, validation, use test, data entry and data checking.

A bank should also assign a specific staff at sufficiently senior level, for instance, the Chief Credit Risk Officer, to bear the responsibility for the overall performance of the IRB systems. This staff must ensure that the systems and their components, including rating assignments, estimation of risk factors, data collection, system controls and oversight mechanisms are functioning as intended. If these components are distributed across multiple functions within the bank, this staff will need to ensure that the parts work together effectively and efficiently.

19.3.4 Independency

Independency is another important element of a proper control mechanism for the IRB systems. A bank is required to have a sufficient level of independency in the rating approval process and in the review of the IRB systems and risk quantification.

To ensure objectivity and accuracy in the assignment of risk ratings, functions responsible for approving ratings and transactions must be independent of sales and marketing. For example, the credit risk officers responsible for rating approvals should have independent and separate functional reporting lines from sales and marketing staff. The bank should establish well defined performance measures for these credit risk officers, such as adherence to policies, rating accuracy and timeliness. For the cases where the rating assignment and approval processes are highly automated and do not involve human judgement, the bank should have at a minimum a process of verifying the accuracy and completeness of data inputs.

A bank should develop an independent system review process in which the reviewing functions are independent of the staff and management responsible for developing the IRB systems and performing risk quantification activities. Such review activities may be housed within one function of the bank or distributed across multiple functions in the bank.

For a bank which does not have sufficient in-house expertise to review its IRB systems, the bank may employ external specialists, such as consulting firms, to review the bank's IRB systems. In general, regulators prefer a bank to use external specialist reviewers even through the bank has equipped the necessary in-house skills and resources, as external specialist reviewers may have broader perspectives on reviewing the IRB systems in different institutions and jurisdictions, and may have more comprehensive data sets to conduct quantitative assessments on the IRB systems.

19.3.5 Data quality

Data quality is one of the most important issues for a bank using the IRB approach, especially with the extensive use of model based rating systems. The requirements cover the management oversight and control regarding data quality, technology infrastructure and data architecture, data collection, storage, retrieval and deletion, reconciliation between the IRB and finance data, and other data processing aspects such as data checking and cleansing. In addition, the bank should conduct independent assessment of data quality at least annually, for example, by the internal audit function.

A bank may use external and/or pooled data in rating system development and validation, rating assignment and risk quantification, and has therefore also stipulated requirements on this. For example, the bank needs to check the external and/or pooled data against multiple sources, and regularly evaluate the appropriateness of the continuing use of external and/or pooled data.

A bank often applies statistical techniques, such as sampling, smoothing and sample truncation, when preparing data for rating system development, validation and/or in production. Missing data is another critical practical issue that the bank has to deal with.

19.3.6 Use test

The BCBS stipulates in its technical paper that for a bank using the IRB approach to calculate its capital charge for credit risk, the internal ratings and default loss estimates must play an essential role in the credit approval, risk management, capital allocation and corporate governance functions. Specifically, the internal ratings and risk estimates are expected to be used for pricing, individual limit setting, portfolio limit setting, assessment of risk appetite, formulating business strategies, monitoring of higher risk borrowers, reporting of credit risk information for review by the Board and senior management, determining credit provisions, and assessment against profitability and performance targets.

Regulators understand that the scope of use test will be limited during the first few years of implementing the IRB approaches. Therefore, during the first few years, a bank may focus on its overall usage of internal ratings and default loss estimates, rather than the comprehensive use of internal rating systems in all major areas. As a minimum, a bank should demonstrate the use of internal ratings in at least three areas: credit approval, credit monitoring and reporting of credit risk information to the Board and senior management. In addition, a bank should have a timeline for extending the internal usage to the preponderance of the other areas specified, taking into account the bank's specific circumstances. A bank should develop a plan for internal implementation, subject to the approval from the Board or senior management and the agreement from its regulator.

Compliance with the use test does not mean that a bank has to use exactly the same estimates for both capital charge calculation and all internal operation purposes. Where such differences exist, the bank should document them and demonstrate their reasonableness to the regulator. The bank should justify the differences and demonstrate the consistency of both inputs, including rating criteria and risk factors, and outputs, such as ratings and risk estimates, between the internal ratings and risk estimates of credit risk factors for capital charge calculation and those for the bank's internal operation purposes. The bank should also provide qualitative and quantitative analysis of the logic and rationale for the differences. The justification needs to be reviewed by the bank's credit risk control unit and approved by the senior management.

Some banks may maintain more than one rating model for the same portfolio, for example, one for capital charge calculation and another one for benchmarking. In these situations, the bank should justify the application of a specific model to a specific purpose and the role they have assigned to that model in their credit risk management process. Nonetheless, in assessing whether the use test requirement for an IRB system has been met, consideration should be put on the extent to which a bank uses the system as a whole, rather than applying the use test to individual models.

19.3.7 Benchmarking

Benchmarking is widely used in the regulatory IRB validation. If designed and implemented properly, benchmarking can be a useful validation tool to assure both a bank and its regulator that the bank's IRB systems are likely to be accurate. Nevertheless, benchmarking can take a wide variety of forms, and a standard or common methodology has yet to emerge in the industry.

A bank should obtain benchmarks from third parties, provided that external benchmarks are relevant to their portfolios. The bank should provide justification and have compensating measures, such as back testing at a higher frequency, if they do not use external benchmarks despite their availability.

Where a relevant benchmark cannot be obtained externally, for example, the public benchmark for retail exposures, a bank should develop its benchmarks internally. For example, the bank may use the estimates derived by an old quantitative model to benchmark against those derived by a new quantitative model.

19.3.8 Frequency

A bank should conduct its regulatory IRB validation at least annually, echoing the BCBS's principle that the regulatory IRB validation is an iterative process. Taking into account the industry practice, the bank may conduct a rolling regulatory IRB validation exercise for individual portfolios or components of an IRB system, depending on the design of the bank's regulatory IRB validation programme, provided that the arrangement is justified by valid operational considerations and approved by senior management, and the validation cycle for each portfolio or each component of an IRB system is initiated no more than 12 months and finished no more than 18 months after the completion of the previous cycle.

19.3.9 Internal and external audit functions

The internal and external audit functions have a specific role in the regulatory IRB validation. The internal audit function should review at least annually a bank's IRB systems, including the validation process and the operations of the related credit risk control unit, and report the findings to the Board and senior management.

The internal audit review aims to verify whether the control mechanisms over the IRB systems are functioning as intended. The internal audit function should give an opinion on the continuing appropriateness, relevance and comprehensiveness of the bank's control mechanisms, including the adequacy of staff expertise and resources available to the credit risk control unit.

The internal audit function should verify whether the bank adheres to all the regulatory requirements for using the IRB approach. If independency in the review of the IRB systems and risk quantification cannot be otherwise achieved, the bank's internal audit function needs to scrutinize the whole regulatory IRB validation exercise, including evaluation of the model assumptions, rating algorithms and statistical modelling techniques, and back testing the quantitative models. In this case, the bank's internal audit function will need to be staffed by personnel with sufficient expertise and be supported with adequate resources.

A regulator will evaluate whether the skill sets of internal audit staff and resources have been strengthened suitably, and whether the scope of the annual audit plan has been broadened to include verification of the bank's compliance with the regulatory requirements.

External audit function should assess whether a bank's IRB systems are measuring credit risk appropriately and the capital charges are fairly presented. The external audit function should also seek to assure themselves that the bank's internal controls relating to capital charge calculations comply with the relevant regulatory requirements.

19.3.10 Stress testing

Stress testing does not have direct implications on the performance of an IRB system. Nevertheless, since the BCBS mandates in its technical paper that a bank must have in place sound stress testing processes for use in the assessment of capital adequacy, a bank should demonstrate that its IRB approach can meet this requirement.

In the context of the regulatory IRB validation, certain aspects of stress testing are particularly important, including among others, adequacy of the stress tests in relation to the complexity and level of risks of a bank's activities, appropriateness of the assumptions, oversight by the Board and senior management, and relevance to the bank's current portfolios and prevailing socioeconomic and political conditions.

19.3.11 Quantitative requirements

When a bank applies quantitative techniques to validate the accuracy of the quantitative models which derive the estimates of credit risk factors, the application procedures and assumptions must be documented and applied consistently. A bank should establish internal standards and/or thresholds. Breaches of these standards and/or thresholds should trigger appropriate responses which may range from higher validation frequency to re-development of the rating systems. The internal standards and/or thresholds and responses may vary among different banks, as they should be commensurate with the potential impact on individual banks' financial soundness if the IRB systems perform poorly. Therefore, the bank should take account of factors such as the size of the relevant portfolios, the risk appetite relating to the portfolios and the inherent risk characteristics of the portfolios when setting the bank's own standards or thresholds and responses.

19.3.12 PD validation

Since the PD acts the most important credit risk factor, the PD validation is equipped with further specific requirements. In summary, there are two stages when validating the accuracy of the PD and each stage is equipped with its own quantitative techniques.

When a bank validates the discriminatory power of the PD, the following quantitative techniques should be used:

- Cumulative accuracy profile and Gini coefficient;
- Receiver operating characteristic, receiver operating characteristic measure and Pietra Index;
- Bayesian error rate;
- Entropy measures (e.g., conditional information entropy ratio);
- Information value;
- Kendall's Tau and Somers' D;
- Brier score; and
- Divergence.

When a bank validates the calibration of an internal rating system, the following quantitative techniques should be used:

- Binomial test with a zero CCC;
- Binomial test with a CCC calculated by one of the six CCC formulas; and
- Chi-square test.

A bank may use quantitative techniques other than those shortlisted above, such as proprietary or customized tests. However, the bank needs to demonstrate that the chosen techniques are theoretically sound, well documented and applied consistently. This arrangement provides sufficient flexibility to avoid stifling further development and innovation in quantitative validation techniques.

19.3.13 External vendor models

A bank may commission external vendors to develop quantitative models for its use in the IRB approach. In this situation, the use of external vendor models should be considered as an outsourced activity and the bank should follow the relevant guidelines on outsourcing which cover such issues as a bank's accountability for and control over the outsourced activities. The transparency of vendor models and their links with a bank's internal information will be the focus of the regulatory IRB validation. Therefore, detailed information should be well prepared.

Regardless of the support provided by the vendors, a bank should have the in-house knowledge to understand the key aspects of the models, including model development, validation, use test and limitations. The bank also needs to possess sufficient in-house expertise to support and assess these models on a continuing basis. In addition, adequate training must be provided to staff using these models.

Regulatory Credit Exposures

KEY CONCEPTS

- Debt exposure
- Securitization exposure
- Specialized lending
- Securities finance transaction

20.1   Credit exposures

In banking businesses, the majority of credit risk arises from debt exposures. In addition, credit risk may also be resulted from credit derivatives. They are collectively referred to as credit exposures and subject to capital charge for credit risk.

Exposure	On balance sheet	Off balance sheet (short position)
Debt	Loan	Credit guarantee
	Bond	Single name CDS
	CLN	Basket CDS
	Commitment – drawdown amount	Commitment – undrawn amount
Securitization	CDO	Portfolio CDS

Table 20.1   Major credit exposures

20.2   Debt exposures

Throughout this book, many descriptions have been focused on debt exposures which comprise loans, bonds, CLNs and commitments.

A loan is a private lending placement between a lender and a borrower. The lender and borrower maintain a relationship from the origination to the full repayment of the loan. A bond is a financial instrument issued by an institution for medium to longer term fund raising. The ownership of a bond is free to transfer among investors. Both loan and bond are classified as assets to be registered on the balance sheet. A CLN is also classified as a debt exposure registered on the balance sheet since it works similarly to the worst performer of a basket of reference debts.

A commitment is a promise from a lender to lend up to a certain amount. The drawdown amount of a commitment is treated as a loan. The undrawn amount is subject to the potential withdrawal from a borrower and may result in a default loss in the future. Therefore, both the drawdown and undrawn amounts contribute credit risk and are treated as two debt exposures, with the drawdown amount registered on the balance sheet and the undrawn amount registered off the balance sheet.

The short position in a single name CDS is largely equivalent to the long position in a debt and the short position in a risk-free security. In case a bank acts as a protection seller to issue a single name CDS, the bank is subject to the credit risk of the reference debt. Therefore, the short position in a single name CDS is classified as a debt exposure.

Similarly, the short position in an NTD CDS is largely equivalent to the long position in an NTD reference debt among the members in a debt basket and the short position in a risk-free security. In case a bank acts as a protection seller to issue an NTD CDS, the bank is subject to the credit risk of the NTD reference debt. Therefore, the short position in a basket CDS is classified as a debt exposure.

A credit guarantee offered by a credit guarantor works in a way similar to a single name CDS and is also classified as a debt exposure. The short positions in single name CDS, basket CDS and credit guarantee are classified as off balance sheet items.

20.3   Securitization exposure

A securitization exposure is a financial instrument constructed through credit structuring where the cash flows are generated from:

- an underlying debt portfolio; or
- short positions in portfolio CDSs and long positions in top quality assets that deliver steady cash flows at an extremely high certainty.

These combinations are utilized to service at least two tranches with different degrees of credit risk. By definition, cash flow CDO and synthetic CDO are securitization exposures. A CLN is not a securitization exposure because it exhibits only single level of credit risk.

20.3.1 Capital charge calculations

Under the Basel III framework, a bank investing in a securitization exposure must calculate the relevant capital charge and hold sufficient regulatory capital against the capital charge.

A bank using standardized approach to calculate the capital charges of its debts is mandated to use the standardized approach to calculate the capital charges of its securitization exposures.

A bank using the IRB approach to calculate the capital charges of its debts may choose to use the standardized approach or, subject to the approval from its regulator, ratings based approach to calculate the capital charges of its securitization exposures.

20.3.2 Standardized approach ★★★

Under the standardized approach, the capital charge of a securitization exposure is calculated as the arithmetic product of the principal less specific provision and capital charge ratio.

Capital charge = (Principal - Specific provision) × Capital charge ratio

The capital charge ratio is assigned in accordance with the CDO rating. These capital charge ratios are exhibited in Table 20.2.

CDO rating	Capital charge (%)
AAA	1.6
AA	1.6
A	4
BBB	8
BB	28
Others	100

Table 20.2   Capital charge ratios for standardized approach

If a securitization exposure is rated differently by several credit rating agencies and results in:

- two different capital charge ratios, the larger capital charge ratio is adopted; or
- more than two capital charge ratios, the second smallest capital charge ratio is adopted.

20.3.3 Ratings based approach ★★★

Under the ratings based approach, the capital charge of a securitization exposure is calculated as the arithmetic product of the principal and capital charge ratio.

Capital charge = Principal × Capital charge ratio

The capital charge ratio is assigned in accordance with the CDO rating with modifier, granularity and seniority. These capital charge ratios are exhibited in Table 20.3.

The granularity of a securitization exposure is determined by the effective number of debts in the underlying portfolio, calculated as:

$$\frac{\text{Portfolio EAD}^2}{\sum_{k=1}^{\text{No. of debts in the underlying portfolio}} \text{EAD}_k^2} \quad \text{or} \quad \frac{\text{Portfolio EAD}}{\text{The largest EAD of the underlying debts}}$$

If the effective number of debts in the portfolio is greater than or equal to six, then the securitization exposure is considered as granular. Otherwise, it is considered as concentrated.

If a securitization exposure is rated differently by several credit rating agencies and results in:

- two different capital charge ratios, the larger capital charge ratio is adopted; or
- more than two capital charge ratios, the second smallest capital charge ratio is adopted.

CDO rating with modifier	Capital charge ratio (%)		
	Granular and senior[42]	Subordinate[43] and granular	Concentrated
AAA	0.56	0.96	1.60
AA+, AA, AA-	0.64	1.20	2.00
A+	0.80	1.44	2.80
A	0.96	1.60	
A-	1.60	2.80	
BBB+	2.80	4	
BBB	4.80	6	
BBB-	8		
BB+	20		
BB	34		
BB-	52		
Others	100		

Table 20.3   Capital charge ratios for ratings based approach

20.3.4 Portfolio CDS

The short position in a portfolio CDS is largely equivalent to the long position in a CDO tranche and the short position in a risk-free security. In case a bank acts as a protection seller to issue a portfolio CDS, the bank is subject to the credit risk of the debts in the reference portfolio. Therefore, the short position in a portfolio CDS is classified as a securitization exposure and is registered off the balance sheet. The capital charge is calculated in accordance with the long position in a CDO tranche.

---

[42] The most senior tranche in a CDO family.
[43] Any tranche having seniority lower than the most senior tranche in a CDO family is classified as a subordinated tranche.

20.4 Extensions to standardized approach

Under the standardized approach, the capital charge ratios in Tables 17.3 and 17.4 are applied to:

- retail exposures, including residential mortgages, qualifying revolving retail exposures and other retail exposures; and
- institution exposures, including debts issued by corporations, banks and countries.

In addition, some specific capital charge ratios are set out for debts issued by a:

- securities firm, which is a financial institution licensed by a country's securities authority to provide securities services to its customers;

- public sector entity, which is an institution having a close relationship with the domestic government and providing critical services to the society on behalf of the domestic government for the interests of the general public. These services include, among others, infrastructure, transportation, healthcare and education. To maintain consistency, each national bank regulator sets out explicitly a list of public sector entities in its regulatory rules; and

- sovereign foreign public sector entity, which is an institution incorporated and owned by a foreign country government to undertake commercial activities on behalf of the foreign country in other countries, e.g., to promote trading and tourism. To maintain consistency, each national bank regulator sets out explicitly a list of sovereign foreign public sector entities in its regulatory rules.

Rating	Securities firm (%)	Public sector entity (%)	Sovereign foreign	Investment fund (%)
AAA	1.6	1.6	0	1.6
AA	1.6	1.6	0	1.6
A	4	4	1.6	4
BBB	8	8	4	8
BB	8			
B	12	8	8	8
CCC to C	12			
Unrated	8			

Table 20.4   Specific capital charge ratios

A bank may also invest in an investment fund which consolidates monies from many participants to invest in a large portfolio of assets. This investment fund is also subject to the credit risk of the component assets. Therefore, a specific set of capital charge ratios are set out for an investment fund in accordance with its credit rating assigned by an ECAI.

These specific capital charge ratios for securities firm, public sector entity, sovereign foreign public sector entity and investment fund are listed in Table 20.4.

A multilateral development bank ("MDB") is an institution created by a group of countries to provide financing and professional advising for the purpose of economic development. The MDBs have large memberships, including both developed lender countries and developing borrower countries. The MDBs finance projects in the form of long term loans at market rates, very long term loans below market rates and through grants.

The major MDBs include:

- International Bank for Reconstruction and Development;
- International Development Association;
- International Finance Corporation;
- International Finance Facility for Immunization;
- European Bank for Reconstruction and Development;
- European Investment Bank;
- European Investment Fund;
- Council of Europe Development Bank;
- Asian Development Bank;
- African Development Bank;
- Nordic Investment Bank;
- Inter-American Development Bank;
- Caribbean Development Bank;
- Islamic Development Bank; and
- Multilateral Investment Guarantee Agency.

An MDB is assigned a capital charge ratio 0 percent.

Other performing debts not covered by any one of the above categories are assigned a capital charge ratio 8 percent. A debt overdue for less than ninety days is assigned a capital charge ratio 12 percent.

When a bank invests in the equity of a corporation, the default of the corporation will result in a loss to the bank. Therefore, an equity investment is also subject to the capital charge for credit risk. Under the standardized approach, the capital charge ratio for investments in the equity of a corporation is simply 100%.

20.5   Extensions to the IRB approach

Under the IRB approach, the capital charge calculations described in Chapter 18 are applied to:

- retail exposures, including residential mortgages, qualifying revolving retail exposures and other retail exposures; and
- institution exposures, including debts issued by corporations, banks and countries.

In contrast to the standardized approach, under the IRB approach, these capital charge calculations are also applicable to:

- a securities firm, which is treated as an institution or a large financial institution;
- a public sector entity, which is treated as an institution;
- a sovereign foreign public sector entity, which is treated as an institution; and
- a multilateral development bank, which is treated as an institution.

When a bank invests in the equity of a corporation, the default of the corporation will result in a loss to the bank. Therefore, an equity investment is also subject to the capital charge for credit risk which is calculated with the following set of simplified IRB treatments to the credit risk factors:

- The EAD is set to the market value of the equity. In case the market value of the equity is unavailable, the EAD is set to the cost of the equity;
- The LGD is set artificially to 90 percent;
- The PD is set to the PD of the corporation issuing the equity; and
- The RM is set artificially to five years.

A debt not covered by any one of the above categories is assigned a capital charge ratio 8 percent.

20.6   Specialized lending

Specialized lending is a loan lent to a special purpose entity ("SPE") incorporated for certain particular financial and operational purposes. The SPE is created specifically to own and/or operate a particular group of assets. In other words, the SPE has little or no other material assets and activities. The lender who lends to the SPE has a substantial degree of control over that particular group of assets and the income generated from that particular group of assets. The primary source of repayment of the loan is the income generated by that particular group of assets instead of the income generated by the SPE.

There are five major types of specialized lending:

- High volatility commercial real estate lending: High volatility commercial real estate lending is the financing of commercial real estate that exhibits higher loss rate volatility compared to other types of specialized lending. High volatility commercial real estate lending includes:

a. Commercial real estate loans secured by properties that are categorized by a national supervisor as sharing higher volatilities in portfolio default rates;

b. Loans financing any of the land acquisition, development and construction phases for properties in such jurisdictions; and

c. Loans financing the land acquisition, development and construction phases of any other properties where the source of repayment at origination of the loan is either the future uncertain sale of the property or cash flows whose source of repayment is substantially uncertain. For example, the property has not yet been leased to the occupancy rate prevailing in that geographic market for that type of commercial real estate unless the borrower has substantial equity at risk;

- Project finance: Project finance refers to a method of funding in which a lender looks primarily to the revenue generated by a single project, both as the source of repayment of and collateral for the loan. Project finance is usually for large, complex and expensive establishments that may include, for example, power plants, chemical processing plants, mines, transportation infrastructure and telecommunications infrastructure. It may take the form of financing of the construction of a new establishment or refinancing of an existing establishment. The borrower is usually an SPE established for the purpose of the project that is not permitted to perform any function other than developing, owning and operating the establishment. The consequence is that repayment depends primarily on the project's cash flows (such as electricity sold by a power plant) and on the collateral value of the project's assets.

- Object finance: Object finance refers to a method of funding the acquisition of physical assets, e.g., taxis, buses, ships, aircrafts and satellites, where the repayment of the loan is dependent on the cash flows generated by the assets that have been financed, pledged and assigned to the lender. A primary source of these cash flows may be rental or lease contracts with one or several third parties.

- Commodities finance: Commodities finance refers to a structured short term lending to finance reserves, inventories or receivables of exchange traded commodities, e.g., metals, energy and agricultural products, where the loan will be repaid from the proceeds of the sale of the commodities and the borrower has no other sources of income for loan repayment. This is the case when the borrower has no other activities and no other material assets. The structured nature of the financing is designed to compensate for the low credit quality of the borrower. The credit risk of the loan reflects its self-liquidating nature and the lender's skill in structuring the transaction instead of the credit quality of the borrower. Such lending can be distinguished from the loans financing the reserves, inventories or receivables of other more diversified borrowers where the lender is able to assess the credit quality of these regular borrowers based on their broader on-going operations.

- Income producing real estate: Income producing real estate refers to a method of funding to finance real estate, such as office buildings, retail shops, residential buildings, industrial premises, warehouse premises and hotels, where the prospects for repayment and recovery on the loan depend primarily on the cash flows generated from the asset. The primary source of these cash flows would generally be lease or rental payments or the sale of the asset. The distinguishing characteristic of income producing real estate versus other loans that are collateralized by real estate is the strong positive correlation between the prospects for repayment of the loan and the prospects for recovery in the event of default, both depending primarily on the cash flows generated by a property.

Most SPEs have no credit rating. Therefore, under the standardized approach, specialized lending is subject to a capital charge ratio 8 percent. Nevertheless, the specialized lending imposes a challenge to the IRB approach because the functional purposes of individual SPEs are unique and the financial structures of most SPEs are extremely complicated. All quantitative credit assessment techniques fail to produce a PD for an SPE. Therefore, under the IRB approach, those IRB formulas cannot be applied. Instead, a specialized lending is first classified into four supervisory grades:[44] strong, good, satisfactory and weak, and a credit provision ratio and a capital charge ratio are assigned to the specialized lending in accordance with the type of specialized lending and supervisory grades, as depicted in Table 20.5.

Ratio	Supervisory grade	Equivalent credit rating	HVCREL (%)	Others (%)
Credit provision	Strong	BBB- or above	0.4	0.4
	Good	BB+ or BB	0.4	0.8
	Satisfactory	BB- or B+	2.8	2.8
	Weak	B or below	8.0	8.0
Capital charge	Strong	BBB- or above	7.6	5.6
	Good	BB+ or BB	9.6	7.2
	Satisfactory	BB- or B+	11.2	9.2
	Weak	B or below	20.0	20.0

Table 20.5   Credit provision and capital charge ratios for specialized lending

The credit provision and capital charge are then calculated as:

Credit provision = EAD × Credit provision ratio
Capital charge = EAD × Capital charge ratio

---

[44] The supervisory grading criteria are set out in Annex 6 of the BCBS guideline "International Convergence of Capital Measurement and Capital Standards," 2006.

20.7   Securities finance transactions

A securities finance transaction is an arrangement for a bank to exchange with its counterparty, on a short term basis,

- an amount of cash, with a liquidly traded financial asset as collateral;
- a liquidly traded financial asset, with cash as collateral; or
- a liquidly traded financial asset, with another liquidly traded financial asset as collateral.

These two parties exchange the cash and/or financial asset at origination and return the cash and/or financial asset to each other at maturity.

Frequently, a securities finance transaction is originated with equal value of cash and/or financial asset exchanged. Since the financial asset is actively traded in the market, the financial asset is marked to market frequently and a regular re-balancing with margin is arranged such that the values of cash and/or financial asset exchanged are largely equal throughout the life of the transaction.

For a securities finance transaction, the Basel III framework adopts the generic principles that:

- The cash delivered temporarily to the counterparty acts similar to a short term loan arrangement. It is supported by the financial asset received from counterparty as collateral; and

- The financial asset delivered temporarily to the counterparty will be returned to the bank in a short period of time. The bank that originally owns the financial asset will continue to be subject to its credit risk.

A bank should incorporate the above generic principles when calculating the capital charge for securities financial transactions.

Agreement	Item delivered to counterparty	
	Cash	Financial asset
Repurchase		*
Reverse repurchase	*	
Securities lending		*
Securities borrowing	*	*
Margin lending	*	

Table 20.6   Securities finance transactions

The most popular securities finance transactions are in the form of repurchase agreement, reverse repurchase agreement, securities lending agreement, securities borrowing agreement and margin lending agreement. They are subject to the following treatments when their capital charges are calculated.

20.7.1 Repurchase agreement

With a repurchase agreement, a bank sells a financial asset to a counterparty in exchange for cash with a commitment to purchase the financial asset at an agreed price on an agreed future date from the counterparty. Essentially, a repurchase agreement is equivalent to cash borrowing with a financial asset as collateral. For a repurchase agreement, a bank should treat the financial asset sold and to be repurchased as the bank's own asset and include it in the calculation of capital charge for credit risk.

20.7.2 Reverse repurchase agreement

With a reverse repurchase agreement, a bank acquires a financial asset from a counterparty by cash, with a commitment to sell the financial asset at an agreed price on an agreed future date to the counterparty. Essentially, a reverse repurchase agreement is equivalent to cash lending with a financial asset as collateral. Therefore, the bank should treat the reverse repurchase agreement as a loan with the financial asset acquired and to be sold as collateral and calculate the relevant capital charge for credit risk.

20.7.3 Securities lending agreement

With a securities lending agreement, a bank lends a financial asset to a counterparty with cash and/or other financial asset as collateral from the counterparty. For such agreement, a bank should treat the financial asset lent as its own asset and include it in the calculation of capital charge for credit risk.

20.7.4 Securities borrowing agreement

With a securities borrowing agreement, a bank borrows a financial asset from a counterparty with cash and/or another financial asset as collateral to the counterparty.

If cash is used as collateral, the bank should treat the securities borrowing transaction as a lending transaction with the borrowed financial asset as collateral and calculate the relevant capital charge for credit risk.

If another financial asset is used as collateral, the bank should treat the financial asset put forwards as collateral as the bank's own asset and include it in the calculation of capital charge for credit risk.

20.7.5 Margin lending agreement

With a margin lending agreement, a bank lends to a counterparty with a financial asset and margin as collateral from the counterparty. A bank should treat a margin lending agreement as a short term loan supported by liquid collateral.

20.7.6 Residual maturity

The RM of a securities finance transaction is subject to a floor of five days and a cap of five years when the capital charge is calculated with the advanced IRB approach. The RM is set artificially to six months when the capital charge is calculated with the foundation IRB approach.

20.7.7 Bilateral netting

It is often for two banks to enter a number of securities finance transactions with each other as counterparty. To minimize the credit risk and capital charge, these two banks may enter a bilateral netting agreement which allows the cash and financial assets to offset among themselves at the default of either counterparty. Under the bilateral netting agreement, the delivered cash and financial asset are treated as loans, and the received cash and financial asset are treated as collaterals. These loans and collaterals are allowed conditionally to offset with each other and result in a net EAD.

$$
\text{Net EAD} = \text{Max} \left[\begin{array}{l} \sum \text{Market value of cash and financial asset delivered} \\[4pt] - \sum \text{Market value of cash and financial asset received} \\[4pt] + \sum \left(\begin{array}{l} \text{Absolute value of net position in same financial asset} \\ \times \text{ Supervisory haircut} \end{array} \right) \\[10pt] + \sum \left(\begin{array}{l} \text{Absolute value of net position in a currency} \\ \text{different from settlement currency} \\ \times \text{ Currency haircut} \end{array} \right) \end{array} \, , \, 0 \right]
$$

The supervisory haircuts follow those in Table 17.5 and the currency haircut is set to 8 percent in most cases.

Under the advanced IRB approach, the effective RM is calculated as the equivalent cash inflow weighted RM of the set of securities finance transactions subject to bilateral netting:

$$
\text{Effective RM} = \frac{\sum_{k=1}^{N} \left(\text{Equivalent cash inflow}_k \times \text{RM}_k \right)}{\sum_{k=1}^{N} \text{Equivalent cash inflow}_k}
$$

where the equivalent cash inflow is either the actual cash flow to be received or the market value of the financial asset to be received. In addition, if the effective RM is below five days, it is adjusted upwards to five days. If the effective RM is above five years, it is adjusted downwards to five years.

Appendix 20.1   Supervisory formula approach

For an unrated CDO tranche where the details of the credit risk factors of the underlying debt portfolio are available, subject to the approval from its regulator, a bank may calculate the capital charge of the entire CDO tranche as the arithmetic product of the total principal of the underlying debt portfolio and a capital charge ratio. This capital charge ratio is derived from a set of supervisory formulas based on the "uncertainty in the loss prioritization model" proposed by Gordy and Jones in 2003. The capital charge of an investment as a fraction of the entire CDO tranche is then allocated on prorate basis, i.e.:

$$\text{Tranche capital charge} = \text{Total principal of underlying debt portfolio} \times \text{Capital charge ratio of the entire CDO tranche}$$

$$\text{Capital charge} = \text{Tranche capital charge} \times \frac{\text{Invested CDO principal}}{\text{Total principal of the entire CDO tranche}}$$

(A)   Portfolio parameters

To apply the supervisory formula approach, there are three portfolio parameters that must be determined, subject to the availability of level of details and certain criteria of the underlying portfolio. These three portfolio parameters are the effective LGD, effective number of debts in the underlying portfolio N and scaled RM-year XCL rate K_{IRB}.

(i)   When the following criteria are satisfied:

- The portfolio EAD of the underlying debts is available;
- The EAD of the largest debt in the underlying portfolio is available and less than or equal to 3 percent of the portfolio EAD; and
- The debts in the underlying portfolio are subject to a single average PD,

the LGD of the debts in the underlying portfolio is set to 50 percent and the effective number of debts in the underlying portfolio N is calculated as:

$$N = \frac{\text{Portfolio EAD}}{\text{The largest EAD in the underlying debts}}$$

Then

$$XCL = \text{Portfolio EAD} \times LGD \times XCDR$$
$$SXCL = 1.06XCL \times MAF$$

$$K_{IRB} = \frac{SXCL}{Portfolio\ EAD}$$

(ii)   When the following criteria are satisfied:

- The portfolio EAD of the underlying debts is available;
- The EADs of the largest Q debts in the underlying portfolio are available;
- The EAD of the largest debt in the underlying portfolio is less than or equal to 3 percent of the portfolio EAD; and
- The debts in the underlying portfolio are subject to a single average PD,

the LGD of the debts in the underlying portfolio is set to 50 percent and the effective number of debts in the underlying portfolio N is calculated as:

$$C_1 = \frac{EAD\ of\ the\ largest\ debt\ in\ the\ underlying\ portfolio}{Portfolio\ EAD}$$

$$C_Q = \frac{Sum\ of\ EADs\ of\ the\ largest\ Q\ debts\ in\ the\ underlying\ portfolio}{Portfolio\ EAD}$$

$$N = \frac{1}{C_1 C_Q + \dfrac{\left(C_Q - C_1\right)Max\left(1 - QC_1, 0\right)}{Q - 1}}$$

Then

$$XCL = Portfolio\ EAD \times LGD \times XCDR$$
$$SXCL = 1.06XCL \times MAF$$

$$K_{IRB} = \frac{SXCL}{Portfolio\ EAD}$$

(iii)   When the EAD, LGD, PD and RM of all M individual debts in the underlying portfolio are available, the effective LGD is calculated as the EAD weighed average LGD of the debts in the underlying portfolio, i.e.:

$$LGD = \frac{\sum_{k=1}^{M}\left(EAD_k \times LGD_k\right)}{\sum_{k=1}^{M} EAD_k}$$

and the effective number of debts in the underlying portfolio N is calculated as:

$$N = \frac{\left(\sum_{k=1}^{M} EAD_k\right)^2}{\sum_{k=1}^{M} EAD_k^2}$$

Then

$$XCL_k = EAD_k \times LGD_k \times XCDR_k$$
$$SXCL_k = 1.06 XCL_k \times MAF_k$$

$$K_{IRB} = \frac{\sum_{k=1}^{M} XCL_k}{\sum_{k=1}^{M} EAD_k}$$

(B) Capital charge ratio

Given the tranche attachment point TAP and tranche detachment point TDP of a CDO tranche, with the above three portfolio parameters, the capital charge ratio of the entire CDO tranche can be derived from the following set of supervisory formulas.

$$h = \left(1 - \frac{K_{IRB}}{LGD}\right)^N$$

$$c = \frac{K_{IRB}}{1 - h}$$

$$v = \frac{K_{IRB}\left(LGD - K_{IRB} + \frac{1 - LGD}{4}\right)}{N}$$

$$f = \frac{v + K_{IRB}^2}{1 - h} + \frac{K_{IRB} - K_{IRB}^2 - v}{1000(1 - h)} - c^2$$

$$g = \frac{c - c^2}{f} - 1$$

$$a = gc$$

$$b = g - gc$$

$$d = h + Beta\left(K_{IRB};a,b\right) - h \times Beta\left(K_{IRB};a,b\right)$$

$$K[x] = (1 - h)\left\{x\left[1 - Beta\left(x;a,b\right)\right] + c \times Beta\left(x;a+1,b\right)\right\}$$

If $x > K_{IRB}$

$$S[x] = K_{IRB} + K[x] - K[K_{IRB}] + \frac{dK_{IRB}}{20}\left\{1 - \exp\left[\frac{20(K_{IRB} - x)}{K_{IRB}}\right]\right\}$$

If $x \leq K_{IRB}$

$$S[x] = x$$

Capital charge ratio $= \text{Max}\{0.0056(TDP - TAP), S[TDP] - S[TAP]\}$

Beta(x;a,b) is the cumulative beta distribution function with shape parameters a and b where x is between 0 and 1.

$$\text{Beta}(x;a,b) = \frac{\int_0^x \tau^{a-1}(1-\tau)^{b-1}\,d\tau}{\int_0^1 \tau^{a-1}(1-\tau)^{b-1}\,d\tau}$$

This function is available in Microsoft Excel as Betadist(…).

Although the supervisory formula approach is highly sophisticated, its applicability is very limited. It is a rare situation where a bank invests in a CDO tranche without a CDO rating assigned by any one of the major global credit rating agencies. A bank that sets up an SPE to originate a CDO family may acquire the unrated equity tranche of the CDO family but such equity tranche must be subject to a capital charge ratio 100 percent without any computation going through the supervisory formulas.

Passwords to open the Excel work example zipped files from the book website:

Part	Password
1	6121947440443012
2	8620816912952548
3	9841890562804059
4	7501260459432635